NO ORDINARY ACADEMICS

SHIRLEY SPAFFORD

NO ORDINARY ACADEMICS

Economics and Political Science at the
University of Saskatchewan, 1910–1960

UNIVERSITY OF TORONTO PRESS
Toronto Buffalo London

© University of Toronto Press Incorporated 2000
Toronto Buffalo London
Printed in Canada

ISBN 0-8020-4437-9

Printed on acid-free paper

Canadian Cataloguing in Publication Data

Spafford, Shirley
    No ordinary academics : economics and political science at the University of
Saskatchewan, 1910–1960

    Includes bibliographical references and index.
    ISBN 0-8020-4437-9

    1. University of Saskatchewan, Dept. of Political Economy – History.
    2. Economics – Study and teaching (Higher) – Saskatchewan – Saskatoon –
History.   3. Political science – Study and teaching (Higher) – Saskatchewan
– Saskatoon – History.   4. College teachers – Saskatchewan – Saskatoon.
I. Title.

    HB74.9.C3S62 2000   330'.071'1712425   C99-932539-6

Publication of this book has been supported by a grant from the University
of Saskatchewan.

University of Toronto Press acknowledges the support of the Canada Council for the Arts and the Ontario Arts Council to its publishing program.

University of Toronto Press acknowledges the financial support for
its publishing activities of the Government of Canada through
the Book Publishing Industry Development Program (BPIDP).

Contents

PREFACE vii

1 A Workman 3

2 Bringing the Wisconsin Idea to Saskatchewan 28

3 An Orthodox Economist 43

4 Retrenchment 62

5 Political Science in Search of Itself 78

6 A Natural Minoritarian 93

7 A New Start 112

8 Three Colleagues 127

9 Wartime 140

10 Union and the New Members 157

11 The Britnell Years 178

12 Conclusion 203

NOTES 213

INDEX 253

Preface

This book is about the academics who taught and did research in economics and political science at the University of Saskatchewan from 1910 to 1960. It had its beginnings in a five-page document found among the papers of the late Mabel Frances Timlin, a distinguished economist who taught at the university from 1935 to 1959. The document was a historical sketch, prepared by Timlin, of teaching and research at the university in her subject. Someone suggested that it might be extended. I had been a student of Mabel Timlin in the late 1950s, and on that rather slender pretext the job became mine, with the idea that the sketch would be filled out with a few more details and made available to her successors in the Department of Economics. A few more details created a need for yet a few more details. The project was expanded to include political science, whose story at the university is intertwined with economics.

The course taken by the two disciplines at Saskatchewan had much to do with the way in which the university itself was conceived. The university was born in the atmosphere of great optimism which accompanied the westward tide of settlers in search of homestead lands. The province of Saskatchewan was only four years old when the university was opened in Saskatoon, a city of barely 10,000, and the new institution had to serve a variety of purposes from the very beginning. The population was made up of newcomers, most of them engaged in agriculture or agricultural services, and the university was seen as an institution which would address their needs. The declaration of the founding president, Walter Murray, that this was a university 'of the people,' placed on the academic staff a heavy burden of responsibility for the survival and prosperity of the new institution and its relations with the community. It was understood that the academic staff would have 'outside' or public service duties in addition to the more conventional duties which professors carried out in the classroom and the study. Of the outside duties of the professor of economics, Murray was to say that they were 'so important that the ordinary academic man may fall far short of requirements.'[1]

Instruction in economics and political science began at the university in 1910 when the university was only one year old, and each subject rated a separate heading of its own in the first calendar of courses. Chapters one to four of the book describe the founding of the university and the beginning of economics; political science is introduced in chapter five; and the two are brought together in chapter ten with the formation of a joint department in 1946. The year 1960 seemed a good place to end for two reasons: first, there is a natural break because the academics whose stories occupy the second half of the book had by then mostly left the scene; and, second, the huge increase in student numbers which began about 1960 changed the university out of all recognition, especially in the social sciences.

Throughout this project, I have benefited from the generous support of many people. In particular, I must mention my special debt to the late Norman Ward, who read an early version of the manuscript and gave it his blessing. Others who were associated with the Saskatchewan Department of Economics and Political Science as faculty or students, or both, have contributed immeasurably with their recollections and comments, among them A.E. Safarian, Kenneth J. Rea, Jack McLeod, John Floyd, Marvin McInnis, Richard G. Rempel, Paul Phillips, June Menzies, Merrill Menzies, Bernard Crick, Hugh Thorburn, and Gordon Thiessen. I am greatly indebted to John C. Courtney, Alan C. Cairns, Richard Simeon, Don Kerr, Stan Hanson, and Michael Hayden, who read parts of the manuscript and gave me many valuable suggestions. Successive heads of department and members of the Timlin Trust, among them Leo F. Kristjanson, R. Glen Beck, Krishan Lal, Robert F. Lucas, Donald J. Heasman, Hans J. Michelmann, David E. Smith, and Morris Altman, have provided support and encouragement as the work progressed. To my husband, Duff, a special thank-you for being my in-house editor and critic for all these years.

I wish also to acknowledge the invaluable assistance of archivist Stan Hanson and the staff of the University of Saskatchewan Archives, and staff members of the Saskatchewan Archives Board, the National

Archives, and the archives of the George Peabody College for Teachers and the universities of Toronto, Queen's, Dalhousie, McGill, Wisconsin, and Rutgers. Support for the project has come from the University of Saskatchewan, the Timlin Trust, and Saskatchewan Heritage 1985.

NO ORDINARY ACADEMICS

1

A Workman

All was in readiness, the staff, eager to be helpful, nervously betting on ten, twenty, or a reasonable number of students – most anxious that Saskatchewan's first enrolment should not fall below that of her one-year-older sister, Alberta. Something seen from the window caught Dr. Oliver's eye. Surprise changed to delight, and he shouted 'Here comes Emmanuel!' (meaning the College of course) as a long, black column of thirty-five bobbing mortar-boards and wind-blown gowns came into sight and advanced over the bridge. The desired registration was in sight.

– Jean Bayer, describing registration day at the University of Saskatchewan, Saskatoon, 28 September 1909[1]

Edmund Henry Oliver, the first professor of history and economics at the University of Saskatchewan, had arrived in Saskatoon, a place he had never seen before, on 18 September, just ten days before this scene in the library took place. He had travelled on the Canadian Pacific Railway from Toronto. In those days, the trip to Saskatoon took from Tuesday to Saturday, two nights and a day spent winding through the seemingly endless rocky expanse of northern Ontario and the woodland of Manitoba to Winnipeg, where the passenger had to alight and stay overnight before boarding the next day a second train, which crossed the flat plains into Saskatchewan, arriving finally in Saskatoon at half-past four in the morning. According to custom, the sleeping car remained quiet on the track while its passengers slept. As dawn rose, Oliver looked out from the window of his berth and could just make out 'a neat, new brick station.' It was a reassuring sight. As he stepped off the train and made his way to the Flanagan Hotel where he was to spend his first few days, he saw around him more examples of new construction, the physical appurtenances of a society beginning to take shape, and he felt a stirring of ambition to be of service in the unfolding of its future. On his first night in Saskatoon, he prayed that 'I may be here in Saskatchewan a workman that needeth not to be ashamed.' He wrote in his diary: 'I go to bed tonight very hopeful of the future ... Can I be an influence for good?'[2]

Oliver was twenty-seven, and the Saskatchewan appointment was his first senior position at a university. He had taught some Greek while still a university student, had taken a doctorate in classical history, had worked for several years as a lecturer in history, and had recently turned to the study of divinity. Before another year was out, he would be ordained a minister in the Presbyterian church.

Oliver had been to the West once before. During the summer of 1904 he had worked at a church mission at Fort Walsh in the Cypress Hills area of the North-West Territories, so he arrived in Saskatoon with some idea of what it was like to live on the frontier. On his first day, as he made his rounds of the city that was to be his new home, he was pleased by its signs of growth and promise of more to come. He thought Saskatoon must surely be 'one of the most progressive towns west of Winnipeg.' There was electric lighting, a telephone system, with long-distance service to Regina nearly complete, and a municipal water supply. Several buildings were of brick or stone, including a court-house, a bank, and two hotels 'swarming with travellers,' but some of the stores were 'pretty rough,' some of the houses 'very small cottages,' and a large number of buildings remained unpainted. There were even a few familiar faces. George Clark, the city engineer, was a chum from the University of Toronto. Both Clark and a dentist, Dr C.E. Smith, whom Oliver had to consult to repair a tooth broken on the train, assured him that the town was 'solid.' He was surprised to find that his former high school teacher from Chatham, J.F. Cairns, had become a leading figure in local political affairs and proprietor of a department store which 'would do credit to a town of 200,000. We did not expect such things of Cairns when he used to teach us grammar.'[3]

Saskatoon – named, so the story goes, after the succulent berries found wild in its environs and used by the Indians to make pemmican – was founded in 1881 by a survey party sent out from Ontario by the Temperance Colonization Society. Though the Temperance Colonization Society was not long-lived, sentiment in the area remained vigorously on the side of sobriety. Growth was rapid after the turn of the century. Cairns came in 1902, attracted from eastern Canada by the prospect of setting up in business in the area. In 1903, the village was duly constituted a town after a census taken by J.R. Wilson, the village overseer, was able to confirm the 450 people required: 'It took less than half a day,' he reported. 'I took everybody in sight ... and enumerated a number of people registered at hotels who had not fully decided to become residents of Saskatoon.'⁴ City status was reached three years later. By the time of Oliver's arrival, Saskatoon had a population of about 10,000, propelled along by a group of strong-willed citizens who were excited by visions of golden business opportunities and impatient to move quickly into the next era of prosperity. Cairns was a good example of what came to be known as 'the Saskatoon spirit' – a mixture of daring and confidence and enlightened self-interest. His contemporary, James Clinkskill, described the 'buoyant feeling': 'All were imbued with an optimism that Saskatoon was destined to become an important centre. Newcomers in business were welcomed and encouraged; everyone pulled together to develop and boom the town; there were no petty jealousies of one another.'⁵

At the southwest corner of Twenty-first Street and Second Avenue stood the Drinkle Block No. 1, a new brick building named after Saskatoon's wealthiest businessman, J.C. Drinkle. Seven rooms on the fourth floor of the block were rented for the use of the university in its first year. The building had an elevator, the first in Saskatoon and, as the university staff liked to claim, the only one to be found at a university in Canada. From the upper-floor windows of the Drinkle Block, staff and students could look out over the town and survey all its bustling activity, with a grand view of the river and the university's intended site in the distance. Outside, the streets were busy and noisy. Across the way, next door to the post office, was Clinkskill's Café, where the best meals in town were to be had; four weeks to the day after registration took place, the university's first official function, a banquet for staff, students, and members of the board – paid for and hosted by the president – was held there. A block or so away in one direction was the Canadian Northern Railway station, and the Flanagan (later the Senator) Hotel about the same distance in the other. And on the other side of the street from the hotel, on an empty lot, a real-estate tent had been erected to accommodate the feverish transactions of the land boom, in which the university staff took a lively interest.⁶

Inside the Drinkle Block, the scene was set for the university's first year of operations. 'Emerging from the elevator,' recalled Jean Bayer, 'one took a few steps to the two class-rooms; a few more steps, and one reached the heart of the University's home: the library, a long narrow room with windows on the right side, and bookshelves, an inner office, and more bookshelves on the left. At the far end, beside a door, was the Secretary's desk, and through the doors and across a tiny corridor was the President's office. The so-called library did duty also as students' lounge, faculty common-room, and waiting-room for visitors. Here all the typing of the University was done, students were registered, text-books sold, library loans checked, mail sorted and distributed, and the electric bell rung for classes.' A 'hole-in-the wall office' was given over to Mr Greig, the superintendent of buildings, which Bayer said 'might well have been called "the prophet's chamber," for here on blueprints were the buildings that were to be, with samples of brick and stone.' The larger classroom was fitted out with a piano and used for 'sing-songs, meetings of the Students' Representative Council and the Young Men's Christian Association, debates, mock Parliaments (where on one occasion the House of Lords was enthusiastically abolished), lessons in boxing from the Professor of English, and social gatherings.' The classroom also became a popular place for the people of the town to gather on many an evening to hear lectures presented by the new professors.[7]

In these crowded and somewhat austere accommodations, students and staff mingled with ease, optimism, and resolute enthusiasm for all the important first decisions of the new institution. The students orga-nized a glee club, athletic council, and literary society. The university shield, depicting three wheat sheaves and an open book, was duly agreed upon. A university yell, a masterpiece of student creativity, replete with bits of Latin, was composed and practised with the degree of high seriousness suited to the occasion. The university colours were chosen, remembered Bayer, on 'a late afternoon, when the students had gone and the library had become a faculty room ... Alberta had already pre-empted the obviously right colours for a prairie university, the colours of wheat in leaf and sheaf. On Mr. Greig's design pennants had been made in various combinations of colours, and were spread on the table. There was a moment's silence, and then Professor Bate-man stepped forward and touched the green and white.' The pres-sident said: 'The Irishman has spoken. So be it.'[8]

In the first year, student registration reached seventy, surpassing that at Alberta, which had started a year earlier with forty students. Only two students were born in the environs; most were from eastern

Canada and British by extraction. Twelve were women, and half had transferred from Emmanuel College in Prince Albert, the Anglican forerunner to the university. The thirty-five capped and gowned men from Emmanuel whom Oliver saw bobbing their way along to register on the first day were a welcome addition indeed, for it meant that the enterprise could begin without the worry of denominational rivalry.[9]

Part way into its second year of operations, the university was forced to abandon its downtown location because of a fire in the Drinkle Block (destroyed altogether by fire in the 1920s). Temporary space was found across the river at Victoria elementary school. Before Christmas the university moved once more, to the second and third floors of the newly completed Saskatoon (later Nutana) Collegiate, for the remainder of the school year and all of the next. The first convocation ceremonies took place at the collegiate in the spring of 1912. In the fall, at the start of its fourth academic year, the university finally settled at its permanent site on the east side of the South Saskatchewan River. There, 292 acres of land had been set aside for the university campus, an adjoining parcel of 880 acres for a university farm, and another 160 for experimental plots. It was an ideal setting for a university – a place of natural beauty and homely prairie serenity, within walking distance of the town's centre but away from its traffic and bustle, and spacious enough to accommodate expansion well into the future.

Oliver had walked alone to this site shortly after his arrival in Saskatoon. On his walk he saw Emmanuel College in the course of construction, 'two little churches and a bunk-house,' and, beyond, only open prairie. 'I confess I felt a bit lonesome or homesick and yet I have great faith that we shall have a great university here someday,' he wrote in his diary that night. The next Sunday the president and some others called for him in a carriage and they drove together to the university grounds, where Oliver helped with the taking of levels for the first building. 'The President,' wrote Oliver, 'was quite jolly this afternoon, driving over the land that is to be the campus at a spinning rate that made the carriage touch only the high spots. He told us of seeing two wolves on the ground when the Property was selected. I ventured to prophesy that those 2 wolves would be the occasion of annual presidential reference.'[10]

The staff was young and high-spirited. Jean Bayer, who had moved with the president from Dalhousie to be his secretary and later was appointed professor of English, described the euphoric mood: 'Each felt himself an important and responsible part of a joint enterprise and was fired by an almost fanatic loyalty to the common cause. The town was proud of the University, and the University was proud of the bustling progress of the town ... The Province was young; Saskatoon was young; the staff were young; and the University was just born. All were buoyed up by youth, hope, courage, and the conviction that they were in the springtime of something that would grow to be very great.'[11]

Oliver was favourably impressed by the men who would be his university colleagues. George Ling in mathematics, the future dean of arts and science, was thirty-five, bespectacled, married with a fifteen-month-old baby, and 'systematic, painstaking, and cool,' 'a man of integrity rather than of popular gifts.' Arthur Moxon in classics was Oliver's age, a Rhodes scholar who had read law at Oxford, 'an able man possessed of rare ability, a gift for administration, but cynical.' Reginald Bateman in English, a graduate of Trinity College, Dublin, the youngest of the lot, was 'a very likeable chap, is interested in football, has a democratic manner, a sense of humour and a moustache, and evidently very glad to get the position.' But of all the men, the president, Walter Charles Murray, was 'by far the strongest.' 'I regard him,' wrote Oliver, 'as a man of vision, a statesman, a true friend, cautious, yes very cautious, possessed of high ideals, a warm heart, and an almost boyish appreciation of jokes and fun. He is troubled a bit with rheumatism and, I think, rather dislikes the climate. I am sure that he is trusted and loved by every member of the Staff and feared by none. We are all willing to speak our minds freely before him. He lectures on Education.'[12]

Walter Murray was forty-three.[13] Born and raised in Kings County in rural New Brunswick, he retained all his life the strong imprint of his early moral upbringing. His father was a country doctor who raised his family according to strict Scottish traditions of discipline and duty. His mother was no less exacting; one of his sisters remembered how their mother would 'sweep the floor with a Latin Grammar tied to the broom handle.'[14] Walter had a boundless supply of energy and will to succeed. He walked four miles each way to attend a country school and took a large share of the labours of running the family farm. As a student his record was outstanding: he received the top marks in every class he attended at the University of New Brunswick, received first-class honours in classics and mathematics upon his graduation from the university in 1886, and a year later came first in Canada in examinations for the Gilchrist Scholarship, the most prestigious award of the day. The news that he had won the Gilchrist reached him at work in

the hay field, where, it is said, he 'immediately threw down the pitch-
fork and proclaimed, "That's the last load of hay I'll ever pitch."'[15] The
scholarship enabled him to study at the University of Edinburgh and
to entertain ambitions of an academic career. In 1891 he graduated
from Edinburgh with a master's degree and first-class honours in philosophy, spent a summer of study in Germany, and then returned to
Canada where he was appointed to the chair of Mental and Moral Philosophy and Political Economy at the University of New Brunswick.
The year following, at the age of only twenty-six, he was named to the
George Munro Chair of Philosophy at Dalhousie University in Halifax.
    Murray spent sixteen happy years in Halifax. In 1895 he married
Christina Cameron, who had been his student in New Brunswick. He
had a wide circle of friends drawn from the city, the clergy, and the university and helped to start an informal club called the Round Table,
which met regularly at the homes of its members for huge turkey din-
ners and spirited discussion on topics of the day. Among its members
were former classmates from Edinburgh, Robert A. Falconer, a Gilchrist
scholar from the West Indies, Arthur Silver Morton, a friend of the Falconer family from earlier missionary days in Trinidad who was to join
Murray at Saskatchewan, and Clarence Mackinnon, later a prominent
theologian. All except Murray were ministers of the church; Falconer
became principal of Pine Hill, a theological college in Halifax, and the
others, including Murray, came to be associated with the college as faculty or board members. They formed a harmonious group, fortified by
their Scots Presbyterian heritage and shared view of the world. Murray
was its sage and peacemaker, 'family mentor' to Mackinnon, and
'Uncle Walt' to the children of Robert Falconer, who became Murray's
closest friend. The relationship between Falconer and Murray, nurtured
throughout by letters, visits, and shared family holidays, was based on
deep affection and respect and provided sustenance for each of them
when they became fellow presidents of universities.[16]
    Dalhousie was a small institution when Murray arrived, with a
teaching staff of ten and about 200 students, and only twice that when
he left. For most of the period, he was the only teacher of philosophy,
conducting five, sometimes six, courses each year, and was, by all
accounts, an outstanding teacher. Over the years he was to become
prominent in the affairs of the city as well as the university. He was a
leader in the Presbyterian church, president of the Halifax Curling
Club when it entertained the first Scottish team to visit Canada, and a
prodigious researcher and writer of articles on university, city, and

church history. In 1905 he was elected to the Halifax city council, where he became known as a Liberal and progressive, but he grew increasingly disheartened, in civic as well as university politics, by the slow pace of change and the barriers to progress put up by the old guard. After his term was up he decided not to run again, and the prospect of the presidency of Dalhousie, which would likely have been his had he remained, was not enough to hold him. When his chance came at Saskatchewan, he was ready to move on.

Early in 1908, a selection committee canvassed university leaders in Britain, the United States, and Canada and asked them to recommend candidates for the presidency of the new University of Saskatchewan. Two such appointments had been made in Canada the year before. Robert Falconer was installed as president of the University of Toronto, and Henry Marshall Tory, a mathematics professor from McGill University, was named to head the new University of Alberta in Edmonton.[17] Falconer, as head of the country's leading English-speaking university, was in a unique position to influence the choice for Saskatchewan. In his reply to the committee, Falconer said that 'the only opinion that will be really valuable to you is one based upon personal acquaintance.' He placed Murray at the head of his list and offered this account of his worthiness: 'His splendid common sense, tact and clear sightedness make his judgment of uncommon value. He is not perhaps an eloquent speaker, but he is effective and has a fine conception of educational ideals and is a leader among men.'[18] Of those recommended, six were sent letters inviting them to let their names stand. The letter described the requirements of the position, the salary, to be no less than $5,000 a year, and the situation of the university, which as yet had 'no buildings erected, no staff, and no equipment.'[19] At the top of the list drawn up by the committee was Adam Shortt, head of the Department of Political Science at Queen's University. Murray was second.[20] Shortt, who was soon to be named to the Civil Service Commission in Ottawa, declined to let his name stand.[21] Murray let his name go forward, and in his letter of reply set out an articulate and remarkably prescient vision of what a university in Saskatchewan should be. In July a committee of three men travelled to Toronto to meet candidates. They decided to recommend Murray, and a month later he was on a train heading west to Saskatchewan for formal ratification of the appointment.

Murray arrived in Regina, the province's capital, in the very early hours of an August morning of 1908 and was being taken for breakfast when he and his host chanced to meet the premier, Walter Scott, rushing on his way to catch the train on which Murray had arrived. Scott's words were few but, to Murray, inspiring: 'This is a great country. It requires men with large ideas to do it justice.'[22] The next morning, as he recalled, he was directed to the city hall and assigned to a spare office where the paint was barely dry: 'I was given a small desk, a chair, a copy of the University Act and told practically to "hop to it" to create a University.'[23] There was never any doubt that the right man had been found. 'The choice of Dr. Murray as President was a very fortunate one,' concluded Clinkskill, a member of the first board of governors; 'he is a man of the highest character, a sound scholar, a great organizer and a most indefatigable worker.'[24] J. Francis Leddy, a later dean of arts, called Murray 'the most effective university president in Canada' during the first thirty years of the century in Canada.[25]

While Murray stayed on in Saskatchewan to assist with the early organization of the university, his wife, Christina, had remained behind in Halifax to see to the sale of their house and the transfer of their belongings. Now, with the university's first fall session about to open, she joined him in rooms at the Flanagan with their three young daughters, as they arranged for more permanent lodgings and waited with anxious anticipation, along with the other participants, for this extraordinary adventure to begin.[26]

I

In 1905, the provinces of Saskatchewan and Alberta were fashioned out of the vast area of the North-West Territories, and each began to fill with homesteaders lured by the promise of free land. When Murray moved west, he had every reason to think that Saskatchewan was where the potentialities of western settlement were to be realized at their fullest. The business and community leaders of the province never tired of saying as much, and soon they would be able to point to official census reports to back up their claim. The census of 1911 recorded Saskatchewan's population as just under 500,000, making it the third most populous province of Canada, behind Ontario and Quebec. Saskatchewan remained the third most populous province in the census of 1921 and again in those of 1931 and 1941. Murray believed that the province of his adoption was of some standing and consequence on the national scene, and that it required a university of some standing and consequence as well.

One of the first acts of the Saskatchewan legislature, after the incorporation of the province, was to provide for the establishment of a university. But between the passing of the University Act and the opening of the university, its location became the subject of great dispute between Regina, the capital city, and Saskatoon, the rapidly growing market town to the north, with the smaller centres of Moose Jaw, Battleford, and Prince Albert creating meanwhile such clamour as they could to have their claims heard. In the end, on 7 April 1909, Saskatoon was chosen for the site, but the decision did not put the issue to rest. Edmund Oliver saw Murray being accosted in the rotunda of the Flanagan Hotel by an officer of the North-West Mounted Police who insisted in his capacity as a citizen of Saskatchewan that the decision should have gone to Prince Albert. Oliver also noted that Regina folk were 'acting nasty and want to keep their children from the university.'[27] Even Walter Murray, who strongly believed that the university should be close to the seat of government, was unable to conceal his disappointment when Saskatoon was picked, and he nearly resigned in consequence. Nevertheless, he stood by his conviction that Saskatchewan should have only one university, and in succeeding years the principle of 'one province, one university' remained firm, even in the face of fierce lobbying from the citizens of Regina. In 1925 Regina College achieved the status of a two-year junior college, and in 1934 passed from direct control by the United Church of Canada to the University of Saskatchewan, but not until 1974 was it finally transformed into a full-fledged university independent of Saskatoon.[28]

Still, the controversy over the location of the university was not the only difficulty to be overcome. Secondary education in the province was itself at a formative stage of development, so many students had to be admitted to university before completing senior matriculation. In Saskatoon itself, a permanent building for the first high school was not completed until the university was in its second year of operation. The task of maintaining standards would not be an easy matter for an institution which prided itself on accessibility and service to the community. In the early years, many allowances had to be made, especially for students from the farm who would present themselves for classes only after the harvesting season had ended.[29]

And, finally, there was the whole problem of financial support and the relationship between the university and the pioneering community. The universities of eastern Canada, most of them established with the support of churches or by means of private endowment, had been plagued throughout their history by sectarian bitterness and political interference. Murray was relieved to find that the government of Saskatchewan, following the precedents of the University of Toronto Act of 1906 and university enactments of the previous Territorial government, had decided to assume responsibility for all capital and operating expenditures and to leave all decisions concerning the use of operating funds to the university's board of governors. The Saskatchewan legislation, as Murray described it, ensured 'that there would be only one degree-granting institution, that it would be state-supported, non-sectarian, and open to men and women on equal terms.' A unique characteristic of the legislation was its attempt to keep the university free from political interference; until 1946, Saskatchewan was the only university in Canada to have fewer than one-half of its board members appointed by government. A further provision prescribed that all academic decisions were to come under the jurisdiction of the university senate, a body separate from the board of governors and elected by convocation, an assembly of university graduates of the province. Murray called the arrangements 'non-political and yet democratic.'[30]

But could the people of Saskatchewan, many of them homesteaders undertaking the arduous and risky business of farming, be persuaded to support such an expensive enterprise when their own government stood so aloof from the decisions which it made? Murray saw from the beginning that a university in the West, without private sources of wealth to call upon, could not survive for long without the goodwill of its constituency, and its constituency was, in the first instance, the people who paid its bills – notably the plain homesteaders. When he and his committee of board members made a tour of university campuses in the United States in the fall of 1908, before the opening of the University of Saskatchewan, Murray was particularly impressed by the universities he visited in the Midwest. The American state university, which he later described as 'the scientific arm of the state for Research, for carrying the benefits of Science to all and sundry in the state and for the supply of information to Legislative assemblies and their Executives,' became the example he set out to follow, in contrast to the Oxford model, 'a place for Liberal Culture and preparation for the Learned Professions.'[31] Service to the community became his credo: 'there should be ever present,' he wrote in his first *Report*, 'the consciousness that this is the University of the people, established by the people, and devoted by the people to the advancement of learning and the promotion of happiness and virtue.'

What is the sphere of the University? Its watchword is service – service of the state in the things that make for happiness and virtue as well as in the things that make for wealth. No form of that service is too mean or too exalted for the university. It is as fitting for the university, through correspondence classes, extension courses, supervision of farmers' clubs, travelling libraries, women's institutes or musical tests to place within the reach of the solitary student, the distant townsman, the farmer in his hours of leisure or the mothers and daughters in the home the opportunities for adding to their store of knowledge and enjoyment, as it is that the university should foster researches into the properties of radium or the causes and cure of swamp fever.[32]

To best serve the needs of the community, he believed, it was important to develop strong and practical professional colleges and extension services, particularly in agriculture: 'In a province destined for many years to be predominatingly agricultural, the Provincial University should place the interests of agriculture in the forefront, or renounce its title to provincial service.'[33] To the president of the University of Alberta, Henry Marshall Tory, with whom Murray struck up a cordial and cooperative relationship, he wrote: 'I think it would be wise ... to have the staff and equipment reach its full strength earlier in our Faculty of Agriculture than in any other faculty. If our plans turn out all right, within two years we will have a fairly well equipped College of Agriculture and Faculty of Arts, but relatively the Faculty of Agriculture will be the more complete. Not only do the practical needs, but also the necessity of allaying the suspicion of the farmers by demonstrating to them the goodwill and utility of the university, urge us to move in this manner.'[34]

Though not everyone agreed with the emphasis given to agriculture, Murray's position eventually won out, and the College of Agriculture at Saskatchewan became the first of its kind in Canada to be established as part of a university. At the University of Alberta, which opened in 1908, one year before Saskatchewan, President Tory decided to start instead with an emphasis on arts and science; agriculture was added later, in 1915.[35] In Saskatchewan, the educational services of the Department of Agriculture and responsibility for the supervision of agricultural societies were immediately transferred from the province to the university, which allowed the university's extension department to form close connections with the farming community from the beginning. In Alberta, on the other hand, agricultural programs remained with the provincial department of agriculture, which meant that extension programs at the University of Alberta fell more generally into the area of adult education.

Murray and his staff waited anxiously for the legislature to approve the expenditures for new buildings on the campus. When approval came, construction proceeded quickly. The main classroom building, a graceful greystone structure adorned with stone carvings of gargoyles, and – for a local touch – *spermophilus richardsonii*, the 'gopher,' had its cornerstone laid by the Prime Minister of Canada, Sir Wilfrid Laurier, on 29 July 1910, and was ready for the opening of classes in the fall of 1912. It included rooms for milk testing, butter making, and grain analysis, with a central meeting room, Convocation Hall, made large enough, at the request of the dean of agriculture, to accommodate large gatherings of farmers. The original plan was to turn the building over to agriculture and build a new one for arts and science, but funds were short, and instead agriculture moved out. Also constructed were 'a cathedral like Stock Pavilion' (so described by Oliver), a main barn with a loft floor of granite, sheep barn, piggery and poultry house, granaries, dormitories for students – Saskatchewan Hall (for women), and later Qu'Appelle Hall (for men) – as well as a stone residence for the dean of agriculture, another residence, less grand in design, for the professor of field husbandry, and some frame houses for the farm workers and foreman.[36] The president's house on campus, envisaged by the architects as 'rising from the riverbank like a castle on the Rhine,' was approved by the board of governors and completed by 1913 at a cost of $44,615. Murray, who objected to its size and expense, was overruled on the matter, though he remained sensitive to any criticism that the house was too lavish.[37]

The style of architecture chosen for the president's house and other major buildings on campus was Collegiate Gothic, a style reminiscent of the college buildings of Oxford and Cambridge and used extensively in the United States for university construction. On their tour of universities in the United States, the president and his committee had particularly admired the buildings of Washington University in St Louis, which was the example they chose for the architects to follow. The architects, Brown and Vallance of Montreal, were selected because of their experience in working with Collegiate Gothic. The Saskatchewan buildings were faced with a local limestone, found in abundant quantity nearby, which weathered to a soft variable grey and gave the university a dignified and unified appearance.

The University of Saskatchewan emerged with a look and feel very different from those of its sister institution in the province of Alberta.[38] Collegiate Gothic was firmly rejected by Alberta as (so one observer put it) 'an exotic affectation which would soon pass out of fashion.' While the University of Saskatchewan went with greystone and a traditional look, Alberta's buildings were constructed of red brick and white stone in an 'elastic free classic style ... with modified English traditions.'[39] In the matter of student life, too, Saskatchewan and Alberta developed different traditions. Tory and Murray both worried over what to do about 'the evils of the clique.' At Saskatchewan, provision of residences for students on campus and an insistence on egalitarian ways, shared by faculty and students alike, discouraged fraternities and sororities, and they never took root. Alberta students at the beginning were made to pledge on registration forms never to join a 'secret society,' but as student demand grew, fraternities became established at Alberta as at most other universities in Canada.[40]

For as long as he was president, the selection of faculty, as well as all other university appointments, was Murray's prerogative alone, and one which he exercised with the utmost caution and sense of purpose.[41] He preferred the American system of recruitment, which meant inquiring after suitable candidates, to the British system of advertising for applications. 'The American system,' as he put it, 'avoids the objectionable canvassing which the best men decline to undertake; and for the vague and sometimes misleading testimonial it substitutes the personal interview and the candid estimates of reliable judges.'[42] He would write to his wide circle of acquaintances, both within and outside Canada, and when he turned up some interesting candidates would probe into their suitability in surprising detail. He once asked, with characteristic directness, the following questions of a prospective candidate in agriculture: 'Is he self centred and self seeking? What is his attitude to others? Is it generous and cooperative? What about his wife?'[43] Though he was personally attracted to robust personalities, he was aware that too much vividness of character could cause disharmony in a small university community. A candidate could be forgiven the lack of a publication record if his academic attainments were high in other respects, but any sign of laxity in personal conduct could not be so easily overlooked. For the beginning at least, Murray wanted to find men (rarely, women) of proven ability and strong character who could be counted upon to submerge selfish interest for the sake of common purpose and endure the inevitable hardships of starting a new institution. 'Mere scholars will not do,' said Murray, writing to a professor at Harvard in 1908. 'The personal qualities in the man,' he explained to another, 'are far more important for success and efficiency than scholastic training, or productive scholarship' – though he wanted training and scholarship too.[44] He looked for youth, vigour, and promise – in short, the kind of person who could grow with the university and some day become a strong head of department and a leader in the community.

Murray knew he would have to compete for staff with the University of Alberta, but he thought that together the two universities would make a more attractive field for appointment and promotion than would one university by itself. He discussed this candidly with President Tory early on: 'I think ... it would be well for us to have an understanding in this matter of appointments. It seems to me only fair to the men to let it be known that those occupying junior positions, or in fact those who desire a change can with perfect propriety consider a change from one University to the other ... I think it is to our interests that the men who come to the west should feel that they have a fairly large field for advancement.' Tory agreed, and 'furthermore,' he added, 'such an exchange might give us each an opportunity of unloading on the other some undesirables.'[45]

Another worrisome matter for the president was the setting of salaries and rank, for here was fertile ground for personal jealousy and intrigue. 'The salary question is to me one of the most troublesome,' wrote Murray in 1908. 'Apparently the system of individual bargaining prevails almost everywhere. I confess that I detest it. In a University the spirit of staff and student is surely the most important thing. This system seems to be fatal to a right University spirit.'[46] A salary schedule, which set out various grades of professorships with stated floors and ceilings within each grade, similar to schedules in use at Toronto and Harvard, was introduced at Saskatchewan in 1918. 'We believe,' he explained to one correspondent, 'that it removes inequalities, and while all men are not absolutely equal in ability or in capacity as teachers and investigators, the attempt to adjust salaries to individual demand leads to intrigue, jealousy, ill will, etc.'[47] To another, he wrote: 'The aim is to make the highest grade of salary available to any man who is doing research work or is publishing work recognized abroad.'[48] In practice, the salary schedule served these good intentions only imperfectly. There were no fixed committees; although Murray consulted with others from time to time, he believed it essential to have a free hand in such matters. With budgetary constraints always prompting the president to make contracts as advantageous as possible for the university on the one hand, and his desire to reward those who served the institution well on the other, the salary schedule became more an administrative device than an assurance of academic justice.

Murray had four academic appointments to make to get his university started. One of them was to be in the field of history. His first choice for the position was Edward A. Kylie of the University of Toronto, who had an established reputation as a historian. After Kylie turned down an offer, Murray turned to Edmund Oliver, who had studied not only history but also economics, a subject Murray was anxious to place on the curriculum from the beginning. Oliver, as it turned out, embodied all the qualities Murray looked for in a faculty member. He had an excellent academic background combined with a rugged but unimpeachable character and an almost evangelical desire to do good. All that he lacked, since senior appointments were in such short supply, was the opportunity to show off his unusual talents. Two of Murray's most trusted informants, President Falconer of Toronto and James Brebner, the Toronto registrar, both urged him to offer an appointment to Oliver. It took Murray only a short time to realize that Oliver was indeed an exceptional find. When Murray wrote again and asked Brebner to recommend more of the same, Brebner replied, 'Oliver is a rare, and I fear we cannot send you many of them.'[49]

II

Edmund Oliver was born on 8 February 1882 in Eberts, a Scottish settlement in Chatham Township, Ontario. From an early age he showed a singular devotion to his church and a marked precocity in his studies. He attended Chatham Collegiate and graduated at the age of only sixteen with the Edward Blake Scholarship for the highest marks in the province in mathematics and classics. He then enrolled in classics at the University of Toronto, took a bachelor's degree with high honours and the McCaul Gold Medal, and continued on at Toronto for two more years as the holder of the Alexander Mackenzie Fellowship in political science. During these years he kept busy with church activities, organized a young men's club at Westminster Presbyterian Church, and had his first taste of missionary work during his summer at Fort Walsh in western Canada. In 1904 he won a fellowship to attend the School of

Political Science at Columbia University in New York.[50] Oliver took courses in economics, sociology, and history, and encountered in Edwin R.A. Seligman, the head of the economics department, a forceful and articulate individual who was one of the first academic economists to serve in an advisory role to government officials. Oliver's doctoral thesis, 'Roman Economic Conditions to the Close of the Republic,' supervised by Seligman, was an elegant piece of work based on Latin sources; 650 copies of the thesis were published in 1908 by the University of Toronto Library, in fulfilment of a requirement of the Columbia school that all dissertations be published, at the candidate's expense if necessary.

After completing his degree at Columbia, Oliver returned to Canada and began to lecture in history at McMaster University, then a Baptist-supported institution in Toronto. In his third year at McMaster he enrolled as a part-time student of divinity at Knox College, a Presbyterian theological school affiliated with the University of Toronto, and continued to devote his holidays and spare time to religious work. He spent the summer of 1908 on an extensive tour of religious settlements in Germany, Italy, Greece, Palestine, and Turkey, which he described on his return in an article in the *McMaster University Monthly,* and the next year attended a summer session at the divinity school of the University of Chicago.[51]

Early in 1909, during his fourth year of teaching, Oliver had before him three offers of work – one from a mission in China, a second from a Christian college in Smyrna he had visited on his travels, and a third from Saskatchewan. He was tempted most of all by the thought of going to China, having always had a desire to do missionary work in some distant land, but he was also worried about finishing his degree in divinity. The majority of his friends, Falconer and Brebner among them, thought he would do the most good in the West and prevailed upon him to accept Murray's offer. In the end, when an arrangement was struck which allowed him to teach until Christmas and take leave in the second term to complete his studies at Knox, the matter was settled in favour of Saskatchewan. 'If I go west,' Oliver wrote to Murray, 'I desire to throw my whole life into that work and I should not desire the interests of my department to suffer through my absence for so long a time.'[52] For his part, Murray had no doubt that Oliver would do well. 'I believe,' he wrote in reply to Oliver, 'that not only among the students will your influence be most beneficial but that as a lecturer through extension courses & otherwise will you become a most powerful factor in forming public opinion & taste.'[53]

A faculty meeting on 20 September introduced the new professor of history to the business of setting up a university. 'What seems to me most wonderful,' noted Oliver after the meeting, 'is that academicals [academic robes], mostly patterned on Cambridge, have already been adopted, although our first graduate is possibly two years off.'[54] President Murray read and discussed the statutes of the senate relating to the faculty. The minimum passing grade was set at 40 per cent. Junior matriculation, or Grade eleven, was established as the requirement for admission.[55] There was a lengthy discussion of classes to be given the first year, the schedule having been made more complicated by Oliver's plan to return east in the new year. In the end, Oliver was assigned to do double duty in history in the first term. Economics came up for discussion, and a motion was passed that it would be given 'four hours a week till the Christmas recess.'[56] But the next day the subject came up again when Oliver, Murray, and Ling had a 'tussle' over the timetable and economics was set aside for the time being: 'Economics comes when it can be agreed upon later,' wrote Oliver in his diary. 'I don't feel very sure about my capacity to teach Economics. Murray understands that I am a History man so shall do the best I can.'[57] Another tussle took place over Latin, where Oliver and Ling joined forces in favour of Latin as a compulsory subject against Moxon, Bateman, and the president, who preferred it to be optional. For the first few years, Latin was made compulsory, but later it was changed to one of several languages other than English of which students were required to choose two.

Oliver had the distinction of delivering the first lecture at the university, one in history. His diary records his dismay at finding his students rising from their seats to pay him respect whenever he entered or left the room. After a few such episodes, he 'told them that no person could be more appreciative of a courtesy that was manifestly prompted by kindliness of heart, yet I was a very young man, and a very ordinary mortal and I feared that in the days to come some young lad might feel a barrier between himself and me and my helpfulness might be impaired. These remarks were well received and later, I was glad to note, acted upon.' 'Obeisance,' he added, 'is still done Bateman.'[58]

To help win the goodwill of the community, Murray had arranged for members of faculty to deliver public lectures in Saskatoon and many smaller centres throughout Saskatchewan. The subjects were wide-ranging: imagery (Murray's contribution), Oxford, Omar Khayyám, Shakespeare, Samuel Johnson, animal husbandry, soil fertility, scientific prediction of the weather (a special interest of Professor Ling's), the Industrial Revolution, and other topics relating to European history. Oliver was responsible for the public lectures in history, nine or so during the course of the term, and his first effort, by his own account, went off rather badly: 'Expected from 10 to 15 people present but the room was packed, 50 to 75. Spoke an hour on "Rome." Got off with a fair start but fell down lamentably towards the end. Found it a heavy strain. Scarcely slept all night by reason of the humiliation. Why can't I keep cool ... I fancy Murray is disappointed in the lecture but delighted with the attendance.'[59] But such thoughts were mostly a sign of the trepidations of youth and the high standards Oliver set for himself. His contemporaries described him as a compelling speaker and an industrious worker. In faculty meetings, as one of his colleagues recalled, 'Oliver rarely intervened unless a matter of some significance was under discussion and then usually exhibited a natural eloquence and facility with words which ... always seemed surprising in a man who in physical appearance resembled a prize fighter rather than an academic.'[60] A colleague, who remembers Oliver as having extraordinary powers of concentration and devotion to duty, reports that he could 'sit at his desk for fifteen hours a day and never idle five minutes.'[61]

After the Christmas break, Oliver returned as planned to Toronto where he finished his studies in theology at Knox College and was ordained as a minister. With this accomplishment behind him, he and his sister Mary, whose education he had undertaken to support, left for a summer in Europe. It was a pleasant sojourn. They spent most of their time in Berlin, met many friends, and took many trips and excursions. Oliver enrolled at the University of Berlin (where classes began at seven o'clock in the morning) for several weeks of lectures in church and modern history; his sister, a member of the first graduating class of the University of Saskatchewan who later taught in the English department, went to a nearby school. 'I am at present reading Bismarck's letters during 1870–71,' he reported back to Murray. 'My plan is to get my German lectures in shape for that 2nd year course in European History. My aim is to write the French ones up in France next year perhaps and then, possibly at Oxford or London, work out that course on the Empire.'[62] But by the following year his plans had changed. He married Stella Marguerite Cowling, whom he had met in Toronto the year before, settled in a new house at 822 Broadway, and turned his attention to an extensive study of western settlement.

The subject of western settlement had captured Oliver's interest from his first weeks in Saskatoon when he had taken lodgings at the home of Mrs Margaret E. Copland on Spadina Crescent, next door to the newly constructed Knox Presbyterian Church. Mrs Copland had many interesting tales to tell of pioneer life; with her late husband, Thomas Copland, she had settled in Saskatoon in 1882, just after the arrival of the first group of Temperance Colonization Society settlers, and they had homesteaded on land later occupied by the university. Murray, looking ahead to the start of a provincial archives, urged Oliver to start on the collection of archival materials and suggested that he might spend his summers on the study of western settlement. Oliver began his search for documents immediately. Only a month after his arrival, he wrote excitedly in his diary about a North-West Mounted Police officer who handed on to him a 'genuine' autograph of Louis Riel, the Métis leader of the North-West Rebellion. The autograph read: 'Louis "David" Riel. We are Christians; let us not forget to pronounce the Holy Name of our Lord Jesus Christ, always very respectfully and religiously. Regina Jail, August 5th, 1885.'[63] As he became ever more intrigued by the prospects of further historical discoveries, Oliver decided not to return overseas but instead spent the summers of 1911 and 1912 in Ottawa, where he zealously tracked down materials on the development of western Canada. In the course of his research he came across the minutes of the Council of Assiniboia from 1835 to 1861 which were thought to be lost. His labours resulted in an important documentary collection entitled *The Canadian North-West, Its Early Development and Legislative Records*, which was published in two volumes in 1914 and 1915 by the Dominion Archives. In 1914 he also contributed chapters on Alberta and Saskatchewan to *Canada and Its Provinces*, the monumental series of twenty-three volumes edited by Adam Shortt and Arthur G. Doughty.[64]

Oliver was hired to teach history and economics, but the demand for history teaching took precedence over the needs of economics. He taught economics only twice. The first course was given in 1910–11 to seventeen students and covered basic economic principles and the development of economic thought. The textbook prescribed, *Outlines of Economics*, by the noted Wisconsin economist Richard T. Ely, was one in current use in most places in North America. In 1912–13, Oliver gave a course entitled 'General Economic Theory.' The course requirements included two essays, one on homesteading and the other on socialism; thirty-seven students enrolled and all but one passed. By this time he was in his fourth year of teaching, and each year his responsibilities had grown more onerous. Since there was no professor of German and Oliver was fluent in the language, he became the instructor in German in addition to his other duties. His timetable showed a solid block of classes each morning from Monday to Friday, and some in the afternoons as well. He wrote in his report to the president that the burden of grading assignments 'dampens the enthusiasm of the Professor and spoils the quality of his work.' As for the condition of the library, he noted that 'for Economics 1 we had practically no books at all,' though the students were evidently 'keenly interested in this important subject.'[65] Not so the professor, who was now engrossed in historical studies and whose diffidence about teaching economics took a turn towards outright aversion. It was a subject, he confided to his diary, 'I cordially hate.'[66]

Still, not all the duties which fell to him as university economist were as repugnant to Oliver as those which had to be carried out in the classroom. When he was appointed in 1913 to two commissions of inquiry, one on agricultural credit, the other on grain markets, he threw himself into the work with an obvious relish. The commissions, headed by John Heber Haslam, had one other member, the young manager of the Saskatchewan Co-operative Elevator Company, Charles Avery Dunning, later premier of Saskatchewan. The three men toured Europe and visited credit institutions, after which Oliver was set to work to write the final reports. The agricultural credit commission recommended, among other things, the fostering of cooperative effort and 'financial institutions of our own, with sympathies for our own problems and control by our own people.'[67] The proposals of the agricultural credit commission were enthusiastically endorsed by the Saskatchewan Grain Growers' Association at its next meeting. One of the proposals led to the passing of the Agricultural Co-operative Societies Act in 1913 and the opening of a special branch in the Department of Agriculture to administer it, but the commission's main recommendation, a cooperative credit scheme for farmers, was set aside for the time being.

In 1915 Oliver, along with a member of the legislature, J.F. Bole, was appointed to a commission of inquiry curiously entitled 'Royal Commission to Inquire into and Report upon the System of Liquor Dispensaries Which Recently Existed in South Carolina (under State Control).' The issue of liquor control had generated a heated debate in Saskatchewan, in the course of which the South Carolina system was brought forward as a possible model for reform. The Banish-the-Bar

movement was strong and growing throughout the province, especially in Saskatoon where the founding settlers had been strongly wedded to temperance. A local option vote to ban the sale of liquor in
Saskatoon, held in 1910, was defeated by a narrow margin of 848 to 698
votes but did not include the votes of women, who had not yet gained
the right to vote in elections. Oliver and President Murray were among
the powerful voices aligned on the side of temperance. In a final report,
written by Oliver, the liquor commission recommended an immediate
removal of the bar from Saskatchewan and in its stead the establishment of government liquor dispensaries. These were to be without dec-
oration or advertisement, mirrors, or pictures, and off limits to 'minors,
intoxicated persons, drunkards or women.'[68] The government, in
response, closed 406 bars, 38 wholesale liquor outlets, and 12 clubs, and
replaced them with 23 dispensaries. It was estimated that liquor consumption was cut by 90 per cent.[69] Before long, the dispensaries themselves were shut down as well. On 14 March 1916 the Saskatchewan
legislature enacted legislation which granted women the right to vote,
and the new electoral voice was to prove a mighty force.[70] Near the end
of the year, a provincial plebiscite taken on the liquor issue revealed
overwhelming public support for complete prohibition. For the next
eight years Saskatchewan went completely dry. New legislation introduced in 1924 brought back a government-controlled system of liquor
stores, but it was a decade before the legislation was extended to allow
hotels to apply for licences to sell beer by the glass. Even then, licences
were notoriously difficult to get and the beer parlours, as they came to
be known, admitted only men and were obliged to close in the evening
by ten o'clock. The university reflected the prevailing mores: there was
no liquor served at university functions during Murray's time, and any
students caught drinking alcoholic beverages were called in and chas-
tised by the president himself.

In these years, as Saskatoon historians Don Kerr and Stan Hanson
describe, 'the leadership of the city passed to a new kind of man ... a
man capable of providing not financial but rather moral and social
advice and guidance.'[71] Murray and Oliver were prime examples of
the new leadership. Together they engaged in many crusades – for prohibition, for educational reform, for church union.[72] Both men believed
passionately in public service, in moral example, and in the essential
role of education in the development of a society. In addition to his service on three commissions, Oliver was the first chairman of the Saskatoon Public Library Board, a trustee of the Saskatoon Public School

Board, and vice-president of the Public Education League, an organization devoted to ensuring that all Saskatchewan children were educated
in the English language.[73] He was a powerful writer and speaker, from
the public platform as well as the pulpit, uplifting and progressive in
his tone, and well in tune with the growing spirit of western dissent.
His message was unequivocal, as in his call to students during wartime: 'We are students of the Western Universities and heirs to Athens.
We are also men of Canada and sons of Britain. We must learn the double lesson of the old Greek legend and the new colonial relationship.
There must be fiery zeal and stern self control. In our personal lives
there must be good discipline and no slackness. We must live at attention ... In the political and in the moral life alike only the self-controlled
and the self-governing will triumph.'[74]

Oliver's emphasis on the importance of church life and the need for
a sense of public morality was received with gratitude by the many citizens eager to move beyond the greed and excesses of frontier society,
his Christian message intermingling comfortably with the economic
theme of cooperation as the only sure way to overcome the injustices
visited on the West by the commercial interests of the East. After the
report of the agricultural credit commission was tabled in the legislature, Oliver appeared frequently at public meetings exhorting the
farmers to organize. 'In the world of modern business relations,' he
said, 'the organized industries prey upon the disorganized.'[75] In the
language of the agrarian radical, he spoke of 'those middlemen who
fatten in our midst,' and asked: 'Are we to contemplate the continua-
tion and the permanence in our national life of a class whose personal
interests are always leading them to fleece both producer and consumer alike?'[76]

III

After the fall of 1913 a full-time economist was hired by the university,
and Oliver, much to his relief, no longer had to worry about teaching
economics. But soon he was to leave the security of his position at the
university for an entirely new challenge. Oliver had been asked in 1910
to join the faculty of theology at the University of Alberta but turned it
down, and President Murray, eager to keep him, promised that he
would be named the head of a new college proposed for Saskatchewan.[77] Murray, who was active in the reform movement in the Presbyterian church and in promoting the integration of church colleges

with the university, began a campaign to raise funds for the college on campus. Oliver joined in the campaign, and in 1914, while the college was still an uncertain venture existing only in name, with little money behind it and no building, he resigned as professor of history to become its principal. The college started out in a frame rooming-house at 209 Albert Avenue, while Oliver carried on at the university as a part-time lecturer in history in an attempt to raise some of the needed funds. Then in 1916, with the enterprise still lacking the necessary funding, Oliver left Saskatoon to serve as a chaplain with the 196th Battalion in France. Near the end of the war he founded the University of Vimy Ridge for the education of Canadian soldiers, which was later incorporated as part of the Khaki University led by Tory of Alberta.

While he was serving overseas, Oliver was asked to allow his name to stand for the principalship of Queen's University, but he declined, saying that he had work yet to be done in the West. 'The matter about Queen's University has again come to bother me,' he wrote home to his wife on 15 August 1916. 'I expect to write before the end of the week definitely refusing to entertain the proposal. I feel that I am in this work, that I can make some humble little contribution, and that I am not going to be distracted from it till the work is complete.' Nevertheless, the work which lay before him was formidable, and he was depressed by the uncertainty of it all. 'I am not tired of the Principalship,' he wrote, 'but I am sick of it under the old conditions with no staff, no building, no enthusiasm for one's work on the part of our assembly ... and now that the war is on us and Union postponed, no immediate prospect of students.'[78]

After the war, he plunged back into his religious work with renewed dedication. In time, the problems of support for the college were overcome, and by 1924 St Andrew's College, a handsome greystone structure which followed the architectural style of other university buildings, came to be erected at its present site along College Avenue, on the south-western corner of the campus. With the future of his college now assured, Oliver turned his attention to the organization of the church on the prairies. He campaigned vigorously for church union, arguing in writings and at meetings across the country that the prairies could not afford the luxury of a variety of Protestant denominations. In 1925, when the union of Methodist, Presbyterian, and Congregationalist churches was finally achieved, Oliver became president of the Saskatchewan conference. From 1930 to 1932 he served as moderator of the United Church of Canada, the first moderator from western

Canada. During the years of the Depression, which ravaged Saskatchewan more than any other province, he travelled the length and breadth of Canada to raise gifts and donations for the stricken region. Years of drought had turned large parts of rural Saskatchewan into a wasteland. 'What a lonesome countryside,' he wrote. 'No men in the fields. No crops. No traffic. No animals. Not many gophers, but a plenitude of grasshoppers.'[79]

Although his scholarly activities came to be pushed into the background, Oliver remained close to the affairs of the university and its president and still managed to contribute to historical research on western Canada. In 1921 he was elected a fellow of the Royal Society of Canada. Between 1923 and 1935 he wrote nine papers for presentation before the Royal Society, a section on the settlement of the Canadian prairies for the *Cambridge History of the British Empire*, and several books and pamphlets for the United Church of Canada. His most notable religious work, *The Winning of the Frontier*, identified him, according to J.M.S. Careless, as a Turnerian historian who applied the frontier thesis to Canadian religious development.[80]

Oliver received many honours during his lifetime. The University of Saskatchewan awarded him an honorary degree, as did Queen's, the University of Toronto, and the theological colleges of Emmanuel in Toronto, Union in Vancouver, and Pine Hill in Halifax. By the time of his death in 1935, which came suddenly while he was teaching at a mission at Round Lake in Saskatchewan's Qu'Appelle valley, he had become one of the most powerful figures in western Canada. The *Winnipeg Free Press*, in a special editorial, described him as 'a true minister of religion who never had a church, but who influenced the people of his own communion in Canada more deeply than any other clergyman of his time, a devoted public man who was never in the legislature but who knew his own province of Saskatchewan better and did more for it than any other citizen.'[81]

2

Bringing the Wisconsin Idea to Saskatchewan

Of all the universities he visited during his tour of American campuses, Murray held none in greater regard than the University of Wisconsin, where the notion of university experts working together with political leaders and others in the community had become known as the Wisconsin Idea.[1] 'If we can follow in your footsteps,' he wrote to Charles R. Van Hise, president of the University of Wisconsin, after his visit there in 1908, 'this Province will ultimately have a University equal to the best in Canada. We were greatly impressed with the way you have conserved the best of the old Universities and have at the same time adapted yourselves to the changing needs of the state.'[2]

The Wisconsin Idea had two essential elements: that university experts should devote themselves to furthering the prosperity of the state and general well-being of the community through assistance to legislators and other public officials, and that the university should extend its services to every resident through practical training, publications, and extension programs. Both elements commended themselves to Murray. In his first annual report, he devoted an entire section to the University of Wisconsin, describing it as 'an admirable example of a University whose watchword is service of the State. In the University of that State there is a happy blending of the best of the old and the new – a harmonious combination of the Liberal Arts and Pure Sciences with the Sciences applied to Agriculture and the Professions. Culture and Utility receive equal emphasis; both inspire Research and are in turn strengthened by it.' 'If Wisconsin,' he asked, 'accomplished so much in forty years is it madness to expect that not a few will live to see in this Province a University as strong and as efficient, as abundant in service and as potent in influence as the great University of that

State?'[3] In the next year, Murray began to look ahead to developing the important role of the social sciences in the service of the state: 'In the University of Wisconsin excellent results have been obtained from the prominence given to History, Economics, Political Science and allied subjects. It is recognized that it is a duty of the State University to provide special facilities for the study of social conditions and the problems of government. In this University, it is hoped that similar provisions will be made ... Public opinion requires the guidance of the expert. It is the duty of the University to provide it.'[4]

With economics (or political economy, as it was also known), Murray had some acquaintance. He had studied the subject when he was a student of philosophy at the University of Edinburgh and, on his return to Canada in 1891, when he was appointed to the chair of Mental and Moral Philosophy and Political Economy at the University of New Brunswick, he began an extension program and taught the university's first course in political economy. In Saskatchewan, Murray quickly reached the conclusion that, if there was to be any economic progress in the province, a solution to the problems of agriculture and how it was to be financed had to be discovered; without economic progress the university itself would surely starve.

From the very beginning Murray was drawn into the circles of government in Saskatchewan. His first invitation came in December 1909, when Walter Scott, the premier of Saskatchewan, decided to set up a commission of inquiry to look into the establishment of a publicly owned system of grain elevators and asked Murray to suggest someone to head it – preferably 'one thoroughly versed economist to act with the Grain Growers' representatives who will necessarily be appointed.'[5] The elevator issue had dragged on for more than a year, after the Saskatchewan Grain Growers' Association, in unison with farmers' organizations from Manitoba and Alberta, had begun to campaign for adoption of the Partridge Plan, calling for a system of publicly owned elevators on the prairies and named for E.A. Partridge of Sintaluta who first conceived it. The government of Manitoba responded immediately by going ahead with a government system of elevators. The government of Saskatchewan was more cautious, and Premier Scott turned to the device of a commission of inquiry. Murray submitted to Scott several names of possible commissioners, among them Robert Magill, professor of philosophy at Dalhousie University, whom Scott appointed to head the commission.[6]

The commission turned out to be an unqualified success. Its final report recommended the establishment of a cooperative system of elevators owned by the farmers and assisted by generous grants from the provincial government. It was accepted – much to the relief of Premier Scott – with amazing equanimity by the grain growers. Scott wrote to Magill, 'I want to say to you most heartily and sincerely that I never imagined it would be in the power of any person residing as far from Saskatchewan as is Nova Scotia to perform services for this Province of a kind to place me under such a debt of gratitude as you have done ... The simple truth is that you have saved us from the danger of being forced into a course pointing to dissatisfaction and possibly disaster.'[7] To President Murray, the masterly way Magill handled the complex elevator issue was proof of the good a university expert in social and economic matters could do in Saskatchewan.

I

The subject of economics, declared Murray in his *Report* for 1911–12, 'is of the very greatest importance to this province. Already we have had to face economic problems of the most intricate and difficult character, – problems of transportation, problems of an international market, tariff problems, problems of government ownership and management, financial problems involving provincial credit for private enterprises. Other problems no less troublesome will appear in the future. The University department of Economics should not only provide expert opinion, but should give the young men of the province who are preparing for public life an opportunity to obtain correct notions of economic principles and their application to present day problems. Similar departments in the larger State Universities, such as Wisconsin, have been of the greatest service to their States.'[8]

The chance came early in 1913, when Fred Engen, a Saskatoon district farmer whose land had been purchased for the university site, made a gift to the university of $5,000 for 'research in the pure sciences.' Murray, taking a broad view of pure science, resolved at once to use the money for a chair in economics. As he set out on a search for someone to fill the position, it became clear that he had in mind no ordinary academic. 'There are a number of very difficult economic problems emerging in this province,' he told John R. Commons, the Wisconsin economist, in a letter setting out his requirements. 'They relate to the handling of grain, to the control of public utilities, to rural credit, and later we expect the question of taxation to become acute.

The public interest in these questions is very keen. The farmers are organized into the Grain Growers' Association, and are very active and radical in their views. We wish a man who will sympathize with them, and will at the same time be independent in his views and discreet in his public utterance. The position has prospects of great public service, and we are anxious to secure a man whose influence will be lasting as well as strong.'[9]

Under the leadership of Richard T. Ely, the University of Wisconsin's economics faculty had grown by 1911 to be the largest in the United States, with six full professors and eleven assistants.[10] Commons, one of its most influential members, had helped to draft several pieces of reform legislation for the state and had attracted a band of bright students to his causes. He lost no time in presenting Murray with a candidate, Lewis Cecil Gray, a twenty-nine-year-old lecturer in agriculture and economics, 'the ablest of the young men who had been in our courses in recent years.' Murray immediately set to work to find out more about the candidate. He asked a Canadian he knew at Wisconsin to look into 'Dr. Gray's personal qualities and his success as a teacher; whether he is married or not, for it is much harder to transplant a woman to this western country than a man, and any information which you think would be of service to us.' 'I am so anxious,' wrote Murray, 'to get a man who is sure to become a leader in public affairs, and whose judgment would be perfectly reliable and sound.' His correspondent reported back that Gray was regarded as 'very pleasing personally with an attractive family,' an able researcher with some notable work on southern agriculture to his credit, and a 'good, though not brilliant' teacher; he was not considered likely to succeed in work outside the university, and he was 'not a mixer.'[11]

Murray, when he heard this last comment, began to have doubts, as he put it to President Van Hise, about Gray's 'ability to impress the people and to lead in the formation of public opinion.' He said that Dr Commons had spoken highly of the candidate but other reports were less encouraging, and reiterated that he was looking for someone 'who would undertake a considerable amount of investigation work as well as teaching, and should have some gifts for public speaking so that he could present his ideas to the people and mould public opinion.' He added: 'We look to Wisconsin University as the nearest approach to the ideal State University.' Van Hise replied by sending on several testimonials from other members of his faculty, including one from Henry C. Taylor, an economist of considerable reputation who became acknowledged as the father of the study of agricultural economics. Taylor hoped that Gray would eventually be hired at Wisconsin and had this to say of his abilities:

> Mr. Gray is thorough in his research work and unusually intelligent in sensing the value and interpreting historical materials. But while Mr. Gray has shown unusual ability as a research student using the inductive method, he is one of the strongest students of economic theory we have had at Wisconsin in many years. He has a philosophical type of mind. Straight thinking is one of his strong points, but while he has the logical type of mind, he also appreciates keenly the importance of seeking further facts and looking for new hypotheses. His ability to combine the inductive and deductive method makes him unusually strong in research work.
>
> Gray is as good a public speaker as is consistent with his tendency to fundamental thinking. I would not count him of the type which will succeed best purely as an extension man. On the other hand, he is capable of expressing his results forcibly, either in writing or orally. If the one thing they want in Canada is primarily a research man and one who can get out and meet people and make an occasional speech in connection with the work he is doing, Gray is first-class; if what they want is someone to be out making speeches a good share of the time with little opportunity for research work, Gray would not accept the position at any price.

Van Hise in his reply did not directly address Gray's virtues or lack of them, but he was not about to let Murray's special requirements pass by without further remark: 'I regard the fundamental qualities of scholarship and effective teaching, which of necessity imply fair ability as a speaker, as far more important than those more effusive qualities which are often associated with so called public speaking ability. Of course, public speaking of a high order of ability is, as you know, very rare and is extremely difficult to combine with the fundamentals above mentioned which are essential for the professor.'[12]

Murray, none the less, held stubbornly to his conviction that conditions in Saskatchewan called for this very combination of qualities, rare though they might be. In his next and final letter to Van Hise, he wrote: 'We do not want a man for Extension Work, and we had in mind primarily a man whose abilities and energies would be devoted to research, but owing to the semi-political character of his work, we feel it necessary that he should be able to defend his opinions on the public platform as well as in the public press. Our Grain Growers are very amenable to wise and capable leadership. One or two public addresses before their meetings would mean more than a ton of literature in directing their actions rightly.'[13]

From all that Murray could see, the ideal man for the position was Oscar Douglas Skelton, successor to Adam Shortt as the John A. Macdonald Professor of Political Science and Economics at Queen's University. Murray, in the midst of his correspondence with Wisconsin, made an earnest appeal to Skelton. Would he consider coming out to Saskatchewan to take up a research appointment? He could expect $2,700 to $2,800 in salary, $500 to $700 for books, the balance of the $5,000 Engen grant for travel and other expenses of investigation, and a teaching load of no more than four hours a week. Skelton politely declined. He liked Queen's, Kingston, the work with his students, most of his colleagues, and, though he did not say so, his proximity to affairs of national importance. However, his rejection of the offer did not prevent him from sending to Murray a continuous stream of advice on the men he should and should not consider for the position. In the course of the next two years, Skelton was to become Murray's most important source of information about prospective candidates in economics.[14]

Skelton began by congratulating the University of Saskatchewan 'on being the first Canadian university to realize what it owes the country in the way of scientific research into its economic as into its other problems.' But he in no way approved of Murray's attempt to find an economist in the United States. 'So far as Commons goes,' cautioned Skelton, 'I should not have very much faith in his judgment and should emphatically want to have the opinion endorsed by someone outside the University of Wisconsin, which has a reputation for log-rolling, before committing myself very far to this candidate.' Skelton proposed instead a Queen's graduate, Hector MacPherson, now at the Oregon Agricultural College, 'the only man whom I could recommend unreservedly for such a position.' Murray was impressed by what Skelton had to say of MacPherson and heard from several of his confidants who also spoke well of him. But when the candidate himself wrote to Murray and described his own merits in fulsome terms – there was, he said, 'not one man in five hundred who has had a better training and experience for the work' – Murray took no further interest in his application.[15]

Skelton next recommended a professor from his own department, William Walker Swanson, whom he described as 'a better man than your Wisconsin chap from what I heard recently of him.'[16] But Murray paid little attention to this suggestion – at least for the present. By now he was deep in negotiations with the Wisconsin candidate, whom he arranged to interview in Madison in May. Murray, after the meeting with Gray, immediately recommended his appointment as Engen Professor of Economics. Gray's salary was set at $2,500, and no mention was made of the generous expense allowance offered earlier to Skelton. Skelton, in the meantime, had come up with yet another name for Murray, this time of a person of vague acquaintance who was also said to be far better than the Wisconsin man, but by then it was too late.

II

Lewis Cecil Gray, the University of Saskatchewan's first full-time economist, was born in Liberty, Missouri, in 1881 and took his bachelor's and master's degrees at William Jewell College in his home state. He spent two years as principal of a high school, three more as a professor of history and economics at Oklahoma Agricultural and Mechanical College, and two summers of study at the University of Chicago before entering the University of Wisconsin's graduate school in 1908. For the next five years he studied and taught at Wisconsin. His teachers were Richard T. Ely, F.J. Turner, John R. Commons, and Henry C. Taylor, all of whom had a profound influence on Gray's development. Historian Richard S. Kirkendall has noted that Gray's work reflected several Wisconsin traits: 'the historical approach that was a characteristic of Wisconsin's institutional economists ... the Turner thesis; the Progressive philosophy that the government needed to attack social and economic problems, including problems in the use of natural resources; and the idea that intellectuals should devote themselves to affairs of importance outside of the academy, serving in government offices when necessary.'[17] It was at Wisconsin that Gray first took up the study of the development of agriculture on southern plantations before the Civil War, which became the subject of his doctoral project. He was awarded the PhD in 1911 and subsequently received financial support from the Carnegie Foundation to write a book on the subject. He hoped to have the work out of the way by the time he took up his position in Saskatoon, but in fact it would take him another twenty years to finish it.

Before Gray left Madison with his wife, Pearl, their three small children, and his wife's sister of high-school age, Murray thought it would be well to caution him about the possible difficulties of moving a family to Saskatoon without first securing proper accommodation. His own family, he said, had learned the hard way: 'We spent six weeks after our arrival in a hotel, and have not yet forgotten the experience.'[18] For the Gray family, it was not an easy move. And for Gray himself, the academic environment at Saskatchewan, with its tiny faculty and few courses, was far from what he had known before. Shortly after his arrival he wrote an article for the *Sheaf*, the student paper, in which he expressed something of the intellectual isolation he felt: 'It is no small privilege to organize the first department of economics in a great province like this one and in a new university whose future greatness it requires no prophetic vision to anticipate. It is no small responsibility to have the whole vast field of economics to oneself after coming from a university where every subdivision of the science is in charge of a specialist ... And with the feeling of unbounded opportunity there is no small sense of loneliness as if one were standing in the midst of a vast and fertile prairie which he might possess at will, but with no neighbors to cheer by their sympathy and to aid by their advice.' He went on to describe the approach he took to his discipline, which he said was 'both an applied science and a pure science.'

> As an applied science economics is close neighbor to applied politics and applied ethics. It seeks the amelioration of the conditions of human life in so far as they are dependent upon the production, distribution, and consumption of wealth ...
>
> Pure economics comprises the investigation of those relations of co-existence and sequence in economic life which are not only less obvious, but also more general in their application, than the phenomena which fall within the sphere of applied economics. The goal of pure economics is the determination of economic laws ...
>
> It is frequently assumed by the practical social reformer that pure economics is hopelessly abstract and unreal – that its generalizations are mere academic toys to amuse those who are of philosophical inclinations. There is sometimes justice in this view; but in general no conception could be more mistaken. Many a fine and superficial scheme of social reform has been wrecked through a failure to ground it upon the elementary truths of pure economics. Indeed, the fundamental difficulties of many modern economic problems are difficulties whose solution appears to depend largely upon future progress in economic theory.[19]

In designing a program of studies for the new economics department, of which he was the sole member, Gray drew upon the economics curriculum of the University of Wisconsin.[20] His first list of courses appeared in the *Calendar* for 1914–15 as follows:

> The Elements of Economics. An elementary consideration of general economic theory and of certain fields of applied economics, including monopolies and trusts, the labour problems and socialism. Ely, *Outlines of Economics*.
>
> Money, Banking and International Exchange. Scott, *Money and Banking*.
>
> (a) Corporation Finance. Meade, *Corporation Finance*. (b) Elements of Statistics. King, *Elements of Statistical Methods*.
>
> Agricultural Economics. A preliminary study of elementary economic principles applicable to agriculture, followed by a study of the principles of farm organization. Particular attention is given to the economics of rural organization, especially as involved in co-operation. Carver, *Principles of Rural Economics*; Taylor, *Agricultural Economics*.
>
> Public Finance. An introductory study of the general principles of public expenditures, revenues and indebtedness followed by a discussion of the concrete problems of Canadian finance. Plehn, *Introduction to Public Finance*.
>
> History of Economic Thought. Haney, *History of Economic Thought*.

There was, in addition, a 'seminary' devoted to special topics in economics and open only to 'advanced students of mature judgment.' The following year, two other courses were added:

> Rural Economics. A study of agricultural problems from the social point of view, designed to equip the student for intelligent leadership in rural life. Consideration is given to agricultural production, prices, distribution, tenancy, credit, marketing, co-operation and community life.
>
> (a) Socialism. Skelton, *Socialism: A Critical Analysis*. (b) Labour Problems. Carlton, *History and Problems of Organized Labour*.

Gray's schedule of courses remained as the core of the economics curriculum at the university for the next forty years. He also developed what was called the 'special' program in economics. While not as rigorous as the honours requirements introduced more than twenty years later, the special program called for more specialization than did the usual pass program. It obliged a student to complete five courses in economics and a sixth in either economics or political science, write a thesis on an approved subject, and pass an examination on one of the following topics: economic theory; industrial evolution; problems in money and banking; business organization; railway problems and public utilities; the trust movement; agricultural economics and rural organization; public finance; international exchange and international commercial policies; the labour movement and socialism.[21]

Gray started out in the fall of 1913 by teaching two courses, one in elementary economics to 28 students and another in money and banking to 12 students. The next year he gave the same two courses and added a third in agricultural economics. Registration in his economics courses grew quickly, from a total of 40 students in 1913 to 104 the following year, and the future of his department began to look rosy. As Gray looked forward to expansion, he suggested to the president, in the spring of his second year, that another instructor should be hired to share the work of the department.[22] But his plans turned out to be premature. Gray spent a good part of the summer of 1915 in Madison recovering from major surgery and never returned to teach at the university. He sent word of his resignation by telegram late in August: 'am offered professorship peabody college nashville ... salary three thousand dollars and valuable perquisites.'[23] It was an attractive offer – a much larger salary, a lighter work load, and the opportunity to be nearer the research materials he needed for his studies on southern agriculture.

III

Gray had worked to fit in at Saskatchewan, even trying his hand at curling, the favourite winter sport of President Murray and other members of the staff. He was a sensitive, thoughtful man with an attractive young family and obvious intellectual qualities. He was a good teacher who had won the respect of his colleagues and many of the townspeople alike. On campus, he had started up an Economics Club and took an active role in the Debating Club, and it would be some time before the department would again have on its staff someone as successful in awakening the students' curiosity about current economic problems. The *Sheaf* printed an article written by Gray on 'The High Cost of Living' and also reported on three lectures he gave to the university chapter of the Young Women's Christian Association:

> In his first lecture on the subject of 'Poverty,' Dr. Gray opened up a new avenue of thought to us. The conditions in which the industrous poor of Europe live are to us almost unbelievable. For his second lecture Dr. Gray took the subject of 'The Social Consciousness of Woman' – a lecture which contained material for a great deal of sober reflection. On the evening of March 30th, Dr. Gray spoke on 'The Social Mission of Woman.' In this he sought to correlate his previous lectures. It is especially a woman's sphere, Dr. Gray believes, to elevate the tone of the existing social consciousness. This improvement can find its roots only in religion which involves three especially important factors, viz: belief in a Higher Power, selflessness (its correlate sympathy), and faith. With this dynamic it is woman's privilege to set a higher standard of life. The girls are very grateful to Dr. Gray for his interesting and helpful addresses.[24]

When Gray went to Nashville, he at first missed the collegial ties he had known in Saskatoon. He wrote to Murray that 'in the first loneliness that one feels in a new place, I find myself longing for Saskatoon and thinking of it as *home*.' And Murray wrote kindly that 'I do not know what the curling club will be without you.'[25] There is no doubt that Murray genuinely liked the shy American, and in his official report of the resignation he spoke highly of Gray's contribution to the university and his popularity with the students. Nevertheless, he could not have been altogether surprised to see him go. It was obviously the wrong environment for Gray. His wife had difficulty adjusting to the unfamiliar surroundings and harsh climate, and Gray himself felt cut off from the intellectual supports he had known before.[26] To make matters worse, Gray suffered from poor health during much of the time he spent in Saskatoon, particularly in his second year. 'I realize that you and the University Governors showed great forbearance during these periods of illness,'[27] he told Murray. Poor health was no doubt part of the reason for his not getting out among the farmers as much as Murray had hoped. There is only one recorded instance of Gray's appearing before the Saskatchewan Grain Growers' Association. In a talk he gave in the spring of 1915 to the Warman Local of the association, Gray chose as his theme the dangers of utopianism and overambitious undertakings on the part of the farmers' movement. While he gave the farmers credit for their success in marketing standard, bulky commodities through local cooperatives, he warned them to be wary of expansion into other lines of retailing where gains would be smaller. 'The immature and unscientific proposals that are given serious consideration from time to time show clearly that the limitations of the farmers' movement are not sufficiently appreciated,' he said. 'The pathway of social progress is strewn with the wrecks of farmers' organizations, and agrarian history in America has been a long record of unintelligent leadership and irrational enthusiasms.'

Unlike Edmund Oliver, who had spoken of 'the middlemen who fatten in our midst,' Gray described the farmers' long-standing quarrel with the middleman as 'characteristically a blind unintelligent hostility rather than a result of careful analysis of the weak points in the system of marketing and credit.' He urged the farmers to organize carefully on a foundation of strong local groups rather than 'a vast centralized system with local ramifications' and to concentrate their attention more on 'the improvement of the technical methods and the business methods of the average farmer' than on 'the mechanism of marketing and credit ... For every dollar to be saved by the improvement of this mechanism, there are ten dollars to be saved by improving the methods of the individual farmer on his own farm.' According to the farm paper which reported on the meeting, the farmer audience seemed nonplussed at Gray's remarks, especially at his apparent lack of sympathy for their cause. Several of those who commented on his speech afterwards were critical of the way he had described their organization. There was no danger, said one, of the farmers' movement in Saskatchewan becoming as overextended as Gray had described, while another declared that the farmers had not shown blind hostility towards the middleman: 'We have only opposed the superfluous unnecessary middleman.'[28]

Gray had started out at Saskatchewan with the intention of carrying out research on economic problems in Saskatchewan. Before his arrival in Saskatoon, he wrote to Murray: 'I shall try to give advice concerning any problem that may now be uppermost. However, prior to careful investigation, and especially in my ignorance of Canadian conditions, any opinion I could express would necessarily be very general, and, I think, very conservative. I agree with you that investigation should come first, if possible. That is the "Wisconsin Idea."'[29] As these words of his suggest, Gray was inclined to be thoughtful, methodical, and painstaking in his approach to research. His history of southern agriculture proved that his method could produce excellent results – in time. He was not a man to be hurried.

Soon after he came to Saskatchewan, he started an investigation of the provincial economy with a study of the uses and costs of farm machinery. He canvassed farm machinery companies and farmers on the question and then began the work of collating the data with the intention of publishing the results. After he resigned his position at Saskatchewan, Gray wrote to Murray that though the investigations of a royal commission on farm machinery had rendered his own study less important than originally, he still intended to finish it, and Murray planned to have it printed as a university bulletin. The two continued to correspond on the matter for most of a year. In November 1915 Gray wrote to apologize for the delay: his new work had left him with no time for research; he would send the manuscript 'as soon as possible.' But the correspondence eventually petered out with no sign of the promised manuscript. The next Murray heard from Gray was in March 1933, when he received a copy of Gray's history of southern agriculture. Gray, who duly acknowledged the University of Saskatchewan in the preface to the book, sent along a note which read: 'As you may recall, when I was connected with your faculty I spent a good deal of my spare time on this task.'[30]

Gray had also made plans for a 'rural social survey' to be conducted by some twelve to fifteen students he had organized into a Social Problems Club. During the summer of 1915 the students were to collect data from various farm families to show, among other things, the extent to which they had developed 'a community consciousness.' Gray described the venture in some detail in an article written for the *Sheaf*. 'Such a study,' he said, 'should present not only a picture of the external features of the community life, – geographic, demographic, ethnographic, institutional, – but also a subtle appreciation of the social psychology of the community ... If ... the investigation is conscientiously carried out, we should be in possession of twelve or fifteen pictures of the external social life and organization of some ten or fifteen representative Saskatchewan rural communities. When the facts are accurately depicted on township maps, it should be easier for us all to visualize the conditions of rural life in the Canadian West as a starting point for future investigations.'[31] When Gray did not return to the university in the fall, this project, too, fell by the wayside.

IV

What Murray could not know was that in Gray he lost an economist of an uncommonly innovative bent.[32] In 1914, while at Saskatchewan, Gray published an article, 'Rent under the Assumption of Exhaustibility,' in the *Quarterly Journal of Economics*, which had carried another (and related) article of his, 'The Economic Possibilities of Conservation,' the year before. The worth of the two papers came to be recognized only with the development of modern resource economics some fifty years later.[33] The article bearing his Saskatchewan affiliation was cited in fifty-six journal articles between 1966 and 1996.[34] In 1967, it was reprinted in *Extractive Resources and Taxation*, along with papers presented at a symposium on the economics of extractive resources. The editor, Mason Gaffney, concluded that 'Gray manages in this little work to foreshadow many of the issues of this conference, to build an analytical foundation consistent with the most polished ones at the symposium, to link current with classical thinking, and to lead us toward policy conclusions consistent with what most conferees reached by more sophisticated means.'[35] Anthony Scott refers to Gray as the 'pioneer economist in the conservation field.'[36]

Gray's next major publication, apart from a textbook on agricultural economics he wrote in 1924, was his *History of Agriculture in the Southern United States to 1860*, a book of 1,086 pages, published in 1933. The book was very well received, but once again a work of Gray's had to bide its time before its full significance was to be appreciated. In 1958, the publication of an article by Alfred H. Conrad and John R. Meyer, 'The Economics of Slavery in the Ante-Bellum South,' prompted a scholarly exchange in the course of which Gray's hypotheses and data came under close scrutiny.[37] In 1967, in a historiographical survey, Gray's work was said to be 'beyond question, the greatest single contribution to antebellum southern history,'[38] and it was to figure prominently in the controversial book *Time on the Cross* by Robert W. Fogel and Stanley L. Engerman, which came out in 1974.[39] Gray emerged from this re-examination of his work as a scholar whose facts were rarely in dispute and whose judgment was usually sound, and as a pioneer in the use of statistics in the interpretation of historical events.

After leaving Saskatchewan, Gray taught for five years at the George Peabody College for Teachers in Nashville. Though he continued to write articles for scholarly journals, he spent the remainder of his career not in academic life but in the United States civil service where he became a leading figure in the New Deal administration. In 1919 he joined the Department of Agriculture as head of the newly created Division of Land Economics and in 1937 was appointed assistant chief in the Bureau of Agricultural Economics. He helped to shape agricultural policies and was responsible for directing a vast program of land reclamation in which large numbers of farmers were moved from submarginal lands to areas of greater productivity. His interventions, which signalled an abrupt end to the back-to-the-land movement in the United States, were based on his fundamental belief in the principles of sound economic analysis and the important role of social science in the framing of agricultural policies. He was dismayed by traditional expansionist policies which had led to an inefficient use of lands and maintained a condition of hopeless poverty for those who lived on them. 'Gray was convinced that the nation had too much farm land and too many farmers,' wrote Richard S. Kirkendall. 'Above all, he hoped to place land policy on a scientific basis involving efficiency and democracy as well as profit in its aims. In short, this "New Deal" effort to break with the past had one of its roots in the rise of a scientific point of view in agricultural circles.'[40] His former teacher, Henry C. Taylor, described him as 'a brilliant scholar and a man of action' who gave 'a vision, an inspiration, and a dynamic to the work in land economics.'[41] Paul W. Gates, a historian who knew him well, remembered Gray as 'a lovable, gentle, thoughtful man who seemed to belong more in the library than in charge of the planning of a great program of land retirement.'[42] In 1940 Gray suffered a cerebral haemorrhage that forced an end to his active career. He died in 1952 at his home near Raleigh, North Carolina, with much of his reputation as an economist still to be made.

3

An Orthodox Economist

'I am possibly more anxious about the chair in Economics than any other one, because of the great opportunities there are for the right kind of man,' President Murray wrote to O.D. Skelton in September of 1915. 'I think the opportunities are greater in the West than anywhere else, and the chances of failure are greater. The outside duties of the Professor of Economics in this country may become so important that the ordinary academic man may fall far short of requirements.'[1] His new professor, he had decided, would have to be better acquainted with western Canadian conditions than the last. Again Murray asked: would he, Skelton, come out to investigate some of Saskatchewan's special problems, perhaps for a year? Again, the answer was no. Skelton was not about to leave his position at Queen's University, at least not for one in the West. But he quickly assured Murray that he had suffered no great loss in Gray and 'should have no trouble replacing him with a better man.'[2] Murray was now ready to heed Skelton's advice. 'Personally,' he told Skelton, 'I value your opinion very highly and would take your judgment of the professional qualities of the men before that of any other economist that I know.'[3]

It was not surprising that Murray, given his current views on what an economist at Saskatchewan should do, would turn to Queen's. Although the University of Toronto had an established program in economics, its faculty at the beginning showed no special desire to make of economics something peculiarly Canadian. 'Toronto,' writes K.W. Taylor, 'relied heavily on imports from the United Kingdom to supply its teaching staff, and while some of these ... became thoroughly Canadian in their outlook and interests, the Toronto production of studies directly related to the Canadian scene, prior to the middle 1920's, was

quite small. Queen's, on the other hand, under the leadership first of
Adam Shortt and later of O.D. Skelton, was a thoroughly Canadian
department eagerly investigating Canadian development and Canadian problems.'[4] Murray, in any event, had his own reasons for not
seeking advice from Toronto's head economist, James Mavor. Mavor
had visited Saskatoon in 1904 as part of a western tour to study its
wheat-growing potential, but his sympathies towards the West were
regarded by Murray with some suspicion. Mavor was vehemently
against government ownership and intrusions into economic activity;
when he ventured to suggest to Murray that the proposals of the
Saskatchewan Commission on Agricultural Credit were having 'a very
bad effect upon the credit of the province,' Murray rose swiftly to the
defence of the western farmer. 'Our people,' he replied, 'have been
reckless in many things, and they have been exploited by interests outside the province. Already one notices a decided improvement in the
caution of the people, and a general feeling that the time has arrived
when they must cultivate more self reliance. The demand for free
wheat and the resistance offered by the milling and transportation
interests, supported by other eastern interests, is only one illustration
of the way things work out against the western farmer. He is watching
these matters, and the day of reckoning is to come.'[5]

'I think the man we want,' began one of Murray's entreaties to Skelton, 'must have not only good ability and excellent common sense, but
he must have a very pronounced sympathy with the underdog in the
tussle. In fact I would like a man who may be described as a "big
human," thoroughly democratic in spirit.' Once more, Skelton recommended his second in command at Queen's, William Walker Swanson.
Swanson had 'a good academic training, is a fluent speaker, an industrious investigator and gets on very well with our students.' Moreover,
Swanson was more than willing to move. His opportunities for
advancement at Queen's, with Skelton, a person of his own age, in the
chair, were limited. Skelton urged Murray to act quickly – the Queen's
department could 'make shift, possibly' and he did not want to stand
in the way of Swanson's promotion. On 2 September, he sent Murray a
telegram: 'doubt whether you can do better next year than this believe
Swanson best man in sight.' This was followed a few days later by a
letter in which he mocked Murray's overweening desire for the perfect
academic:

Swanson has his faults, like most of the rest of us, but Perfect Paragons of
Professors are scarce. On his first appointment, he was somewhat trou-

bled with swelled head, but experience has cured him of that common complaint. As for the 'human sympathy' side, while he's not of the crusader or missionary type, he has sound democratic sympathies, both for the individual and for the man ... and in the favouring atmosphere of Saskatchewan should develop the 'human sympathy' side as well as any man ... I can only say, as a friend of Saskatchewan, that I do not see that you can do better than take Swanson. He's not perfect, but are the professors of economics at Manitoba, Toronto, McGill, New Brunswick or even Queen's perfect? Compared with any of these institutions, you would have nothing to regret, I believe, if you took Swanson, and it's with actual occupants of other chairs & not with your Presidential Platonic Ideal of the Perfect Professor (for $2500), you should compare the candidates.[6]

Nevertheless, Murray refused to be hurried. 'It is probable,' he said, 'that Dr. Swanson falls no farther short than the occupants of similar chairs in Canada,' but he was not prepared to make a decision just yet. There were still two others in the department at Queen's for Murray to consider: William Clifford Clark and Humfrey Michell. Clark, who had a bachelor's degree from Queen's and three years of graduate study at Harvard, was younger than Swanson by ten years and less experienced. Nevertheless, Murray at first was far more interested in Clark. In a telegram to Skelton after Gray resigned, he was ready to make Clark an offer: 'Wire me fully about Clark. Greatly attracted by reports of him and his work. Is he available for us this year? Possibly Governors would wish to make conditional appointment if Clark's teaching experience has been slight.' But Skelton stopped Murray from further pursuit. Clark, said Skelton, had shown signs of brilliance as a student, but 'at our last interviews it seemed to me he had stopped growing and lacked somewhat in personality.' Swanson was less of a risk, 'a more practical and executive type than Clark.' As for Humfrey Michell, he was 'a rather queer beggar in some ways' and would not, in any case, consider anything but a permanent appointment; besides, both he and his wife disliked the West. Neither Clark nor Michell bothered to correspond directly with Murray. Swanson, on the other hand, had actively sought the appointment since 1913 with letters, telegrams, supporting documents, and letters of reference. As was his way, Murray took all such testimonials advisedly. 'I am not sure that Swanson is the man we want unless he has changed in the past two years, though he may be the best available,' he told Skelton. 'I have a feeling that Swanson's superiority is due to his longer experience and age, that in the matter of ability and some other qualities he is not superior to Clark or to some others.'[7]

Were there no others to choose from? Hardly any, it would seem, and none who held any appeal for Murray. Those few Canadians who were taking graduate studies in economics or had recently graduated were nearly all off to war. Murray made inquiries of his friends at other Canadian universities, but they had little to offer him. President Falconer of Toronto said only: 'I suppose you would not like to take Swanson of Queen's. He was anxious to come to us.'[8] Gray, when he resigned, had suggested two names: James A. Estey at Purdue, formerly a lecturer at Dalhousie and a graduate of Wisconsin, and Duncan MacGibbon, who was teaching at Brandon. The first man Murray ignored altogether; MacGibbon he had known before. MacGibbon had written earlier to Murray and wrote again when he heard of the opening. He was thirty-three, a Quebec-born former newspaperman with a BA and MA from McMaster, Toronto's Baptist college, where Edmund Oliver had been one of his teachers. He was well regarded at the University of Chicago, where he had lately received the PhD with great distinction and won the Marx, Shaffner and Hart Award. But Murray had come to the conclusion, as he told Skelton, that MacGibbon, though 'in many ways a very attractive fellow,' was 'not ... a man of first class ability.'[9] Skelton declined to comment.

Murray's ability to judge candidates was astute but not infallible. He was usually to be found on the side of candidates with youth and promise who were not yet set in their ways. In this instance, he was hampered by the slow development of Canadian economic studies and a deficiency of candidates with an interest in such studies. He was also led astray by his own fierce empathy for the plight of the farmers. His assessment of the good an economist could do in Saskatchewan, which led him to exaggerate the importance of assertiveness and the ability to speak in public and to underestimate other qualities he ordinarily valued in an academic, was probably at the root of his swift rejection of MacGibbon's application and his lack of persistence in pursuing Clark. Judging from their later careers, both men were good prospects. It is probably true that Clark could not have been persuaded to move West. He did not stay long in academic life and later followed Skelton to Ottawa where he served as deputy minister of finance from 1932 to 1952. MacGibbon, on the other hand, would have liked the appointment. He was, in fact, one of the few economists of his day who preferred to work in the West and who had a genuine interest in its problems. He was to be the author of one of the first studies of the prairie economy, *The Canadian Grain Trade* (1930), instrumental in the resuscitation of the Canadian Political Science Association in 1929 and the establishment of its journal, president of the association in 1935, and later chairman of the Board of Grain Commissioners for Canada. During the 1920s, after MacGibbon had become head of the Department of Political Economy at Alberta, Murray had occasion more than once to ask his advice, which turned out to be good, and it may even have crossed his mind that he had been too hasty in passing over MacGibbon in 1915.

As the time for fall registration was drawing near, Murray decided to take on two young law graduates, J. Wilfred Estey and Andrew S. Sibbald, to carry on the teaching of economics for the coming session. At this point, the rapid exchange of letters and telegrams between Skelton and Murray came to a close, and there the matter rested. In the following summer, when the time of appointments rolled by once again without any new prospects having come to his notice, Murray made up his mind to go with 'experience and age.' On 6 July 1916, several days past the starting date of university contracts, he wrote to Swanson to offer him an appointment as professor of economics. The offer was promptly accepted. Murray's last communication to Swanson, before the latter left for the West, suggests that his major concern was that his second economist should not repeat the mistakes of the first: 'One thing of great importance here is that you should get into a thorough sympathy and understanding of the Saskatchewan people's attitude toward economic problems. If they are wrong in their opinions there is only one way to correct it and that is to secure their confidence; if they are right they will resent dictation very strongly. Many of them for years have been fighting the powers that be in finance and transportation and they are very strong in their feelings.'[10]

In Saskatoon, Swanson settled into a two-storey house at 106 Eighth Street with his wife, Grace, and two, soon to be three, daughters. He became the second head of the Department of Economics and its only member. His starting salary was set at $2,500. There were no other emoluments. The Engen research professorship had since passed to the chemistry department and was soon to be discontinued altogether because of a reversal in the fortunes of its donor. The loss of the Engen money was one more sign of the deepening gloom from war and recession which threatened the roseate promise of the university's beginning.

I

William Walker Swanson was born on 15 December 1879 in Thurse, Scotland, and as a child moved with his family to Canada. He took his high school education in Oshawa, Ontario. One of his most cherished memories was of a Greek Testament his mother had given him when he was in high school. From this he taught himself to read Greek. 'For two years in a rural village it was my chief companion ... ' he recalled. 'I read most of it before I entered Queen's and was astonished to find that the boys in theology there had much finer editions, with abundant notes and glossaries ... however: I knew the *Greek* and the larger part of them in John Macnaughton's class only knew the *notes*.'[11] For his major course of study he chose economics, taught then by Adam Shortt, who inspired in Swanson, as in his other students, a large measure of affection and respect. In 1905, he left Queen's with a BA and MA in economics and went on to the University of Chicago, where he had been awarded a fellowship for the study of economics. There he joined O.D. Skelton, a Queen's graduate in classics who had turned to the study of economics and political science.

Swanson spent three years at Chicago and found life there stimulating and instructive. He was active in the Political Economy Club, worked for the university's *Journal of Political Economy*, and played a little tennis with Skelton. In his last year, he taught a course in the financial and tariff history of the United States. In a series of long letters to Adam Shortt, Swanson recorded his impressions of the professors he encountered: 'I find that Adam Smith is yet very much in esteem with the Chicago Economists; they seem to lay more stress upon him than upon Mill.' 'Mr. Veblen is both interesting and thorough. He has a peculiar streak of humor in him; and enjoys a laugh as well as anybody, altho' he looks grave and taciturn.' J.L. Laughlin, who had established the Chicago department before the turn of the century, 'is a bright, clear-headed Scotchman; who gives you free use of your own views but ends in obliterating them with his own!'[12] Laughlin gave Swanson a private seminar on banking and supervised his doctoral thesis, 'The Establishment of the National Banking System,' of which a chapter was subsequently published in the *Journal of Political Economy* under the title 'The Crisis of 1860 and the First Issue of Clearing-House Certificates' (1908). The thesis itself was published in 1910, first as a pamphlet by the University of Chicago Press and then in hard cover by the Jackson Press in Kingston, and drew the following notice in the inaugural issue of the *American Economic Review*: 'the general conclusion is that the research is thorough and practically exhaustive; that the writer's statements are fortified with abundant references; that the whole performance is not only creditable, but that we have here a valuable contribution to the literature of the subject.'[13]

In 1908, the year he received his PhD degree, Swanson looked hopefully towards Queen's, where Shortt, who was rumoured to be leaving for Ottawa, had promised him a place. When no news came from Queen's, Swanson accepted the offer of an instructorship at the University of Washington. He was at home in Oshawa preparing to leave for Seattle when he received a telegram from Skelton, who had joined the Queen's department the year before, reporting on Shortt's appointment to the Civil Service Commission of Canada. Skelton was promoted to the John A. Macdonald Chair of Political Science and Economics and Swanson was asked to fill the vacancy Skelton's appointment had created. Quickly passing on his apologies to the University of Washington, he made for Kingston instead. For the next eight years Skelton and Swanson were the department's only senior members, with Skelton taking the politics side of the teaching duties and Swanson the economics.

Swanson was active in research and writing in his years at Queen's.[14] The Queen's course in banking, instituted in 1914 at the behest of the Canadian Bankers' Association and conducted by correspondence across the country, was prepared by Skelton and Swanson together and comprised more than eight hundred pages of text.[15] Swanson taught the first course in the financial history of Canada to be given at a Canadian university.[16] He also prepared two studies, *Canadian Bank Inspection* (1912) and *The Financial Power of the Empire* (1915), which were published as Queen's *Bulletins*, an important outlet for publication of Canadian studies before the regular appearance of a Canadian professional journal of economics. He had two articles in the *American Economic Review*, 'The Revision of the Canadian Bank Act' (1913) and 'Present Problems in Canadian Banking' (1914), and a note on 'Money, Prices, Credit and Banking' (1913). In addition, he wrote frequently for the *Queen's Quarterly*, the *Journal of the Canadian Bankers' Association*, the *Monetary Times of Canada*, and two popular reviews of the day, the *Canadian Magazine* and the *Canadian Courier*. In 1914 he revised a text on money and banking which had been written earlier for correspondence school students in the United States by Earl Dean Howard of Northwestern University. Howard's original work had provoked an unflattering review from the economist Wesley Claire Mitchell, who, in what he termed 'this ill-considered venture,' detected 'gross carelessness,' 'slovenly English,' and 'misstatement of facts,' in addition to 'many other offenses against the English tongue.'[17] Swanson's revision was one of eighteen texts issued for the Canadian market under the general title *Modern Business*. Besides correcting the errors cited by Mitchell, Swanson performed a neat bit of surgery on the original work by inserting a piece on the Canadian monetary system in place of a chapter on bimetallism and adding about one hundred pages on Canadian banking at the end, an operation which allowed the pagination of the book and the bulk of Howard's writing to remain unchanged.

Swanson's other projects included a study of inland water transportation for the Montreal Harbour Commission and a summer's work for the Ontario Royal Commission on Unemployment. He also worked for a time on the *Journal of Commerce*, edited by the Hon. W.S. Fielding, minister of finance, who offered to Murray a brisk comment on Swanson's social views: 'Without being a Radical, he is I believe sufficiently progressive to place him in sympathy with reasonable liberal sentiment. More than that I do not suppose you would desire.'[18]

II

On first coming to Saskatchewan, Swanson had a flurry of publications, mostly projects undertaken while he was still at Queen's. In 1917 he reviewed the report of the Royal Commission on Transportation for the *American Economic Review* and had brief articles published in the *Journal of the Canadian Bankers' Association* and the *Journal of Commerce*. In that year, too, he wrote a piece on Ukrainian immigration for the *Canadian Courier*, which was advertised as the first of a series by the Saskatchewan professor who 'promised to study humanity out west for our benefit.'[19] But no other articles by Swanson appeared in the *Courier*, nor, for the next six years, with the exception of brief notes in the *Monetary Times Annual* in 1918 and 1920, in any other publication. Murray may have been disappointed at the lack of publication by his new professor of economics, but his main concern lay elsewhere – in Swanson's ability to earn the confidence and respect of the farmers and their leaders.

The annual conventions of the Saskatchewan Grain Growers' Association were large and important affairs. More than a thousand farmer delegates and several hundred observers would be in attendance, while the remainder of the population gravely followed the proceedings through the daily press and farmers' weeklies. Swanson appeared twice on the convention platform. In his inaugural year at the university, he gave a talk to the closing banquet of the 1917 convention on the subject of education, which was described by the *Saskatoon Daily Star* as 'full of sound sense and humourous twists.'[20] In the following year, he was featured as the main speaker at an evening session. His address, entitled 'The Economic Factors Affecting Western Agriculture,' began with an exposition of the medieval concept of the just price and moved forward to the present era, which he held to be characterized by huge trusts and cartels, paper money of no worth, and ruinous national debt. The farmers, caught in the midst of such conditions, not of their own making, 'must accept a price for their biggest cash crop on a basis determined by mutual agreement – an agreement which concerns itself with the interests of the consumer as well as of the producer – while they are obliged to purchase farm machinery and all kinds of necessary supplies at prices determined by manufacturers and other producers alone.' At the end, the farmer audience was left in no doubt of the professor's sympathies as he called for a reform of policies relating to agriculture: 'It is of imperative importance,' he said, 'that a premium be placed upon agriculture, that all economic disabilities under which it, at present, labours be removed, that foreign markets and shipping and transportation connections be organized in the interests of farming; and that, above all, agriculture be furnished with abundant, and cheap capital for long periods. In a word, it is the time to consider the farmer both as producer and borrower, as well as the interests of the lending class.'[21]

So far so good; but when events in the 1920s and 1930s divided economists into two camps – on the one side, reformers, on the other side, conservative or 'orthodox' economists – there was no question at all about which camp Swanson belonged to. Swanson made known in the early 1920s his vehement opposition to the creation of a central bank in Canada, and when the matter came to decision in the 1930s, it was as a self-declared orthodox economist that he renewed his opposition, to the great irritation of the farm leadership in the West. Murray, for his part, seemed to draw back from the advocacy role he had once espoused for the department and no longer expected that its members should lead and mould public opinion. He became, as time went by, more and more fastidious about keeping the university apart from politics or indeed from identification with any particular interest group. He also drew back from his emphasis on agriculture at the university. Where once he had spoken of the College of Agriculture as 'the sheet anchor of the university,' he chose a new metaphor in his report for 1917–18, according to which the college was 'thumb' to the university's hand:

> In our endeavors to emphasize the importance of one phase of University work, we may appear to ignore or fail to appreciate the value of the other branches. For example, we have in the past said so much about Agriculture that not a few people have come to believe that the University does nothing else, values nothing else. In reality, the College of Arts and Science must always be the centre of the University, be the palm of the hand whose fingers are the professional schools. Agriculture may in utility rival the thumb; but the thumb apart from the hand is lifeless. So now, in our discussions of the importance of Science and Scientific Research, we must not be understood as being neglectful of or indifferent to the Humanities. In emphasizing the utility of scientific discovery there is no intention to imply that other subjects have no utility.[22]

In the spring of 1923 Swanson was called before the House of Commons Select Standing Committee on Banking and Commerce. He was the only Canadian economist besides Adam Shortt to be summoned, a sign of his standing in Canada as a financial expert, no doubt because of his early research on the banking system. In his testimony Swanson revealed himself as a staunch upholder of classical economic doctrines, so much so, in fact, that William Irvine, the labour MP from Calgary and a member of the committee, interrupted him at one point to say there was little point in questioning him further. 'The professor,' he said, 'has presented such orthodox views on this matter that it is not worthwhile. Perhaps it would be superfluous for me to have him reiterate what we have heard one hundred times already.'[23] Allowed to continue, Swanson put forth his case so emphatically that, in Irving Brecher's account of monetary thought in Canada, he is singled out for having 'the most outspoken – if not the most clearly formulated – views among the Canadian economists' on the matters being considered by the committee.[24] Swanson declared himself firmly in favour of the gold standard and against alterations in the credit system, except for the provision of intermediate credit for farmers, a matter which he suspected was outside the scope of the committee in any case. World

conditions, not the banking system, accounted for the recession of
1921. He warned that a managed currency or government regulation of
credit to prevent price fluctuations could be 'a very dangerous thing.'
It should be left to bankers to manage credit so that loans were made
for productive purposes only. 'What we need to do,' he said, 'is to
check speculative factors, the boom conditions, where profits are taken
without real service being given to the community or to the nation – in
other words, that the banks and financial institutions shall loan to the
producers and not to gamblers.' On the consumption side, the problem
was due to 'a great deal of luxury spending to-day that cannot be justified.' He went on to explain that 'though a great many people are com-
plaining about poverty they are suffering from what I would call
psychic poverty; that is, they cannot get those things that they got during the war. There are a great many people operating automobiles and
the like, and talking about poverty.' Improvements would only come
from such things as 'an increase in population, a reduction in the burden that is being carried by the farming interests, a development of our
resources.' The real solution, however, lay in individual effort: 'we will
find economic salvation only by working harder.'[25]

Swanson's ideas on the importance of a sound and stable medium of
exchange based on gold were further expounded in 'Credit and Expansion,' an article written for the *Saskatchewan Farmer*, in which he said
that historical evidence proved 'that paper money which bears no relation to gold, and is not payable on demand, can produce nothing
except the illusion of prosperity.' According to his analysis, the abandonment of the gold standard by some countries already had led to
chaos in marketing and falling prices; the farmers, as a result, had to
suffer a poorer standard of living and heavier financial obligations. He
recommended that credit be extended to farmers using new methods –
'provided such operations are free from paternalism and political control' – but offered no specific proposals.[26]

Swanson by this time had settled into the community as a prominent
citizen. His name appeared with increasing frequency in the local
press, and he was in constant demand as a speaker. He served on the
provincial transportation council, the Saskatoon Public School Board,
the board of St Andrew's College, and a board of arbitration constituted to determine milk prices in Saskatoon. In 1927 he was chairman
of the Saskatchewan Royal Commission on Overseas Livestock Marketing, which toured extensively through Europe. Swanson made a
special excursion to Russia, Lithuania, and Latvia, before returning to

Saskatchewan to complete a detailed 425-page report for submission to the government.

III

Swanson did not set out to make any major changes to the economics curriculum devised by Lewis Gray. At first, he introduced only one new course, rail and water transportation, added his own revision of the Earl Howard book to the money and banking course, and changed the introductory text from the one by the Wisconsin economist Richard Ely to *Principles of Economics* by the Harvard economist F.W. Taussig. He usually taught four classes each year, sometimes five, and often conducted a summer session as well. In addition to his heavy schedule of teaching, the administrative burdens of the department fell on his shoulders. Not until after his retirement did the department have a secretary all to itself. As for a departmental telephone, such a luxury was unheard of in his day. He never took a full year's leave from the university until it was forced on him by illness. Otherwise, he was absent from his teaching only when he was called away on government business; after one such mission, he handed over to the university bursar from his contract earnings enough to cover any expenses incurred while he was gone.[27] Students looked upon him as a good lecturer and teacher, perhaps a little on the stern side, but no less respected for that. Those who joined him later as colleagues in the department were not quite so respectful. They were younger, eager for change, imbued with some of the more current notions in economics, and doubtful about Swanson's claims to scholarship. He, on the other hand, was solidly wedded to the classical view of economics, and insistent on strict protocol and observance of the academic hierarchy. He expected from his junior colleagues the same fidelity that he paid to his own superiors.

Enrolments at the university, which had slipped during the rush of enlistments for military service, began again to climb near the end of the war when some of the veterans returned home. In the spring of 1918, after he had completed two years of teaching at the university, Swanson suggested to the president the hiring of additional staff. In 1919 some relief came in the person of J. Courtland Elliott, a graduate of Queen's, who was appointed a temporary instructor and paid $125 a month for eight months. During the academic year 1919–20, eight courses were given: introductory economics (now divided into two sections with a total registration of 98 students), rail and water transportation, public finance, agricultural economics, socialism and labour problems, a seminar in the history of economic thought, and an additional evening class in introductory economics. The evening class was part of a new program introduced by the university and turned out to be a popular innovation with the townspeople. 'All types were registered,' reported Swanson, 'from the University graduate to the Mechanic, and the keenest interest was shown by one and all.'[28] At the end of the term, Elliott left Saskatoon to study in Paris. When Elliott wrote to President Murray in 1922 to see if he could return to the university, he was told that no assistants were being hired. 'As you know,' replied Murray, 'financial conditions in Canada ... have been very bad this year, and we are curtailing rather than expanding, in all our departments.'[29]

In the meantime, Murray decided to add a new permanent member to the economics department, and this time canvassed in Great Britain for a suitable candidate. In the light of recent events in Russia, he was especially concerned to find someone with no tendencies to extreme social and political views. The man he settled on was William A. Carrothers, a thirty-two-year-old Irishman known as Pat, who was recommended as 'a man of strong character and attractive personality who could be trusted to perform with the utmost conscientiousness any duties which he may undertake.'[30] His supervisor, J. Shield Nicholson, assured Murray that he had talked with Carrothers and found his attitudes on social and political questions to be much like his own. They had agreed, reported Nicholson, 'that especially in such a country as Canada it was most important that the University should not support extreme views in the direction of socialism. I understand from him that in some of the Canadian Universities a change in the staff was made necessary by the propagandist efforts of some of the teachers.'[31]

Carrothers was educated in Ireland at the Methodist College, Belfast, and in Canada at Wesley College and the University of Manitoba, where he studied philosophy and took a bachelor's degree. During the war he served overseas first with the Canadian army and then with the Royal Air Force. After his discharge, he went to the University of Edinburgh to study political economy, economic history, and political science, and during his final year at Edinburgh lectured part-time in political economy. He completed a study of immigration for his PhD, which he received in 1921. Though he also had the offer of a joint appointment at Wesley College and the University of Manitoba, the proposal he received from Murray attracted him more. 'I am very much interested in Economic History and the fact that the Saskatchewan appointment is concerned largely with Economic History has made it appeal to me,' he told Murray.[32] Carrothers was named 'Junior Professor of Political Economy' and his salary set at $3,200.[33] During his time at Saskatchewan, which lasted nearly a decade, he became a popular member of the university and the community at large, serving as an alderman on city council and a member of the boards of the hospital and public library.

In the fall of 1923, Swanson and Carrothers were joined in the department by a third member, Robert McQueen, the son of the Reverend David George McQueen, a pioneer minister and prominent citizen of Edmonton, who was known to President Murray through his Scots Presbyterian connections.[34] By virtue of his birth in Edmonton in 1896, McQueen could claim to be the first economist born on the prairie. He attended the local schools in Edmonton and then registered at the University of Alberta, where he first came to be called Pete, a nickname that attached to him for the rest of his life. At university, he had difficulty deciding what course he should take. He started in engineering, changed over to architecture, and then settled on philosophy. But before he had made much headway in philosophy, the war intervened to darken his undergraduate years. Duncan MacGibbon described him as one who 'shared deeply the general malaise and sense of futility common to many young people after the war.'[35] He served with the Royal Air Force for two years, after which he returned home to complete his bachelor's and master's degrees in philosophy at the University of Alberta. In the course of an additional year at Alberta when he lectured in philosophy, his interests shifted once more, and finally, to the study of economics. He began to take courses in economics on the side, forming in the process a lifelong friendship with MacGibbon, who had become the head of the economics department. When the final term was over, he enrolled in a summer session at the University of Chicago and obtained a bursary to study the following year at the London School of Economics and Political Science. His father financed him to a second year there, and it was through a letter from his father that he first came to the notice of President Murray. Murray at first said there was no vacancy in economics, but after he received a letter from MacGibbon setting out McQueen's exceptional attractiveness and ability for teaching, Murray changed his mind and decided to hire him.

The rest of the twenties were relatively untroubled years at the uni-

versity both financially and academically. There was moderate growth
in all areas. The subject of economics appeared to be growing in popularity, and there was a revival of interest in the Economics Club, which
held debates and brought in speakers. J.S. Woodsworth, the labour
leader, addressed the club in 1924. The number of students enrolled in
economics courses rose from 250 in 1923 to 339 in 1928, at which time
the department had a published list of sixteen courses. A clear pattern
of courses in economics began to emerge, the practice of offering some
subjects in alternate years allowing the small department to spread its
resources over a wider area.

Carrothers and McQueen each taught a section of elementary economics. Carrothers took responsibility for courses in business administration, corporation finance, the history of economic thought, and
economic history. Three courses in economic history were set out in the
Calendar: the economic history of the British Isles to 1763, the economic
history of the British Empire from 1763, and the economic development of France, Germany, and the United States in the nineteenth century. There was no doubt that it was the presence of Carrothers which
helped to establish the department's reputation in this area; Harold
Innis, in a 1929 survey of the teaching of economic history, especially
complimented the University of Saskatchewan for its ambitious program in economic history.[36] In addition to his other courses, Carrothers
taught a section of elementary economics in the evening: 'This is a difficult class to conduct,' he complained, 'as a number of those who register have only a popular interest in the subject and may have little
time to study, while a number take the lectures with a view to receiving
regular credit for their work on the university standard.'[37] McQueen,
for his part, taught courses in socialism and labour problems (later
called comparative economic systems), industrial relations, and (for
students in the College of Agriculture only) agricultural economic
problems. He later took over from Carrothers the course in corporation
finance, and in 1930 introduced the department's first course in international trade.

Swanson took the remaining and apparently largest share of the
course load and had the major responsibility for the supervision of students undertaking graduate studies in economics. His courses were
money and banking, rail and water transportation, economic geography, public finance, cooperative production and marketing (the first
university course in cooperatives to be given in Canada, introduced by
him in 1923), agricultural economics, and rural economics. This last

course, first advertised, though never taught, by Lewis Gray, proved a popular offering; in 1922, for example, it had an enrolment of fifty-nine, the largest of the economics classes that year.

During the 1920s there were six successful candidates for the master's degree in economics, each of them completing theses on topics of regional interest: W.G. Coates, 'A Survey and Study of Economic and Social Life in the Ethelton District' (1921); Annie Bell Sherriff, 'Agricultural Cooperation in Saskatchewan' (1923); A.W. Mahaffy, 'The Machine Process in Agriculture with Special Reference to Western Canada' (1923); Pauline Creighton, 'Taxation in Saskatoon' (1925); Clive B. Davidson, 'Price Determining Factors in the Wheat Market' (1925); and Vernon C. Fowke, 'Economic Realities of the Canadian Coal Situation' (1929), of whom more will be heard later. The first recorded thesis in the department, 'The Law of Employers' Liability and Workmen's Compensation in Canada,' was submitted in 1915 by John Weir, not for a master's degree, but for a bachelor's degree with honours. Weir was Saskatchewan's first honours graduate in economics and a Rhodes scholar, and later became the first dean of law at the University of Alberta. Before 1920 the only other student in the department to receive a master's degree from the university was John G. Diefenbaker, later Prime Minister of Canada, who had been a student of Edmund Oliver and Lewis Gray in economics and of Ira MacKay in political science. Diefenbaker received a master's degree in 'political science and economics' in 1916 but apparently did not submit a thesis. The omission of a thesis though uncommon was not irregular, since university regulations (until 1930) allowed the granting of a master's degree without one. As for further expansion in graduate studies, the university's general policy was not to offer a doctoral program until the staff was larger and better equipped. 'It would be folly,' pronounced President Murray in 1923, 'for Saskatchewan to add another feeble graduate school to the many that encumber the land.'[38]

A major problem for undergraduates as well as graduate students was the condition of the library. The holdings of the library, 'the laboratory of students in Economics,' as Swanson called it, were woefully inadequate to accommodate the needs of the larger classes.[39] The paucity of library materials, as well as the sorry state of the accommodations themselves, had been the subject of complaint since Oliver first began teaching economics in 1910. In 1914 it was recorded that Lewis Gray had spent about $150 on acquisitions and had started subscriptions to several journals, but progress since that time had been disappointingly slow. Nevertheless, the library's collection of historical materials was greatly enhanced in 1918 with the purchase of Adam Shortt's library of Canadiana, said to be 'second only to the public collection in Ottawa.' The price was $5,000, a nominal fee even at that time. Shortt, who had declined to let his name stand as first president at Saskatchewan, retained a warm feeling of attachment towards the university and for several years afterwards continued to search out and add to the materials.[40] The purchases formed the nucleus for a collection that remains one of the best in the country.

As the Department of Economics grew, so too did the scope of its service role, both to the community and to the rest of the university. The University of Saskatchewan was the first in Canada to set up an extension department with a full-time director.[41] Programs such as Better Farming Trains, Farm and Home Week, 4-H Clubs for young people, Homemakers' Clubs, a bulletin service, and numerous fairs and competitions extended the reach of the university to every part of the countryside. In his annual report for 1923, Murray reviewed the work of the university's extension service and estimated that its programs reached 120,000 people in the province each year.[42] Other colleges and departments on campus were called in to help extend the university's service to the community. There were many demands for speeches by members of the economics department from farmers' locals and other organizations. Short courses for farmers and other groups in the community, such as loan inspectors and life underwriters, were introduced in 1924; and, starting in 1929, correspondence courses were offered for credit. In addition, the department provided economics courses for students enrolled in the professional colleges. The university's policy was to have one department for each subject, but in the face of pressure from the professional colleges the policy sometimes fell by the wayside. In one controversial case, the College of Agriculture in 1926 decided that the courses provided by the economics department were insufficiently practical for students in agriculture and set up its own department for economics instruction. This department was first called farm management, and later, agricultural economics.

IV

In the fall of 1928, W.A. Carrothers went on sabbatical leave to the London School of Economics and Political Science to continue his studies on immigration. C.E. Dankert, a graduate student from the University of Chicago, took his place at Saskatchewan for the year. During his year away, Carrothers reported to Murray that he had made splendid progress in his work and had travelled with Mrs Carrothers to Ireland, Scotland, and the continent. His researches resulted in an article of 1929 in *Queen's Quarterly*, 'The Immigration Problem in Canada,' in which Carrothers explained that, as migration to North America had progressed during the nineteenth century, 'the peoples drawn in were more alien to the original stocks on this continent in race, language, religion, history, traditions, customs and political institutions.' 'Canadians,' he said, 'generally prefer that settlers should be of a readily assimilable type, already identified by race or language with one or other of the two great races now inhabiting this country and thus prepared for the assumption of the duties of democratic Canadian citizenship.' In the absence of French-speaking migrants, this meant that 'the great bulk of the preferred settlers are those who speak the English language – those coming from the United Kingdom or the United States.' Next came the Scandinavians or the Dutch, who were acquainted with democratic institutions. Not readily assimilated were settlers from southern and eastern Europe, and 'less assimilable still, according to the general opinion of Canadians, are those who come to Canada from the Orient.' 'We confer the privileges and rights of Canadian citizenship much too easily on the non-English-speaking immigrants,' Carrothers concluded.[43] The article was followed in the same year by *Emigration from the British Isles*, which was published in Britain.[44] The book was particularly commended for the thoroughness of its research and established Carrothers's reputation as an economic historian. C.R. Fay, writing in the *Canadian Forum*, called it 'the best among several recent books on this all-important subject ... It is well proportioned and abounds in the correct emphasis.'[45] Helen I. Cowan, who reviewed the Carrothers book for the *Canadian Historical Review*, had high praise for 'his sounder grasp of economic history and his wider familiarity with government reports than that of any previous investigator in this field.'[46]

After returning from his sabbatical, Carrothers taught at Saskatchewan for only one more year. In the spring of 1930 he accepted an appointment as professor of economics at the University of British Columbia. During the 1930s he served as an adviser to the government of British Columbia and prepared the province's brief to the Rowell–Sirois Commission (the Royal Commission on Dominion-Provincial Relations). He later left the university to become president of the Public Utilities Commission of British Columbia, remaining in this position for thirteen years until his death in 1951.[47] His book, *Emigration from the British Isles*, was reissued in 1965.

The timing of Carrothers's resignation from the University of Saskatchewan was a stroke of ill luck for the economics department. The sunny years of the late twenties had drawn to an end. Now the department, as well as the university, had to suffer a decade of reversal. So meagre were the university's resources that President Murray never was able to make a serious effort towards filling the vacancy left by Carrothers, and it would be many years before the department would again have its full complement of senior staff.

4

Retrenchment

The economic depression struck the Saskatchewan economy with particular ferocity and had profound effects on the university. There could be no thought of new appointments. 'We are retrenching in every way possible,' wrote Murray to one rejected applicant in 1932.[1] An arts and library building to be called Haultain Hall, scheduled for construction at an estimated cost of $800,000, was initially approved but never built; at the last moment when it heard of the estimated cost the government refused to sanction the project.[2] The building was to provide accommodation for classes in arts and science, household science, and education; offices for the president, dean, registrar, bursar, and students' societies; rooms for physical training for women; and a library, museum, and lecture theatre to seat four hundred. Instead, the library continued to be housed in the Administration Building until 1956, when the Murray Memorial Library was finally erected, while an arts building, envisaged by Murray as early as 1913, had to wait until 1960 before becoming a reality. The abandonment of construction for Haultain Hall had serious repercussions. 'No decision,' wrote Walter P. Thompson, a later president, 'could have had a more profound effect on the nature and development of the institution. It severely handicapped the humanities and social subjects and directed development towards the sciences and professional training.'[3]

But the loss of its capital budget was not all. During the Depression the university's operating grant from the government was reduced by 40 per cent. As a result, about one-third of the faculty, those without family responsibilities, were given leave of absence without pay, while all those remaining suffered some salary reduction which varied, according to putative need, from 20 to 30 per cent. At its optimistic beginning, the university administration had hoped that soon it would do away with tuition fees altogether, but now fees began to edge upward. By 1934, the annual rate for a full-time registrant had reached $90, three times what it had been in 1930. Nevertheless, there was no sign of slackening in enrolment, though the university often had to accept promissory notes for fees and stories of hardship were common. 'In times of unemployment many young men and women make great efforts to attend the University rather than remain idle,' the president reported in 1933. 'This year, as never before, have they practised economies. Some have managed to keep their expenses for food and rooms within three dollars per week.'[4]

The Depression served to focus attention on economic problems and to stimulate inquiries into the nature of Canadian economic development. The Canadian Political Science Association, which had been allowed to lapse during the war, came to life again. W.W. Swanson was present at the first meeting of the association at the Château Laurier in Ottawa on 23 May 1929, and he was one of a group which gathered a few weeks later at the Manitoba Agricultural College to organize the Canadian Society of Agricultural Economics. In 1932 he was elected to a two-year term on the executive of the Canadian Political Science Association.

I

During the decade of the thirties, Swanson turned his hand to writing books on economic topics for the general reader. *Wheat*, a collaborative work by Swanson and P.C. Armstrong, a specialist in agriculture, was published in 1930. The book describes how wheat is grown, harvested, and marketed. It also describes, with eastern Canadian readers clearly in mind, the people and society of the West. The people were resourceful and democratic in spirit. They took public issues seriously, but were reasonable and well-educated, and their taking up of radical doctrines from time to time should be understood by outsiders as a more or less natural by-product of pursuing an occupation, farming, which was subject to so many vicissitudes of weather and markets. In any case, 'steady growth in wealth and in comfort of living softens the asperity of the most discontented.' There was much misunderstanding to be cleared up. Farmers were not selfish, 'unable to see the broader national interest,' as was sometimes alleged; nor was it true that any number of western farmers wintered in California. Again, it must be understood that agriculture was an important industry, to Canada as well as to the West. Indeed, it could be said that agriculture 'is the only industry in the end ... Modern civilization is merely a highly developed specialization of agriculture, with great factories to replace the little workshop on the farm or at the crossroads, with bankers to enable us to postpone the bringing home of the goods for which in primitive society the farmer exchanges his crops, and with hospitals to replace by organized effort the goodwill of individuals to each other in sickness.' But there was misunderstanding on the other side too. The western farmer believed that the railways and banks were 'indifferent to his struggles, if not actually predatory'; but it was 'probable that this is a very erroneous impression.' Further, it could be held that the Winnipeg Grain Exchange, for so long the object of the farmers' ire, 'may never have deserved attack.' The authors suggested that there was in the West, 'perhaps too much talk of currency reform and of minor adjustments in the economic and social structure, and not enough thought of the inevitable and basic changes in the whole structure that must be produced by such events as the coming exhaustion of the natural soil fertility.'[5]

   Wheat received a generous response from its reviewers. Robert England gave it an enthusiastic review in the *Queen's Quarterly*.[6] Holbrook Working of the Food Research Institute at Stanford wrote in the *Journal of Farm Economics* that the book's 'many controversial points are suggestively developed and discussed with balance and moderation.'[7] Harold Innis reviewed the book twice, once for the *Canadian Historical Review* and again for the *Canadian Forum*. Professor Swanson, he wrote in the first, 'by virtue of his position in the foremost wheat-producing province, of his wide experience on commissions investigating its problems, of his association as joint author with a technical agriculturist, and of his training and tradition ... has been able to produce a volume which will take an important place in the literature on the subject. This important book gives an excellent description of the stages in the production and marketing of wheat, and an analysis of the chief problems of this staple industry and, incidentally, of other staple industries in Canada.' 'It is, perhaps, unfair,' he added, 'to complain that the implications of the argument have not been worked out and that the volume consequently contains incomplete statements.'[8] In his second review, Innis discussed, besides *Wheat*, the new book by Duncan MacGibbon, *The Canadian Grain Trade*, and used the occasion to launch an important plea on behalf of a Canadian economics attuned to Canadian conditions. 'In some sense,' he said, 'these books represent the height of academic achievement in Canadian economics.'

Whereas Dr. MacGibbon fails in his effort to link the evolutionary and the classical point of view, Professor Swanson fails in his effort to link the sociological and the classical point of view ... The classical analysis is of fundamental importance, but it carries the economist far short of his goal of scientific explanation. Both economists have supplemented the classical analysis, in the one case with reference to the evolutionary and the institutional aspects, and in the other case with reference to the sociological and perhaps the introspective aspects. The advance is significant, but inadequate. If economists are to make important contributions to the science of economics from the standpoint of Canadian material, they must build on such valuable work as has been done in these volumes, they must draw on the whole range of social sciences, and finally they must invent their own technique for handling their own problems. We may eventually, through such work, understand the significance of wheat to Canadian institutions and Canadian cultural life.[9]

In 1930, Swanson was appointed chairman of the Saskatchewan Royal Commission on Immigration and Settlement. The commission, which included four other members, held sittings throughout the province and was kept busy from January to June 1930, examining 476 witnesses and collecting fifty-two volumes of evidence. In a final report, prepared by Swanson, the commission urged the government to exercise improved control over immigration and recommended the carrying out of a provincial soil survey to determine lands suitable for further settlement. The commission set no quotas but strongly urged that British immigrants be given priority over others. In a review of publications on immigration in the *Queen's Quarterly*, Robert England, who deplored the increasing restrictiveness of Canadian policies and the closing of frontiers all over the world, called the Saskatchewan report 'authoritative and ... reasonably full' and commended the commission for its affirmation of the need for immigration, its ample appendices in support of the case, and, most of all, for not yielding to the pessimistic Malthusian conclusions in vogue among most economists. The problem confronting the province of Saskatchewan was 'unique,' he said, 'because of its racial composition of nearly fifty per cent. non-Anglo-Saxon; its seventy per cent. rural population; its lack of large cities; its youth (nearly forty per cent. still in its elementary schools); its curious acceptance of older party allegiance despite a certain susceptibility to radical as well as reactionary programmes. Agrarian, it has remained immune from direct farmer government, unlike Ontario, Alberta and Manitoba; polyglot in population, it saw the rise and quiescence of the Ku Klux Klan; pioneer, yet maintaining highways, railways, schools, churches, community halls and a first class university comparable with anything to be found in older provinces.'.[10]

Swanson had hardly time to recover from the strenuous labours of the immigration commission when, in September 1930, he was on a steamship bound for London, along with Duncan MacGibbon and R.H. Coates, the Dominion statistician, as part of the Canadian delegation to the Imperial Conference. The selection of the three was interpreted by Harold Innis to be an indication of 'the increasing prestige attaching to the work of economists.'[11] Swanson, along with other members of the delegation, was settled in at the Mayfair Hotel. The conference itself, besides being a marathon of its kind, turned out to be a highly posh affair, more so than many of the colonials had come prepared for. A.J. McPhail, president of the Saskatchewan Co-operative Wheat Producers (later the Wheat Pool), who was invited along to take part in the discussions on wheat marketing, wrote back to Violet McNaughton, the women's farm leader, that he and some of the others had been unable to attend the first evening's function – a government dinner followed by a gala reception put on by the British prime minister at Lancaster House – for lack of proper evening wear. The next day, McPhail, in company with Swanson, MacGibbon, and J.I. McFarland, manager of the farmers' Central Selling Agency, went shopping for dress clothes. 'As a result,' wrote McPhail, 'I have enough clothes of a certain kind to do me the rest of my life time, probably more.'[12]

The remainder of the conference, which went on for another six weeks, was full of event. For Swanson, there were summonses at all hours from Prime Minister Bennett, memoranda to prepare, and committee meetings to attend, besides the interminable sessions of the conference itself. In addition, there were social functions to go to almost every day, including a pleasant party one afternoon at Buckingham Palace. Most of these functions, as he related to President Murray, he turned down 'for I find that otherwise I cannot do my work. It is a little hard, at times, for I was really worn down by that Immigration investigation at home – but it is a wonderful experience which I hope to make use of for the benefit of our students in time to come.'[13] Many Canadians, especially those in the West, had hoped that the conference would help to bring down the wall of protection which had been erected after the war. But in the end its results were disappointing. McPhail commented wryly that 'the more of the meetings I attend the more respect I have for our farmer board members.'[14] One farm publication, disgusted at the lack of progress made at the conference, hailed Swanson as a 'wonder worker' and 'the prairie magician' for his part in keeping up the trade barriers while professing at the same time to act the role of a 'born free trader.'[15] Two years later, when the next imperial conference came up, Swanson informed an official in the Department of Finance that he was ready to be of service.[16] The message was duly passed on to the prime minister, but this time no invitation was forthcoming.

At the end of 1932 Swanson brought out a second book, *Depression and the Way Out*, a small polemical volume addressed to the general reader. In the *Canadian Historical Review*, the only academic journal to give it any attention, it was described as 'controversial in style and conservative in outlook,' but the reviewer, H.A. Logan, said that its title was 'a misnomer' since 'there is no adequate analysis of the depression and few definite suggestions as to remedy.' Some readers, he said, 'will fail to agree that the present economic dilapidation is chiefly due to a lack of individual industry and will ask why it is necessary to accept a radical decline in standards of living in an era of unprecedented production capacity.'[17] A.S. Morton, of the Saskatchewan history department, took note of the book's arrival in a letter to a former student: 'Swanson has a new book out on the economics of depression. Other people are doing it so why should I not, he says. It affords another occasion for him to sit on the fence.'[18]

In the book, Swanson traced the origins of the economic collapse of the 1930s to extensive borrowing by governments to finance the war. This had resulted in a dangerous expansion of the national debt and a rate of accumulation which could not be sustained. As he put it, 'We have built up a social and economic machine so complex that we cannot even permit it to slow down much below the speed for which it is designed without a great disaster.' While he conceded that a moderate increase in borrowing might be necessary to keep the economy functioning and made clear the unfortunate had in some way to be protected against unnecessary suffering, it was his view that interference in the complex economic machine was ultimately self-defeating. 'If we attempt booms,' he wrote, 'we shall merely magnify the collapse.' The economist could do little save to say, like the physician, that 'nothing can cure past excess except present pain.' Living standards had to come down and remain there until 'that thrift and industry which have created all material progress for the race had allowed sufficient accumulation to restore standards of living.' By his reckoning, a reduction of about 10 to 20 per cent in the standard of living of the average citizen would accomplish what was necessary to restore the economy to health. He was encouraged by signs around him that people were seeing the error of their ways: 'Men and women are learning to abandon vain chasing after easy wealth and careless amusement. Men and women are learning once again the folly of building on shifting sands.' Again, he saw no reason to abandon his *laissez-faire* position in the present crisis: 'My original statement was that the economic position of our society is still, as ever, chiefly dependent on thrift and industry. If that is correct, then any troubles of the present must, in great part, be due to lack of those simple virtues. I believe that every economic ill of the moment is plainly traceable, in chief part at any rate, to the attempt to create and maintain standards of living in some quarters beyond the actual capacity of our society to maintain.'[19]

Yet something had to be done about agriculture, whose recovery Swanson believed to be crucial to the recovery of the economy as a whole.[20] In June 1931, the local newspapers reported on a plan submitted by Swanson to the federal government and the three prairie provinces for the reorganization and consolidation of farm debts. His plan called for extending farm debts without interest for a period of three years and debts excluding mortgages to be repaid at the end of the period by bonds purchased by the farmers, the federal government, and the provinces. The waiting period, he suggested, would allow time for a more permanent solution to be found for dealing with mortgages. He also recommended the establishment of a federal council to consider the problem of unemployment and the immediate undertaking of public works and other forms of relief to help those in distress. The only public response to the plan were two comments solicited by the *Star-Phoenix*: one from Arthur Moxon of the College of Law, who said he failed to understand why 'solvent and provident citizens' should be asked to assume responsibility 'for credit recklessly given,' and another from Frank Eliason, the secretary of the United Farmers of Canada, who thought the plan 'entirely too kind to the creditor section of the community.'[21]

In July 1932, Prime Minister Bennett invited twelve economists across the country to comment on a memorandum on monetary reconstruction which had been prepared by Swanson's former colleague at

Queen's, W.C. Clark, who had just been appointed deputy minister of finance. Swanson was among those canvassed and, like the others, received an honorarium of $100, but his reply, if ever sent, has not survived. Of the seven comments that did survive, six supported the establishment of a central bank.[22] There is no doubt that Swanson would have taken the minority view. By the following year, when the Macmillan Commission on Banking and Currency held its hearings across the country, it became clear that most experts had indeed come to support the principle of central banking and that Swanson was one of the few who remained opposed to a managed money supply. He told the commission hearing in Regina: 'this so called new economics is not new at all. It is merely a return to the seventeenth and [eighteenth centuries] of mercantilism. You can sum it up all in one phrase that it is based on the belief that the technological improvements that have been made and the advancements of science have proceeded so far that now we have to be afraid of over-production. On the other hand the orthodox economist believes that there is no such thing as general over-production, that what is wrong with the world to-day is unbalanced production and that even commodities under-produced cannot be sold in an unbalanced world.' 'There is no way I see,' he went on, 'that the bank acting in and by itself can raise the price level and stabilize it. Our monetary control is not a simple matter; it is not the mere mechanical manipulation of guaranteeing a credit. The quality of the money and the quality of the credit are really more important than the amount of the credit or the guarantee which may be issued.' On the other hand, he seemed less certain than before of the efficacy of laissez-faire: 'I wish to make it clear,' he said, 'that I do not by any ... means believe that things will right themselves if left [to] themselves.' Swanson had two remedies to offer: increasing the responsibility of the Canadian Bankers' Association and setting up a monetary commission composed of able bankers.[23]

The *Western Producer*, a leading farm weekly, devoted an editorial to the evidence he gave at the commission hearings: 'Dr. Swanson disclosed himself as an antediluvian conservative in all matters relating to finance – in his espousal of a return to the gold standard, his unwavering support of the policies of international financiers, his opposition to even the most innocuous brand of a central bank for the Dominion, and the emphasis with which he advocated and commended the present banking system in practically every single detail.'[24] Not long after, the executive of the Canadian Bankers' Association received a suggestion from one of its members that Swanson be given some con-tract work to do, though apparently nothing came of it.[25]

Swanson's next major undertaking, a study of municipal finance and taxation in Saskatchewan, came at the invitation of the Canadian Pio-neer Problems Committee, headed by W.A. Mackintosh, who had suc-ceeded Skelton at Queen's University. The study later comprised five chapters of *Economic Problems of the Prairie Provinces* (1935), volume four of the series *Canadian Frontiers of Settlement*, edited by Mackintosh and W.L.G. Joerg. Swanson's part in the series owed much to the assis-tance on the project of Neil Herman Jacoby, an honours student in the department, who later became chairman of the Royal Commission on Taxation in Saskatchewan and dean of the School of Business Adminis-tration at the University of California. In a review in the *Canadian Jour-nal of Economics and Political Science*, V.W. Bladen made special mention of the admirable comparative studies relating to Saskatchewan.[26]

Swanson's last book, *Rail, Road and River*, which came out in 1937, contained a denunciation of publicly owned transportation facilities and did nothing to enhance his reputation as a scholar. Only George de T. Glazebrook, in the *Canadian Historical Review*, had anything good to say about the effort, calling it 'an interesting and concise essay,' though somewhat inconclusive in some chapters and lacking in evi-dence in others. W.R. Maxwell, in the *Dalhousie Review*, declared that 'the task ... of recalling to the minds of the Canadian people the service rendered to it by this great company [the Canadian Pacific Railway] will not be advanced by rhapsodies like this.'[27] In the *Queen's Quar-terly*, a reviewer called it 'this racy little book' and added that 'the mass of information which it contains must stand as a permanent trib-ute to the capacity of the author's memory; one may, nonetheless, regret that it was not refreshed at several points before this book was finally committed to print.'[28] In the *Canadian Journal of Economics and Political Science*, he was taken to task for 'errors in fact,' 'misrepresen-tation,' and 'logical inconsistency,' and for his neglect of other studies in transportation of which several were newly published: 'The aim is excellent, the performance leaves something to be desired. Populariza-tion is the most difficult of all the literary arts, and those who attempt it should carry into their writing the marks of full acquaintance with the work of the specialists in the field. The reader is also entitled to know what specialists are followed, and to have differing views, if any, reflected in the footnotes or appendices. This book comes forth naked of either footnotes or bibliography.'[29]

After *Rail, Road and River*, Swanson's participation in public affairs quickly declined. In June 1937 he read a paper on 'The Immigration Problem in the Prairie Provinces' to a meeting of the Canadian Agricultural Economics Society (formerly the Canadian Society of Agricultural Economics) and after that wrote no other papers. He now turned his full attention to teaching economics and to administering the department, where problems of morale and staffing were beginning to reach a critical point.

II

Pete McQueen, Swanson's younger colleague in the economics department, was one of the most popular and gifted economists of his generation in Canada. His fund of stories and asides on the world were much appreciated and talked about by his friends across the country. 'His tastes,' remarked one of them, 'were broad, irreverent, blasphemous, salacious ... The only test of fitness he applied was that they had to be really funny. And they were.'[30] McQueen was liked by everyone, and he and President Murray quickly became friends. In the classroom he was regarded as a very good teacher, who delivered his lectures in a nervous, excited sort of way, sometimes unable to repress his penchant for ribald stories which would both horrify and delight his listeners.[31] Students were drawn by his intellectual detachment and sense of humour, and he became companion and confidant to several of them. With Swanson, it was a different matter. The two men were very unalike, and their differences became more evident as time passed. As McQueen grew in strength and confidence as an economist, he became more and more critical of Swanson's economics and his administration of departmental affairs.

McQueen was among a growing number in his profession to advocate a more rigorous approach to the teaching of economics at Canadian universities.[32] He wanted especially to see a strengthening of economics departments in the West. 'Economics,' he once reflected, 'has not filled the place it should fill in western life and that is largely due, not to lack of facilities or problems, but to lack of competent men.'[33] But with all his teaching duties, the innumerable demands put on the department for public speaking, and the other tedious chores that arose, he found that his work at the university continually sapped his creative energies, and more so after Carrothers resigned. He had a nagging desire to publish but neither the confidence nor the time to write anything of consequence. 'Routine work in a western university is frequently very exacting and laborious, and owing in part to this – but only in part I think – my publications up to date have neither been many nor important,' he wrote in 1935.[34] He had hoped to write a doctoral thesis on the problems of the railways in the Peace River region for presentation to the London School of Economics and Political Science, but he lingered too long on the topic and eventually had to give it up, along with his hopes for a PhD, when the Canadian Pioneer Problems Committee published its series on prairie settlement. He was, in fact, never entirely able to overcome a reluctance to commit to writing the many original ideas in economics which he could express in casual conversation. He never produced a major piece of work, though at one time he and W.A. Mackintosh at Queen's planned together to write a general textbook on economics.

In 1935 McQueen went to Queen's University to take the place of Mackintosh for a year, and while there was asked if he would consider an appointment as head of political economy at the University of Manitoba. At first he said no. The idea did not appeal to him; he had been 'very happy' at Saskatchewan and would miss valued friendships with men such as Murray, Ling, and F.C. Cronkite. 'Frankly, I see a possibility of a better department at Saskatchewan than I do at Manitoba,' he wrote to Murray from Kingston. 'My association with the men in the east here has shown me that being the Head of a Department can be rated much too highly – some of the best economists here have told me they are much more happy in not being heads of the department than they would be if they were and they give very real reasons for saying so.'[35] In reply to Sidney Smith, the president at Manitoba (later president of the University of Toronto), McQueen declared his intention to remain at Saskatchewan. Smith then offered the Manitoba position to Vincent Bladen of the University of Toronto. But Bladen was convinced that McQueen had made a mistake. Bladen later explained:

When A.B. Clark retired at U of Man. the President S.E. Smith invited me to go as head of the department. I knew that Pete McQueen had been offered the job & had turned it down because he thought the offer half hearted. It probably was; SES thought the Chancellor, Dafoe, was pushing his own candidate too hard & he was not going to be pushed around. Knowing this, and knowing that Pete was most unhappy under Swanson at the U of Sask – and believing that he would be an admirable head at

U of M – I replied that I advised SES to invite Pete to W'peg & discuss the possibility of his acceptance. I thought that once they met, they would realise how compatible they were. If Pete refused I said I would take the job. Pete accepted, as I hoped he would.'[36]

McQueen's resignation left the economics department stranded. McQueen was deeply grateful to Murray for having made his time at Saskatchewan such a happy one, and when he heard of the trouble he had helped to cause he was full of remorse. 'Had I known the shake-up that was coming in Saskatchewan, it might well have changed my decision regarding Manitoba. It was so typically fair of you not to mention it,' he told Murray.[37] Murray, it is true, was exceptionally magnaminous in the matter of having members of his faculty taken from him by other universities. Warned by one head of department of a 'poaching expedition' into Saskatchewan territory, Murray replied: 'While we are very anxious to retain good men we would be very wrong to attempt to prevent our men from receiving offers from institutions which would appeal to them.'[38] As conditions of employment at the university worsened during the 1930s, some of his best men were attracted away by better offers.

And so Pete McQueen went, in the fall of 1936, to the University of Manitoba. For the next several years there were signs of his growing maturity as an economist. He introduced 'a more modern and American curriculum,'[39] wrote several articles for publication, and served in several important positions, including membership on the executive of the Canadian Political Science Association, the research staff of the Royal Commission on Dominion-Provincial Relations, and the board of directors of the Bank of Canada. Though he was not entirely content at Manitoba and, with his reputation, could no doubt have moved on to another position, he had reasons for staying put; as he related to a friend, he had 'incautiously bought' when he first arrived in Winnipeg, and 'in the current local market' would be unable to sell the house.[40] But his time was all too short. In 1941 he was killed in a Trans-Canada Airlines crash while he was travelling east to a board meeting of the Bank of Canada. His death, at the age of only forty-six, came as a shock to the economics fraternity and his many friends and admirers in Canada and the United States. In an obituary notice in the *Winnipeg Free Press*, the Chicago economist Jacob Viner wrote: 'McQueen could be absolutely relied on to approach any problem which attracted his interest with an objective and fresh point of view, uncontaminated by, though fully informed of, the standard easy formulae and the routine biases. He was without guile or stratagem, pure of mind and heart. His salty, vigorous and earthy style of conversation was an appropriate vehicle for his honest, straight-forward and courageous thinking, and I recall now how, whenever I have had talk with him the wish would come to me that, without his knowledge, his conversation could be recorded with all the flavour of its pungency, vigor, determined honesty, pertinent wisdom, and goodwill to good men and anger against men of evil ... he still had so much to give.'[41]

III

When McQueen decided to leave for Manitoba, he was unaware that two young instructors in the department, Vernon Fowke and George Britnell, were also arranging to leave. The two were graduates of the department who had been hired to fill in after Carrothers left for British Columbia, and both had received permission to take the academic year of 1935–6 in pursuit of their studies. This left Swanson alone in the department. Having to cast about quickly for temporary help, Murray made three sessional appointments. The first went to John Guthrie, a recent graduate of the University of Manitoba; the second to Benjamin H. Higgins, a Canadian who had studied for six years at the London School of Economics and Political Science and was recommended by his supervisor, Lionel Robbins, as 'a solid sort of person' he was 'prepared to go to bail for;'[42] and a third to Mabel Timlin, secretary of the correspondence courses at the university. Timlin, who had been put in charge of tutorials in economics the year before, was now assigned, in addition to her other duties, to the teaching of a new elementary course in economics designed for students not intending to take further work in the subject.

Swanson was pleased with the new help. He referred to Higgins as 'a smart laddie, and an excellent worker' and handed over to him the job of resuscitating the Economics Club, which he evidently managed very well.[43] But his method of teaching was another matter, according to the following account given by Mabel Timlin: 'To his class in Economics 1, he gives the most involved type of modified Austrian theory, set up in terms of the differential calculus. He teaches them how to find the point of average diminishing returns by dropping a perpendicular from a tangent drawn on a curve showing total returns when variable factors are combined with fixed factors, then just for luck, throws a couple more curves into the same design, positive, and negative, showing the marginal products ... When he gets through he has a very handsome design on the blackboard ... The majority of his students don't know what the score is at all, and I strongly suspect that what he is giving them is material he got in a *graduate* seminar with Dr. von Hayek at London.'[44] When, in addition, he shared lodgings with a woman friend from Britain, to the shock of some of the more conservative members of the university community, his request to be released from his commitment to Saskatchewan after the Christmas break was received with good grace. As it happened, Higgins, on his way to Ontario for the break, had stopped at the University of Minnesota in Minneapolis to talk to an economist he had corresponded with about points of theory; there, out of the blue, he had been asked to teach the next semester. He stayed on at Minnesota another three years to complete a PhD degree. Of his brief time in Saskatchewan he later wrote: 'Saskatoon in the fall of 1935 was hardly London, the University was hardly the London School of Economics. The great depression was still much in evidence on the prairies, and the dust bowl was at its worst. If the wind came from the south the dust would blot out the midday sun. But just because of the magnitude of the problems Saskatoon had a certain wartime gaiety. As with the Viennese during the Nazi occupation, the attitude was, "things are desperate but not serious." So I had a good time.'[45]

A replacement for Higgins at Saskatchewan was found in the person of Walter W. Glaeser, a graduate in business administration from the University of Washington, who had applied for a position some months before. He hurried to Saskatoon and proceeded to rescue Higgins's classes in introductory economics, international trade, and socialism and labour. The Economics Club survived the transition, and at its first meeting of the new year heard two students, Bill Lederman and Gordon Robertson, deliver papers for and against the nationalization of the central bank of Canada.[46] Lederman was later the first dean of law at Queen's University and a leading scholar of the Canadian constitution. Robertson, who in 1938 was the first student to graduate from the four-year honours course in economics, went on to a distinguished career in the civil service.

In the midst of these trials with his provisional staff in economics, President Murray embarked on a search for a senior economist, his first such mission in well over a decade. This time he found no lack of candidates. President Smith of Manitoba offered to send a list he had assembled of twenty-five persons looking for permanent positions in economics. McQueen said that 'good men are going cheaply these days' and suggested three: John J. Deutsch, James Aitchison, and John Stuart Mill Allely.[47] Deutsch did not apply. Nor at this point did Allely. Aitchison, who had grown up in Saskatchewan and graduated from the university before going on to postgraduate studies in political science and economics, did send an application but was rejected. But Murray, as it turned out, was not at all interested in candidates from Canada. What he now wanted was to find someone trained in the new economics currently in vogue in Britain, hoping, it appeared, to introduce new ideas into a department all too dominated by classical notions. Cambridge just then had a strong reputation in theory, owing to the presence there of John Maynard Keynes. As Murray put it, 'the Cambridge tradition is good and very desirable for us if we can secure the right person.'[48] He explained to President Smith: 'We are making inquiries in Great Britain in the hope that we may secure a man unusually well qualified in theory and international trade, and also to bring in some one who is in close contact with developments in the homeland. There is a danger of too much inbreeding in our Universities ... I think it is most desirable, particularly in Economics, to bring in another tradition.'[49]

In the end, Murray's inquiries in Britain came to naught. Only one candidate of consequence turned up, Sidney Friefield, twenty-five, former Torontonian and graduate of the London School of Economics and Political Science, who was currently employed at the London Stock Exchange. Murray deliberated over the matter for some months and, finally, in the summer of 1936, decided to continue with the two men he had hired as temporary help, Vernon Fowke and George Britnell. They were each hired back as assistant professors of economics and offered a salary of $2,100. Swanson was agreeable to this new arrangement and in fact claimed that it was his intervention with the president that had resulted in better terms for the two men. 'I miss both George and you more than I can say,' he wrote in a letter to Vernon Fowke. 'The lads I have are doing the best they can, and doing it, I think, quite well, but it has been a strain on me to have men away so much the past few years.' He said he had managed to get $300 more for each of them: 'I am sorry it could not be more, but I think you know that all increases are at a dead standstill. I think I accomplished this expertly by taking advantage of the President's good will for both of you, and while he was in an expansive mood.'[50]

Britnell and Fowke were both graduates of the university. The year before, Murray had named Mabel Timlin, also a graduate of the university, as an instructor in the department. As things turned out, the three were to be the means by which Murray's wish to build a strong social science department came to be realized.

5

Political Science in Search of Itself

Political science was a step behind economics in gaining recognition as an independent academic discipline in Canada. The term itself was first used in university circles in Canada as a rubric for a somewhat heterogeneous collection of studies.[1] In 1889, W. J. Ashley was appointed professor of political economy and constitutional history at the University of Toronto, under an act of the Ontario legislature which authorized teaching at the university in 'Political Science (including Economics, Jurisprudence and Constitutional Law).'[2] The object in view was the resumption at the university of the teaching of law, which had been earlier interrupted. Ashley's inaugural lecture bore the title *What Is Political Science?* In the lecture, he defined political science as 'systematic knowledge concerning the state or political society, – concerning its constitution, its functions, the organs by which these functions are discharged, its relation to the individual and to other societies,' and held it to include constitutional history, constitutional law, jurisprudence, international law, the history of political ideas, and economics. Economics, he judged, made up the most important part of political science. 'We shall find ... ' he said, 'that most of the movements and forces which cause constitutional changes, still more the political contests waged within the lines of constitutions, are at bottom economic in their character.'[3]

The appointment of a political economist at the university had been regarded as one of some political sensitivity, political economists being known for having views on such contentious matters as the protective tariff, and indeed the appointment went to Ashley only after he had been interviewed by Premier Mowat himself. It is not surprising, therefore, that in his inaugural lecture Ashley was careful to stand well above the fray of political debate by emphasizing the utility and objectivity of his subject. The role of the study of political science, he made clear, was to examine government and its works in a non-partisan way. He warned of 'the perils of an ignorant democracy,' perils that would intensify as the state was called upon to expand its activities. 'It is coming to be recognized ...' he said, 'that the state has a positive duty as well as a negative, and that it cannot limit its action to the protection of life and property. Most of the younger economists ... do not go to the extreme of preaching state action in all departments as the remedy for all their ills. But on the other hand, they no longer accept *laissez-faire* as a general principle. Each case, they think, must be decided on its merits, on a balance of advantages and disadvantages. The state may wisely do some things and not others.'[4] John George Bourinot, clerk of the House of Commons, who addressed the Royal Society of Canada in 1889 on 'The Study of Political Science in Canadian Universities,' saw wisdom in a cautious approach to the subject. 'In no department of study,' he said, 'is there more danger of being deceived and carried away by dangerous theories and delusive ideas than that which leads us to consider political, social and economic problems ... we must be careful not to be deluded by the glamour of republicanism or the social tendencies of purely democratic conditions, and to level those old landmarks which can best lead us in the direction of true social happiness and national greatness.'[5]

At Queen's University, the first courses in politics and economics were offered in 1890 by a department which was known as 'political science' for some twenty-five years. Adam Shortt, the founding member of the Queen's department, defined political science in very generous terms. As he explained in the first issue of the *Queen's Quarterly*: 'the social conditions, means and aims of *civilization* constitute the sphere of modern Political Science. We are compelled to go considerably behind the science of wealth, on the one hand, and considerably beyond the science of government on the other. We have to ask many questions with regard to the nature of man as a social being and the circumstances in which he is placed, and we have to ask many ultimate questions with regard to the final *aims* and objects of society.'[6]

It is important to distinguish the capacious political science of Ashley, Bourinot, and Shortt from the academic discipline which was to assume that name in the twentieth century; the former offers a highly inflated impression of the latter. The former was a collection of largely undifferentiated social and philosophical studies, supplemented, in

Ashley's case, by legal studies. The latter came to mean the study of political thought and the institutions and processes of government, distinct from the study of law, and separate from the study of economics and the other social sciences such as sociology and anthropology. Of the several fields of study listed by Ashley as belonging to political science, only one, the history of political thought, would fall to the discipline of political science as it was to be later understood; all of the others were to find disciplinary homes elsewhere.[7]

Political science as an academic discipline was slow to develop in Canada. Well into the 1920s, at each of Toronto, Queen's, and McGill, the teaching of political science courses represented the workload of about one full-time member of faculty. At Toronto, the discipline was recognized principally as the provider of courses in the history of political thought for law students; teaching about the institutions of government was left largely to the staff in law. The history of the Department of Political Economy at the university records that 'for forty years or more, what later years would call descriptive political science and government were treated by lawyers, in the context of law courses ...'[8] As late as 1936–7, only three courses in political science were taught at the University of Toronto.[9] Disappointment at the progress made by political science in Canada was expressed by O.D. Skelton in 1932, who reported to the Royal Society that 'the study of politics receives far less consideration from faculty or students than the study of economics.' This he put down to 'the less obviously practical trend of the study, its less close relation with the urgent individual and social aspect of the dominating problem of making a living; and in some measure also the slower progress made in putting the study on an inductive basis.'[10].

Political science was much more of a going concern in the United States, where its practitioners promoted and taught it as a discipline invested with an important social purpose: the education of the democratic citizen. Political science was thought there to consist mainly, though not exclusively, of the study of the institutions of government, especially the government of the United States itself. By 1915 the modal course offered in political science in the United States was one on American government, to become before long the standard course introducing students to the subject.[11] In Canada, in contrast, courses devoted to Canadian government, introductory or otherwise, were long in coming. C.B. Macpherson writes: 'The study of its own government is a natural subject for the political science of any country, and its comparatively late appearance, and that of suitable material, may be attributed partly to the late development of a Canadian national consciousness and partly to the fact that the similarity of the Canadian to the English and United States systems of government made a specifically Canadian study seem relatively unnecessary.'[12] At Macpherson's own university, Toronto, it was not until 1937–8 that a course in political science devoted to Canadian government was offered. The course was taught by Robert MacGregor Dawson, recently hired away from the University of Saskatchewan, where he had been teaching courses in Canadian government for almost a decade.

The general practice in Canadian universities was, for many decades, to house political science and economics in one department. The two disciplines also were brought together in the Canadian Political Science Association, a national organization of academics and others interested in economic, political, and social affairs. The association was founded in 1913 and promptly folded with the advent of war; it was revived in 1930 under the same name, which harked back to Ashley's usage. Political scientists made up a very small proportion of the association's membership, and the association felt called upon in 1931 to explain its own name: 'When first organized it was called a Political Science Association because it was intended to promote the discussion of all matters of public policy which may become matters for political action, not because it was to be concerned solely with the science of government. In Canada, those matters of public policy are as yet mainly economic and therefore economic topics predominate in the programs of the annual meetings of the association.'[13] Beginning in 1935, the association sponsored a quarterly journal, the *Canadian Journal of Economics and Political Science*. The association existed until 1967, when it split into two organizations, one for each of economics and political science, each sponsoring a journal of its own.

The partnership in which economists and political scientists found themselves in university departments was one in which political science decidedly was the junior member in point of numbers. Skelton's lament of 1932 was echoed almost two decades later by Burton S. Keirstead and Frederick M. Watkins, who wrote, rather more irritably: 'the tendency has been for Economics to grow and develop, while Political Science has languished, starved for funds, lacking students, staff, and adequate library provision, and denied full and equal recognition in the curriculum.' They went on to take note of some instances in which 'a few courses in Political Science are taught, as a sort of side line, by economists, who appear to regard Politics as something which has no particular method of its own and which can properly be offered to the weaker students – those who could not master the difficulties of Economics – by anyone with some intelligence and spare time.'[14] A view was to emerge in the 1950s that, if it were to develop properly as a discipline in Canada, political science would need to declare its distinctiveness from economics and establish a department of its own at each university. This view had to contend with one to the contrary, which saw collaboration between political scientists and economists to be fruitful from a scholarly standpoint and expressive of an indigenous 'political economy tradition' in the social sciences. This tradition, which resisted the drawing of distinctions between the two disciplines, was associated with the work of the Toronto school of economic history, of which Harold Innis was the central figure, and the kind of interdisciplinary research done under the aegis of the Rowell–Sirois Commission in the late 1930s. That the arrangement which joined the two disciplines in the same department eventually came to an end everywhere in Canada was, as things turned out, as much the doing of economists as of political scientists. Economists turned increasingly to studies of a mathematical and statistical nature, and many of them saw little connection between their discipline and the matters which interested political scientists. The University of Saskatchewan, though it did not combine economics and political science in a single department until 1946, was to be, nearly forty years later, the last to give up the arrangement.[15]

Over the period covered in these pages, which ends in 1960, political science at the University of Saskatchewan, as elsewhere in Canadian universities, was a discipline in search of its own boundaries and a secure and independent place in the university curriculum. The discipline needed first of all to attract students in respectable numbers, and this requisite for a secure place in the curriculum would wait upon the enormous increase in general university enrolment which took place in the 1960s; that the students of that decade were keenly interested in politics made the discipline a special beneficiary of the increased numbers. In the early 1950s the number of full-time teachers of political science in Canada was about thirty; by 1970–1, the number exceeded five hundred.[16] But the search for boundaries, and indeed a disciplinary identity, was one which the 1960s simply renewed in the form of a controversy between 'traditionalists' and 'behaviouralists,' the latter standing for an approach to political science which originated in the

United States and which emphasized political processes over institutions and political thought. The controversy was resolved in a way which was to become characteristic of political science – by making room in the discipline for new approaches while yielding the centre to none, new or old. The discipline emerged as one which was pluralistic in interests, eclectic in method, and, in Canada, subject to the considerable pull exerted by disciplinary practices and norms established in the United States. The controversy over 'behaviouralism' was followed by another over a perceived 'Americanization' of the discipline in Canada, prompted in part by the hiring of many American political scientists by Canadian universities to meet the increase in student numbers. How to make itself indispensable in the curriculum, how to disentangle itself from its sister disciplines, and whether and how to render itself Canadian in content and perhaps also character – these were among the questions which lay before the nascent discipline of political science when it found a place in the curriculum of the University of Saskatchewan in 1910.

I

Although Murray, following the example of the University of Wisconsin, declared in his *Report* for 1910 that 'it is the duty of the State University to provide special facilities for the study of social conditions and the problems of government,' he soon judged that the problems of government in Saskatchewan were chiefly economic.[17] While he strove at the beginning to establish a strong department of economics, political science was relegated to a minor place in the curriculum, where it was designed as a preparatory program for students intending to study law. Murray's first appointment to what he called the Chair of Political Science and Philosophy was therefore made with future developments in mind: 'The appointment is made with the idea of preparing the way for a School of Law.'[18]

His choice for the position was Ira Allen MacKay, a lawyer from Winnipeg and one of Murray's former students. MacKay was born on 5 June 1875 in Boston, Massachusetts, of British parents from Pictou, Nova Scotia, and named after Ira Allen, a colourful politician in New England history. After his parents returned to Pictou, he was sent to school at the Pictou Academy. He entered Dalhousie in 1893, the year after Murray was appointed to the chair of philosophy, and took both his bachelor's and his master's degrees in philosophy. The Dalhousie

University Library still holds an honours essay he wrote for Murray on 'Kant and Idealism,' a bound copy of 115 pages handwritten in its author's ornamental script. On the strength of recommendations from Murray, MacKay was awarded a fellowship to Cornell University, where he completed a doctoral dissertation on the subject of Hegel's philosophy of knowledge and was awarded a PhD. For the next five years, he read law with a Halifax law firm. In 1906 he wrote examinations for the LLB at Dalhousie, married a former Dalhousie student, Margaret de Wolfe, and then moved to Winnipeg to enter the practice of law with the firm of Ferguson and Richardson.

In accounts of MacKay left by his contemporaries and students, a portrait emerges of a man of complex character, able but highly forgetful, known for his dandified style of dress and strong opinions. One of Murray's informants from Winnipeg said that MacKay was 'a very good lawyer' and 'a gentlemanly chap of good appearance and address.'[19] A brief biography of the time describes him as 'ind. in politics; a strong advocate of better and cleaner politics in both Can. parties; a firm believer in the idea of Empire; a Christian.'[20] Edmund Oliver wrote of his new colleague: '[MacKay is] in many respects the most remarkable man on the staff. He is a Philosopher, and absentminded. He got into the wrong house the very first week and has been known to ask the blessing twice in one meal. He is a high Tory, a Scotsman of Pictou, a smoker, an orator. I do not regard his judgment as final. He is often very brilliant, and often only eccentric. He is a popular teacher, not without a touch of the prophetic and poetic.'[21] His success with students was noted in 1919 by A.S. Morton of the history department: 'The work of Professor MacKay's classes in Political Science and International Law, and of a series of history classes has given us in the last three years four very promising young men, intensely interested in the British Empire and the problems of its government, and of its constitutional history.'[22]

One of the promising young men was John G. Diefenbaker, who graduated from the University of Saskatchewan, first in economics and political science, and then in law, and became leader of the Progressive Conservative Party and later Prime Minister of Canada. Diefenbaker remembered MacKay as 'a man often remote from the ordinary things of life.' In his memoirs, he tells the story of how he and some other students took MacKay on a shooting trip, and after hours of waiting finally set their sights on a flock of geese, when MacKay rose up and waxed eloquent about 'poetry in motion,' utterly oblivious to the disappointment of his companions as the startled flock flew out of range. When Diefenbaker joined up, MacKay presented him with William James's *The Principles of Psychology*, expecting him to carry it throughout the war. 'No one had a greater influence on me in university ...' wrote Diefenbaker. 'He was my professor in political science and law, and he had that quality essential to a great teacher, the power to inspire. He was a man of much wisdom and I remember many of his lessons. He judged that a people can never be made good by legislation, a point that many of us never learn.'[23]

Against this encomium must be put the account of another Canadian political leader, David Lewis of the New Democratic Party, who had MacKay as his professor in an introductory philosophy class at McGill. Lewis recounts in his autobiography that he was surprised to find at the end of term that he had failed the course. He sought out his professor for an interview, questioned his grade, and, in return, Lewis recalls, received an outburst of anti-Semitic invective. 'I told him that his words were shameful, that I might have expected to hear such sentiments from an illiterate but not from a university professor.' Lewis then stormed out of the office. He later passed a supplementary examination in the subject. What he had learned from the experience, he said, was 'that bullies should be challenged and that ... education is not a shield against meanness and prejudice.'[24]

In the reminiscences of other students at McGill, MacKay was remembered as 'the kindest and most helpful of deans,' 'the most absent-minded of absent-minded professors,' 'an idealist.' One who talked with him about possible vocations was told: 'Don't worry too much about how you are going to make a living. Get an education and learn *how to think*. An educated mind will help you to make life!'[25]

II

MacKay was eager to join what Murray called 'the noble army of martyrs on the banks of the Saskatchewan in that hot-bed of culture, Saskatoon.'[26] He told the president that his friends in Winnipeg 'think I have made a mistake in throwing away the chance of a much larger income in law' but that he 'cared little for income unless it also brings opportunity.'[27] '"I am with you" to make things a success,' he wrote in a letter full of ideas for the courses he would teach.[28] MacKay became one of eight faculty members hired by President Murray in the first two years of the university's existence. MacKay, who was expected to teach philosophy, political science, and law, suited Murray's need for academics who could be called upon to help in a number of different areas. Murray believed that MacKay's practical training in law would complement the more academic background of Arthur Moxon, the professor of classics and another Dalhousie graduate, who had studied at Oxford as a Rhodes scholar. MacKay and Moxon would form the nucleus for a faculty of law which would be supplemented by lawyers from downtown offices. It was not expected that MacKay would produce anything of importance in the way of scholarly research. Besides fulfilling the requirements for his degrees, he had never written for publication before coming to Saskatchewan, and while there his output amounted to three articles, none of academic interest, published in the *Canadian Magazine*. His later published work consisted of a pamphlet on Canadian citizenship, originally prepared as an address for a service club audience in Montreal.[29]

MacKay's views on education were coloured by his extravagant estimate of the edifying effects of an education in the law. His own training, he once said, 'has taught me ... how far-reaching and interesting are some of those principles which lie concealed in the petty duties or even petty annoyances of practical life. There is for example scarcely a single principle, of Ethics, Economics, or Law which cannot be beautifully illustrated from so commonplace an institution as a Joint Stock Company.' In political science he planned to set out four courses – introductory politics, constitutional government, jurisprudence, and a senior course on current problems of imperial politics – but these four, he believed, were as far as a student should go in political science. As he explained: 'After the standard courses in this subject the proper transition is to a group of standard courses in Law – in Contracts, Torts, International Law etc. These courses are not only more practical but they have a higher cultural value for the general student ... I consider a good course in Contracts the best single course of study which any student can take ... Anson *On Contracts* is the best student's text book extant except Bradley Arnold's *Latin Prose Composition*.'[30]

In devising his programs, MacKay consulted the Wisconsin calendar that Murray had recommended to him but found it of little use. After studying its abundant variety of courses, he came to the conclusion that 'like all U.S. universities, they chop their courses up too much ... I am inclined to think that the reason why the small colleges so often do better work than the large universities is due to the fact that they confine themselves to a systematic course based on the standard classics.'

For his class in ethics, he chose the following list of readings: Seth's *Ethical Principles*, Aristotle's *Ethics*, Marcus Aurelius's *Meditations*, Omar Khayyám's *Rubaiyat*, Mill's *Utilitarianism*, Kant's ethical writings, and Darwin's *Descent of Man*. No intelligent student, he said, could read the *Rubaiyat* and the *Meditations* 'without becoming tainted somewhat with the two great types of Ethical theory and character which *they* represent.'[31]

MacKay's first draft of political science courses had them grouped with philosophy under the general heading 'Philosophy of Law.' But when the calendar for 1910–11 was published, political science showed up with its own heading, separate from law and philosophy. Four courses in political science were offered:

Introductory Politics. The elements of political theory as in Aristotle's *Politics* and in Sidgwick's *The Elements of Politics*.

Canadian Constitutional History and Law. A systematic course of lectures on Canadian Constitutional History with Houston's *Constitutional Documents of Canada* and all other available original sources, and a careful study of the British North America Acts as in Clement's *Canadian Constitution* with selected leading cases from the *Law Reports*.

Elementary Jurisprudence. This course will be of particular value to students intending to enter the legal profession. It is also recommended to students in Philosophy and Economics. Salmond's *Jurisprudence* and Maine's *Ancient Law*.

Advanced Political Theory. Bagehot's *English Constitution*, Dicey's *The Law of the Constitution*, Woodrow Wilson's *Congressional Government* and Bryce's *American Commonwealth*.

During the eight years MacKay spent as a member of the Saskatchewan faculty, the list of courses offered in political science changed from year to year, with some omitted, and a fifth course, international law, later added. The early calendars also set out the requirements for an honours or special course in political science. The calendars, however, often promised a great deal more than could be delivered, especially in the early years of the university when the staff was small.

In the case of political science, all but two of the advertised courses were in fact courses in law which were listed in the arts calendar and, after 1913, in the law calendar as well. Only one or two courses in political science itself were given each year. In his first year, 1910–11, MacKay introduced the course in constitutional government, in which two students registered. Among the matters studied were local statutes and procedure at meetings; classical ideas were brought in, he explained, 'merely for purposes of illumination.'[32] In his second year, MacKay taught two other courses in political science: the introductory course and elementary jurisprudence. In his third year, he again taught constitutional government, this time to a class of twenty-six. In the meantime, he continued to teach courses in philosophy, including ethics, psychology and logic, and modern philosophy.

In the fall of 1913, upon the opening of the College of Law, MacKay's title was changed to Professor of Law and Lecturer in Political Science and his teaching duties increased considerably. In this year he taught six different courses to a total of 165 students: introductory philosophy, introductory politics, a seminar in politics, jurisprudence, contracts, and bills and notes. In his report to the president at the end of the session he expressed general satisfaction at the results of his political science classes and urged that more attention be given to the only department 'designed to expressly recognize the claims of intelligent and conscientious citizenship.' 'Every student,' he said, 'should leave the University prepared to take a leading part in the government of his city, town or municipality.'[33] He took note of the work of two excellent students: Clarence Rife, the first honours student in political science and history, who later studied at Toronto and Yale and became head of the history department at Hamline University in St Paul, Minnesota; and John Weir, the first honours student in economics, who later became the first dean of law at the University of Alberta.

MacKay expected his work in political science soon to draw to a close and leave him with responsibility for only the elementary course in political science, and that only in alternate years. A new man in history, Frank Underhill, was expected to help out in political science and be assigned to teach the courses in the constitutional history of England and the constitutional history of the British Empire. But by the next year the country was at war, and many of the faculty, Underhill among them, had signed up for service. The First World War had a devastating effect on university work in Canada. For MacKay, it meant more work than ever. In 1914–15 he taught a total of 195 students and nine courses in all – two in political science, two in philosophy, one in senior English, and four in law. And with the war, and the crushing

burden of teaching which it visited on him, seemed to come a shatter-
ing of some of his illusions about the university. 'Featureless courses of
instruction, featureless examinations and featureless examination
results, all tend to produce featureless scholars,' he wrote in his report
to the president. 'Unless the University wishes to sink to the level of an
advanced high school these tendencies will have to be corrected.'[34] His
melancholic outlook became even more pronounced the following
year as he described developments within the new law college as 'a
progress down hill' and spoke of a state of low morale caused by the
'makeshift, halting, dilatory, discouraging attitude of the university to
the school ... When I came to the University four years ago I had three
enthusiasms, a department of Psychology, a department of Political
Science or Government, and a school of Law. Three triplets are
still-born ... And yet I conceive all three to be essential to even a small
modern state university. I feel the failure personally.'[35]

III

By 1919, an accumulation of grievances at the university flared into a
full-scale controversy involving MacKay and three other members of
faculty – Samuel E. Greenway, the director of extension, John L. Hogg,
head of physics, and Robert D. McLaurin, head of chemistry, all of
whom were dissatisfied with the administration and hostile to the
president. The whole business lasted for more than a year, adding to an
atmosphere already made cheerless by the grim news of war casualties
and the effects of the influenza epidemic, which shut down university
classes for most of the first term. The trouble started in March when
Greenway, the leader of the group, went directly to the provincial government in Regina with charges against President Murray of mishan-
dling university funds and improper management of the institution.
When news of the accusations reached the university council, all members except for the dissentients responded by declaring their support
for the president, and the Board of Governors decided to issue letters
of dismissal to the four men. But instead of bringing the issue to an end
as it had hoped, the action of the board served to ignite the interest of
the public, the student body, and the newspapers, all demanding a
public inquiry into the matter. At a lively meeting of convocation,
especially convened to consider the dismissals, the board was
reproved for its failure to give any reason for its actions. The students
and the press were strongly on the side of the four men, especially with

Professor MacKay, who, according to a report in the *Saskatoon Daily Star*, delivered an 'eloquent' address to the meeting.[36] John Diefenbaker, in one of the first exhibitions of his vivid oratorical style, also spoke, and in an impassioned plea in favour of the rebels threatened to burn his diplomas in public. In the end, a formal investigation into the charges was launched by the government, using the device of a Visitor as allowed by a special provision of the University Act, and the president was cleared of all the accusations brought against him.[37]

The intervention of the Visitor had helped to bring the crisis to a close, but no one involved in the whole affair emerged unscathed. Although public sentiment was generally in favour of the four men, their careers at the university had been brought to an abrupt end. Morale at the university and the confidence of the public in the university were seriously damaged. By dismissing the men, the board may have acted within its powers, but its action looked high-handed and ill-considered. And the president himself, though found innocent of any wrongdoing, did not escape without injury. The controversy was a blow to Murray's vision of the university as a dedicated community of academics working together towards common goals. He knew he had to contend with the criticisms of those he identified as troublemakers; but as the controversy grew more bitter, he was wounded by the nasty suspicions aroused in people he respected. 'I was not aware of the fact that I had been autocratic,' he wrote to Premier Martin in the early days of the crisis; 'in fact, I thought that I had been too easy going; but probably when people do not get what they wish, they think that those who oppose them are autocratic and wrong.'[38] Murray never had to use the letter of resignation he had prepared, but privately it was feared that he would not have the strength to carry on. In the summer of the crisis, as he was waiting in the Maritimes for events in Saskatchewan to take their course, he suffered a nervous collapse, followed by an appendicitis attack and surgery. Although details of his condition were kept from the public, rumours that he could not continue as president were widely circulated. When he finally returned to the university in mid-January of 1920, he was a changed man with an altered style of administration, ever aware of the hostile elements in his midst.

Murray was especially aggrieved that MacKay, after their long association, should have taken a part against him.[39] He came to suspect that MacKay, like the others, was motivated by deep personal disappointment – in MacKay's case, the loss of the appointment as dean of law, an appointment for which his colleague, Moxon, had emerged as the front runner. Murray would not easily forget, as he said many years later to one of his friends, 'the disturbance that may be caused by an ambitious man who will go around canvassing among his colleagues for ulterior purposes.'[40] By those unsympathetic to him, MacKay was seen as someone who was foolish enough to allow himself to fall in with bad company.[41] 'He has always impressed me as a very clever, impractical sort of fellow, perpetually prancing about with his head in the clouds,' the chancellor of the university, F.W. Haultain, wrote to Murray. 'I fancy that you regard MacKay even yet as an object more of sorrow than of anger. My general impression of him is that he is rather silly and vain and weak. If any distinction could have been made between him and the other three, the proper treatment in his case would have been a good spanking. Nevertheless, he is a clever, likeable sort of child.'[42] MacKay was careful never to express any personal animosity against the president, nor was he as vocal in his criticism as the other three. But he did join their cause in presenting charges directly to the government instead of using the usual procedural channels within the institution, and he declined to take part in the vote of confidence passed by university council in support of the president. He appeared to have been swept along by the remonstrances of the other men, who hoped that his presence would lend respectability to their cause. He presumed, wrongly as it turned out, that his friendship with the president allowed him the privilege of publicly criticizing the university. The letters of dismissal from the board, which had been quietly engineered by Murray, came as a complete surprise to him.

IV

MacKay's career did not suffer any lasting damage from his involvement in the affair. His dismissal, along with that of the other three, was changed to a leave with pay for the academic year of 1919–20, after which he went on to McGill University as a professor of constitutional and international law. Murray wrote a letter in support of his appointment. In 1924, MacKay was appointed professor of logic and metaphysics and dean of arts at McGill, where he exercised a considerable influence on the development of the university.[43] He remained in this position until his sudden death from a heart attack in 1934.

Without MacKay there to promote it, political science at Saskatchewan went into decline. Though courses in political science continued to be advertised each year in the university calendar, none were actually given for three years. Perhaps no one could be spared for teaching political science, or perhaps there were few students interested in studying it. In any case, no one seemed to lament its absence – not, that is, until Frank Underhill, the man hired to replace Edmund Oliver in history, undertook to revive political science and to make it his major interest.

6

A Natural Minoritarian

Frank Hawkins Underhill, the second teacher of political science at Saskatchewan, was born on 26 November 1889 in Stouffville, Ontario, where his father, the son of a cobbler who had emigrated from Britain, carried on a successful shoe-manufacturing business.[1] In Underhill's own view, he had always been 'a natural minoritarian.' 'I was born a North York Presbyterian Grit,' he wrote when he was seventy. 'Something, however, in my heredity or in my environment, whatever it was, did make it certain that I should never belong or want to belong to the Establishment.'[2] When he was in his twenties, he confessed to his mother that he had 'very little religion left in me.'[3] But in his early years there were few signs of a rebellious nature. He was a bookish child with little interest in sports or games, brought up on a regimen of regular church attendance and strict observance of middle-class proprieties, and an exemplary student throughout. He attended the Stouffville Public School and Markham High School, and in 1907 was the top student in university entrance examinations, winning the McCaul Scholarship for study at the University of Toronto. At Toronto, he became the favourite of the history department and was regarded as the best student to have passed through the department in years.[4] After four years of study he graduated with a bachelor's degree and high honours in classics and ranked first in the course styled as 'English and history with the classical option.' His good marks brought him the financial support he needed to go on to further studies; with the Flavelle travelling scholarship to Oxford he was provided a comfortable allowance of $750 a year for two years, and an exhibition from Balliol College later added another £50.

At Oxford, Underhill enrolled in *Literae Humaniores,* or Greats, and got caught up in the intense political debates which formed part of the intellectual atmosphere there. He went often to public meetings where he was able to hear the leading politicians and thinkers of the day. He joined the Fabian Society, of which G. D.H. Cole and Harold Laski were members, and the Russell and Palmerston Liberal Club. On the other hand, his response to the social side of Oxford was only luke-warm. His Toronto seniors were fretful over what William S. Milner, professor of ancient history, termed his 'handicap of great shyness' and suggested that he should study less and entertain more.[5] Edward Kylie in classics sent Underhill a series of fatherly letters, instructing him to 'keep out in the air for hours every day – such air as it is! and fall asleep in your armchair ... take life easily and pleasantly and have peo-ple in for tea constantly,' 'make a speech a week.' 'I should like you to know the Englishman better,' he said; 'don't be afraid to come out of your shell to let yourself go – there is rather the danger that after all this thinking ... you should become too self-centered.'[6]

George Wrong, the head of history at Toronto, replying to a letter from Underhill, worried that he was becoming unduly sensitive to 'the defects of English life' and its 'social injustice': 'Luxury shocks me as I see it shocks you. Yet it may be that a year or two of luxury will do a Canadian youth no harm. I doubt whether the soul is after all much injured by the luxury of good pictures, carved furniture, comfortable easy chairs and beautiful rooms.'[7]

At the end of two years of intensive study, Underhill attained his ulti-mate goal, a first in Greats. For the following year, he rejected an offer of an assistant lectureship at the University of Manchester (for pay of £50) and decided, with the assurance of financial support from his father, to stay on at Oxford to study modern political philosophy. What he should do after this was a matter of some debate, since his maturity and readiness for teaching at this stage seemed doubtful. His tutor, A.D. Lindsay, advised that he should remain at Oxford, join more societies, and 'open out a bit.' 'You'd make a very good researcher as you are now but not yet, I don't think, a very good teacher,' he told Underhill.[8] Pro-fessor Kylie from Toronto suggested he might take a few years in busi-ness with his father 'just to give you a larger experience of men and to neutralise all your abstract thinking.'[9] On the other hand, Milner had intimated to Underhill that a place would be found for him at Toronto; but this was before the University of Saskatchewan had declared its interest. When Milner heard of the Saskatchewan offer, he wrote imme-diately to Underhill, releasing him from any obligation to Toronto and urging that he 'let nothing but the most cruel necessity intervene' in accepting this 'heaven sent' opportunity: 'You will know your country. Saskatchewan is a pivotal province in Canada – *the* pivotal province – in the same way as the Middle West States in the American Republic. Everything in our immediate future will turn upon what happens there. So go if you possibly can. I may say that literally no man in Canada knows our country as well as President Murray. You will find that this is the deliberate opinion of many public men; and he is a glorious man to work with.'[10]

The offer from President Murray was simply too attractive to pass up. At the age of twenty-four and with no experience of teaching, Underhill had the good fortune to move directly into a senior university position. It gave him the status of a full professorship, a starting salary of $2,500, and the choice of a 'chair' in either Greek or history. He chose history and it was understood that he would help out in Greek and political science as well.

I

In the fancy of Underhill's youth, the West was a land of golden opportunity with visions of future Chicagos springing up alongside the new transcontinental railways. His own father had bought title to some barren land in the West upon which he would never set foot, and two of his uncles had gone to Manitoba to make their fortunes. While he was at Oxford, Underhill read in the *Westminster Gazette* a series of letters from Canada written by the poet Rupert Brooke. Brooke dilated eloquently on the differences between East and West, on the austere prairie landscape with its succession of small towns, on the bold attempts of the farmers to form new economic and political organizations (like the Chartists, he said), and on the easygoing manners of the West – 'better than those of the East, more friendly, more hearty, more certain to achieve graciousness, if not grace.'[11] But Underhill heard other stories as well. A family friend living in Regina wrote despairingly of the terrible cold and severe hardships he'd had to endure, and his old school chum, Charles Cochrane, warned him not to take too romantic a view of his new home: 'the river is muddy and the sand blows in your eyes.'[12]

Saskatoon, at the time Underhill first laid eyes on it, had lost some of the buoyant optimism that had swept the community forward from a small settlement to a city of some pretensions. The land boom had left behind a number of imposing structures which remain as the city's historic landmarks, but its collapse at the end of 1913 served as a reminder of the fragile economic base on which the fortunes of its citizens, and that of the university, rested. As a result – a quite unexpected result – the number of full-time students at the university increased in 1914 to 445 from the previous year's record of 382. As Murray, in wise hindsight, explained in a letter to the president of the University of Manitoba, J.A. MacLean: 'hard times, so far as it reduces the openings for young men, tends to drive those who can afford it to the University, and it has also prevented a few from journeying to the eastern universities.'[13] For the President and his young faculty, hard times and the reduction in the government's grant to the university cast a shadow over their hopes for expansion and dimmed their early ardour for the adventure. When a fire started by lightning destroyed part of the business district of Saskatoon and a cyclone wrought devastation in the city of Regina, both during 1912, Murray said woefully: 'I think it would be well for us all to leave this country. It is not fit to live in, so the women say, and probably they are right.'[14] There were few amenities in Saskatoon to remind faculty members of the venerable academic places they had once and all too briefly known. It was not unusual for newcomers – and their families – to suffer problems of adjustment. Walter P. Thompson, a biologist and later president who came from Harvard in 1913, remembered being cautioned by President Murray: 'Do not be appalled at the absence of all you have been accustomed to find in other Universities. We have all had to start with nothing ... You have virgin soil to break.'[15]

For Underhill, a shy, intellectual young man who had become accustomed to the rarefied atmosphere of Oxford, the move to Saskatoon was especially difficult. He thought he had come to a 'back-woods settlement.' He was scandalized by the informal mixing of men and women at the University of Saskatchewan. 'Among various horrors of the Univ hall,' he told his mother, 'there is one unique one – men and women students sit together, two or three women and four or five men at each table. They also play tennis together a great deal, which probably accounts for the fact that the only persons who know how to use a racquet belong to the staff.' During the first term he stayed away from the university dining-hall and its coeducational intimacies by crossing the river twice a day for meals at Cairns's new department store downtown (later the site of the Hudson's Bay store), a round trip of two or three miles a day by his reckoning. When the cold set in, he took his meals at the university, although he found the fare pretty unappetizing and suspected it would make him thin by spring.[16]

At first he found life in Saskatoon terribly lonely and monotonous. 'It is a dull town,' he wrote in one of his letters home. 'There isn't a thing to go to except the pictures and a 5th class stock company, and now the one theatre in town is going into the picture business too. The one relieving feature is the Manitoba Free Press which is simply incomparably better than the Globe.'[17] There were other bachelors on the staff – Louis Brehaut in philosophy, Reginald Bateman in English, and John Eaton in German. The first two soon left the university to enlist in the war, but Underhill formed a close and long-lasting friendship with Eaton, his convivial Irish office mate, who stayed behind. For amusement they would take in a picture show twice a week. From time to time, there would be invitations to the homes of married faculty, or to the president's new place on campus which Underhill fancied had been built for the purpose of entertaining students; he thought it 'quite the finest residence in Saskatoon.'[18] But the occasion of the year that would most stand out in his memory afterwards was his meeting with J.S. Woodsworth, who came to the university to deliver a series of lectures on the subject of immigration: 'I was greatly impressed by his lecturing, especially by the main point that I remember, that we should seek to find out what we could learn from the new European immigrants, and not be too insistent on what they must learn from us. He was given a big tea party one afternoon at President Murray's home, which was attended by all the best people in Saskatoon as well as by a good many professors, and I had quite a talk with him.'[19]

Teaching gave him less satisfaction, his mood shifting between disappointment in the quality and performance of his students and self-reproach at his own inability to excite their interest. 'Out here,' he wrote to his mother, 'education is a matter of getting in a certain number of classes involving a certain number of hours each year, and it is all arranged with the precision of an American factory.'[20] Of the students he taught during 1914–15, only the two who took a reading class from him in history came up to his standards. In his largest class, English history to 1485, attended by eleven women and fourteen men (Underhill always segregated the sexes in his class lists), he found there was little interest in either reading or class discussion.[21] In introductory Greek, the efforts of the students were 'thoroughly unsatisfactory.'[22] Advanced Greek attracted only one student, a 'dull stupid theolog,' who soon dropped out of it.[23] In Greek philosophy, a class given over to Underhill when Brehaut left for the war, the students, with one exception, were 'more fitted to benefit by the agricultural courses which the Presbyterian College prescribes than by any study of philosophy.'[24] At the year's end, Murray had come to the conclusion that his new recruit had turned out exceptionally well, but Underhill, who developed a habit of critical introspection in his early years, thought he had performed very poorly.[25]

II

Toronto, where Underhill went in the summer of 1915 to recuperate from his first year of teaching, was in the midst of feverish preparations for sending troops off to war. Most of Underhill's friends were occupied with some kind of military work, and he became impatient to join in. 'I ought to be doing something, after having spent a whole year as if I were an American neutral. And I'm afraid I'll lose my own self-respect if I put off matters much longer,' he wrote to Murray. He wondered whether he should sign up at once rather than spend the winter 'in more or less useless and uninteresting history work' while he waited for a commission to be offered to him.[26] Finally, in September, he made up his mind to join the 4th University Company, a regiment of the 11th Reserve Battalion of the Canadian Expeditionary Force. His absence from the university was remarked upon in the *Sheaf*: 'It is hard for us to realize what a great sacrifice Prof. Underhill has made. After spending the best years of his life in the best universities preparing for his professorship to be called away at the very outset of his career is indeed a notable case of self surrender.'[27]

It did not take long for Underhill to discover that he had little taste for the life of a private in the Canadian army. He wrote to his mother: 'If ever I am shipwrecked I hope there are no Canadians or Americans among the company with me. Their absolute lack of intelligent interests would drive me crazy.'[28] He had been forewarned by Murray about joining up as a private: Brehaut, his colleague in philosophy, had apparently broken down after a short time in the army and been forced to take a discharge. Obviously, there were adjustments to be made, as Underhill himself described to Murray: 'In college, or in Oxford anyway, you simply cut the men in whom you are not interested or whom you don't like. But here we are crowded thirty men in a hut and you have to get along with everybody. It's made me somewhat more democratic in my ways however much I disliked it at [the] time.'[29] He had confidently expected to be quickly promoted to the rank of officer; when he was not, he felt ineffectual and depressed. Eventually, his Oxford friends managed to bring about his transfer to the British forces, and he was installed as a second lieutenant with the Hertford-shire regiment. On his twenty-seventh birthday, 26 November 1916, just after receiving his new commission, he wrote in his diary: 'In some ways I feel so enormously more mature, as if I had acquired a real indi-vidual judgment; and then again, in matters of practice I find myself as ineffective and as without confidence as ever – so totally unfit to be an officer to have charge of men and so entirely an egoist in the way I habitually view the world that I am always unhappy and miserable when facts make me contrast the actual me with the person about whom I am always weaving fantasies. Well, if I am to make a birthday resolution it must be to give up always thinking about myself and to try and view my surroundings objectively. And I must put more energy into my military work. If I fail in it I shall be no good for any-thing afterwards.'[30]

After spending most of a year training as a Lewis gun officer, Under-hill was posted to France and stationed just behind the front line, where he saw some heavy fighting. The worst came after the Treaty of Brest-Litovsk had confirmed the withdrawal of Russia from the war but before American troops were fully mobilized to help on the western front, when the German Army, led by Ludendorff, mounted its last major invasion of the war and smashed through the British forces. On the second day of the German offensive, on 22 March 1918, Underhill was hit by shrapnel in the back of his leg and had to walk four miles before he could get a lift to the nearest town. He considered himself lucky to get out so easily when so many in his group fared worse. He was removed to a hospital in Plymouth, where he spent eighteen days, and then had several months of convalescence in England. He was pro-moted to lieutenant and afterwards returned to active duty in France, but by then the fighting was nearly over. He became an education officer with his battalion and later was transferred to the Khaki Univer-sity established for the education of Canadian soldiers.[31] By April 1919 he was able to report that he was hard at work correcting papers, read-ing, and preparing for next winter's lectures in Saskatchewan.[32]

Officer's rank with the British forces had made life in the army more congenial to Underhill. There was time for reading, reflection, and argument with his fellow officers. Most of his companions were conser-vative in political opinion and were inclined, he said, to 'regard me and my opinions as an interesting freak.'[33] Yet there were compensations. He ordered his military gear from Hawkes & Co., a Savile Row tailor, and had regular mail deliveries of the *Times Literary Supplement, Nation Canada, New Europe,* and the *Manchester Guardian.* Afterwards, when he returned to the company of Canadians at the Khaki University, he sorely missed some of the pleasures the British camp had afforded. 'There is no afternoon tea or dinner at 7:30,' he noted. 'Instead we have the ordinary Canadian meals, dinner at 12:30 and supper at 5, which I don't like nearly as well. The batmen don't look after you either in the way that English servants do ... There are no drinks to be obtained there and few papers to read.'[34] In an article for the *Sheaf,* written from overseas, he declared: 'I beg to bear witness that one individual, at least, never had a better time in his life than during the period he spent with English officers in an English mess.'[35]

But the experience of the war sowed in him the seed of a Canadian nationalism.[36] In his account of Canada's participation in the war, published in 1923, Underhill eschewed the gadfly style which characterized much of his later writing. He called the efforts of his countrymen 'the noblest example yet given of the ability of Canadians, working in concert with a single inspiration, to accomplish great ends,' and concluded with the following tribute: 'The four years' career of her fighting troops in France forms the real testimony to Canada's entrance into nationhood, the visible demonstration that there has grown up on her soil a people not English nor Scottish nor American but Canadian – a Canadian nation.'[37] When he was older, he reflected on what he had learned from his time with the army: 'I discovered that this Edwardian-Georgian generation of Englishmen made the best regimental officers in the world and the worst staff officers. The stupidity of G.H.Q. and the terrible sacrifice of so many of the best men among my contemporaries sickened me for good of a society, national or international, run by the British governing classes.'[38] Whether by happenstance or design, he never again visited Europe after 1919.

III

Underhill returned to Saskatchewan after the war in time to witness the gathering strength of the Progressive movement. As he said later, and not entirely originally: 'I experienced for the first time what a democracy is like when it is thoroughly alive ... Bliss was it in those days on the prairie to be alive, but to be young was very heaven.'[39] Underhill was swept along by the excitement of the prairie upheaval. He attended as many meetings as he could and admired the vigour of the grassroots members as they protested against their domination by the financial interests of eastern Canada. He was thrilled to hear Aaron Sapiro, the spell-binding exponent of cooperation from the United States, rouse a packed audience gathered at Third Avenue Methodist Church in sup-port of wheat pooling. It was a speech worthy of the great American revivalists: Underhill called it 'the most magnificent that I have ever heard.'[40] He was utterly won over to the side of the farmers and hoped that their rejection of traditional institutions would result in a transfor-mation of the Canadian political system. 'As far as I can see,' he wrote to a friend in Oxford, 'the only hope for a civilization in this country in which we won't all be abject slaves to a few vulgar ignorant money bar-ons in Toronto and Montreal rests with the Western farmer.'[41] Underhill voted Progressive in the election of 1921, along with most other faculty members. By the time of the next election, in 1925, he felt he was almost the only Progressive supporter left on faculty.

Underhill was disappointed when the eastern press took so little account of the momentous developments in western Canada. He tried to persuade Lionel Curtis of the *Round Table* to come out to the West to see with his own eyes 'the Western Progressives in their native habitat and with their war paint on. Your Toronto correspondents are too much in the habit – it is a Toronto habit – of writing about the people of other parts of Canada as interesting pathological specimens ... The fact is that this western movement is the one thing that is alive in Canadian politics outside of the C.M.A. [Canadian Manufacturers' Association] and the C.P.R. and the Roman Catholic Church. In spite of its weak leadership and its many futilities it is a real effort to establish democ-racy in this country against the two sham parties which are dominated by the sinister interests in Toronto and Montreal. At present it is going through the "Chartist" stage and [has] far too many Feargus O'Con-nors attached to it. But it is going to develop trained leaders through the Wheat Pool and such organisations just as the British Labour party did through its Trade Unions.'[42]

Underhill was also disappointed in the way that the western univer-sities reacted to the political events of the twenties. President Murray had sought to create an image of a university that would be as politi-cally neutral as possible. As time went on, he became increasingly scrupulous about keeping himself free from political involvement and expected the same of his faculty; on one occasion, in 1917, he placed a letter of resignation on file before he would consent to act as chairman at a public meeting in favour of union government, where he spoke fervently on the side of the war effort. Underhill knew Murray as a man with a passionate interest in social issues. He once said that Murray was one of the 'few genuine liberals whom I have met among those in high places in Canada in my lifetime,'[43] a remarkable tribute from one who wrote a book entitled *In Search of Canadian* Liberalism. Yet remembering the seething political atmosphere he had experienced at Oxford, he was puzzled that the prairie universities should have kept so aloof from the Progressive movement when there was so much to be gained from a closer association between its leaders and university men. He remarked to his Balliol tutor, Kenneth Bell: 'The Universities exist to make young hopefuls more proficient in the art of making money. They help the farmer a good deal in the technical side of agriculture but they are failing absolutely to provide any of the badly needed leadership in social and political problems.'[44]

IV

In contrast to the political battles being waged outside, the atmosphere at the university during the decade of the twenties was calm and optimistic. The provincial government showed its confidence in the work of the university with generously increased grants. Underhill now drew a salary of $4,000 a year instead of the $2,500 he had received before the war. Full-time enrolments at the university increased from over 700 students in 1920 to more than 1,500 by 1929. In the history department, A.S. Morton had become head. Morton, Murray's former Edinburgh classmate and an ordained Presbyterian minister, had joined the faculty in 1914 as university librarian and lecturer in history, in response to Murray's call for help when Underhill, his only faculty member in history, had gone to war. Morton, who was later named the first Saskatchewan archivist, believed it was his responsibility to see to the province's records and artifacts and to study its early development. 'During the war,' he wrote, 'I was left alone to carry on the work of the Department and became impressed with the duty lying upon the Department of History of a State University towards the Province whose institution it is.'[45] Putting aside his earlier inquiries into church history, Morton began to trace with indefatigable zeal the paths of the early settlers to the North-West. His *History of the Canadian West to 1870–71* was published in 1939. As he neared the end of his task, he wrote: 'Here one is absolutely alone, with a large staff around me, but not interested in the past of the country.'[46]

Morton and Underhill, colleagues though they were in the history department, were almost completely unlike in personality and in their approach to history. Underhill scoured the past for what it would offer in the way of lessons for the present. Morton loved the past as the past. Moreover, he had little use for Underhill's easy tendency to debunk anything which did not suit his tastes. When Underhill later published a searing criticism of Harold Innis's book on the fur trade, Morton privately put down Underhill's review as the jeers of a philistine.[47] Nevertheless, their relations in the history department were always marked with the greatest civility, and whatever they thought of one another they kept pretty well to themselves. Morton taught ancient history, Underhill, British and Canadian, and between them they divided responsibility for the modern period. They worked together in the Saskatoon Historical Society and on the collection of archival materials. Underhill never objected to Morton's taking the headship that almost certainly would have gone to Underhill if he had not gone away to war, while Morton kept his silence when Underhill audaciously established a club of his own (which reputedly barred women members) in competition with one of Morton's.[48]

The smallness of the university gave it a cloistered feeling – 'too damned intimate for one's more mature years' was how John Eaton put it.[49] Many of the younger members of faculty were hoping fervently for appointments elsewhere. 'I mean to try fairly hard to get away from that desert waste of desolation (pace the Saskatonians), for in it I shall be dead within five years,' John Lothian of the English department confided to Underhill.[50] Feelings of isolation were compounded by the smug attitudes of Canadian periodicals issuing from the East. Underhill said that the 'stuff you read in the Round Table and such organs is mostly by pundits who have never penetrated beyond Toronto farther than the surrounding golf links.'[51] Nevertheless, Underhill himself never felt quite at home in Saskatchewan. As he once said ruefully to one of his friends, 'It is easier for a camel to go through the eye of needle than for an Oxford man to fit out here – at least if he is a very young Oxford man.'[52] And he told his former tutor in Oxford: 'The West is not a very comfortable place to live in, or at any rate I don't find the great open spaces particularly alluring to an academic person like myself. We are pretty well cut off from communion with our fellow creatures in the university world.'[53]

To compensate for their remoteness, the more convivial spirits on the faculty formed a club called The Unashamed, which met fortnightly to discuss a new book or play. John Lothian was the secretary, and his moderately libellous rendering of the minutes was one of the prime entertainments of each gathering. Underhill ('admitted on all hands to be essentially the most conservative member of the Club,' according to the minutes) was once chosen to lead a spirited discussion on Lord Hugh Cecil's *Conservatism*, a book which Underhill judged to be both wrong and important.[54] J.A. Corry, who was then a member of the Saskatchewan law faculty, later commented that this club suited his outlook better than any other he had ever belonged to: 'The view was that nothing was so serious that we had always to take ourselves seriously in its company.'[55]

In spite of his peevishness towards his surroundings, Underhill became deeply attached to Saskatchewan both politically and personally. Not long after he returned from the war, he began to develop an acquaintance with an instructor in English, Ruth Carr, who occupied the office next to his in Qu'Appelle Hall and whose family lived in Prince Albert, north of Saskatoon. Their first outing in public was to attend a meeting called to hear the Progressive leader, Thomas Crerar, at the Third Avenue Methodist Church; arriving late, the couple had to sit in the front row of the choir stalls behind the speakers, in full view of friends and colleagues. 'I still remember,' said Underhill later, 'their amused comments on what was evidently happening to me.'[56] They married in 1922 and soon after moved into a house at 815 Fourteenth Street. His new domestic arrangements suited him well. Despite a perennial feeling of impecuniousness and the worry about finding good maids – a problem which seems to crop up fairly often in the correspondence of faculty members at this time – he now felt better able to concentrate on reading and research and teaching than at any time since the war.

V

When Underhill first joined the staff in 1914, it was understood that he would help Ira MacKay with the work in political science. The university *Calendar* had announced that twice a week Mr Underhill would conduct a political science course in the constitutional history of the British Empire. But the scheme never worked out. Underhill went away to war, and MacKay was left to carry on by himself. When

Underhill returned, MacKay was no longer a member of faculty and political science was left to languish.

It was not until the fall of 1921 that Underhill turned his attention to the teaching of political science. He began with a course in introductory politics to which, for the first three years, only upper-year students were admitted (nine, twelve, and seven, respectively, each year). The textbook used was Stephen Leacock's *Elements of Political Science*, and selections from Plato, Aristotle, Hobbes, Locke, and Rousseau were prescribed readings. In 1923 a seminar on comparative politics was added and taken by five students. Though he complained as usual about the quality of the students and their lack of intellectual curiosity, Underhill himself became more and more drawn towards the study of politics. In the spring of 1924 he recommended to the president that political science become a full-fledged department so that students could specialize in the subject. Murray agreed. In the fall of the same year, George Simpson, a former student, was added to the teaching staff in history, and Underhill's title was changed from Professor of History to Professor of Political Science and Lecturer in History. Thereafter, he proceeded to work happily on plans for a new department of political science. He organized a League of Nations Club in Saskatoon, arranged for the acquisition of a number of periodicals for the library (the *Political Science Quarterly* and *American Political Science Review* to begin with), and designed a new structure of courses which would permit students to take political science as a major. With all of this President Murray concurred, except for an expenditure of $100 for publications of the League of Nations to which he objected on the grounds that there were too many other demands to be met.

Underhill expected his shift to political science to be 'more on paper than in reality, at least for the next two years.'[57] By then he hoped to be able to move completely over to the teaching of political science, except for the course he taught in Canadian history. 'I find,' he said, 'that it is problems of government which interest me more and more and therefore I think P.S. is where I belong,' and he liked the idea of having 'a department to myself which I can make or mar by my own efforts.' His aim was to set out a more or less fixed course which all students specializing in political science would have to take, rather than offer too wide a range of options, which he said was 'the curse of the history dept.'[58] His new schedule for political science, consisting of six courses, was described in the *Calendar* for 1926–7 as follows:

Comparative Government. The structure and the working of the governmental institutions in Canada, Great Britain, United States, Australia,
South Africa, Irish Free State, India, France, Germany, Switzerland, Union
of Socialist Soviet Republics.

International Relations. The contemporary political map of the world,
development of international organizations in the 19th and 20th centu-
ries, nationalism and imperialism, the League of Nations.

Classical Political Theory.

Modern Political Theory. The political issues of such men as Bosanquet,
Hobhouse, Webb, Laski, Cole, Russell, Duguit, Krabbe, Wallas, Lippmann.

Contemporary Problems of Democracy in Canada, Britain and the United
States. Government by public opinion, parties and the party system,
direct vs. representative government, big business, imperialism, foreign
policy, the state and the individual.

English Political Thought since 1760. (a) The development of the Empire.
Successive phases of the imperial problem; the American Revolution,
Responsible Government, Little Englandism, Imperial Federation, the
Commonwealth of Nations. (b) The development of the democratic state.
Aristocratic, middle class and labour political ideas since Burke.

In the beginning, political science was not a popular choice for
Saskatchewan students, to whom, as Underhill described it, 'Politics ...
means something the same as patriotism meant to Dr. Johnson.'[59] He
explained the difficulties to a correspondent in Toronto:

The western student who doesn't go in for natural science (the best of
them do) takes most readily to economics on the theory that a knowledge
of economics is what the West most needs. I believe that a knowledge of
government is what it most needs and a study of the methods by which
men combine to achieve their common purposes; but whether I can make
them realize this is another matter. The trouble with the West is that it is
peopled by money making individualists who have never thought about
any of the problems of man in society until the recent hard times have
compelled some thinking. And naturally most of the thinking has been

superficial and in politics they jump at the most obvious half baked solutions of North American democracy ... Until some Canadian university sets itself to produce something like the Oxford Greats school and ... its students to thinking about society as a whole our country will meet its problems without much help from its universities except of the narrowest technical kind. But our Canadian universities have no philosophers – only professors of philosophy.[60]

Underhill sometimes talked about devising a combined course in philosophy, economics, and political science, like the Oxford Greats, but never developed the idea further. Moreover, it is doubtful whether he could have mustered the necessary cooperation from other departments. Underhill's own relations with W.W. Swanson, the head of economics, were noticeably cool. After the 1925 federal election, Underhill remarked privately on one of his reasons for espousing the Liberal cause: 'The head of the Economics department was slated for a job on Mackenzie King's tariff board and we all prayed for a sweeping Liberal victory at the last election but an unkind fate ruled otherwise. So I am afraid we shall have to rely on the same Providence upon which Mr. King relies for the reform of the Senate.'[61] At a later time, he spoke scathingly of 'our economists' who 'have played the humble self-imposed rôle of minor technicians, never questioning the major purposes of the capitalist system in which they found themselves, never venturing any opinions about the general planning of the machine or the powering of its engines, pottering about with their little statistical measuring instruments, doing occasional odd repair jobs on Royal commissions, such as putting new brake linings into the financial mechanism, happy in their unambitious way as the intellectual garage-mechanics of Canadian capitalism.'[62]

Underhill was greatly inspired by the writings of Walter Lippmann – 'the most suggestive writer on public affairs in America at present and worth all the Ph.D.'s in the Universities put together.'[63] He thought of putting together an article on Lippmann's ideas but doubted that he was up to it. A student who was thinking of majoring in political science was advised to read books by Lippmann, Lowell, Ostrogorski, and Bryce, in addition to Cecil on conservatism, Hobhouse on liberalism, and Ramsay MacDonald on socialism. 'No one,' said Underhill, 'should be allowed to graduate as a specialist in the subject who hasn't made a fairly thorough study of the history and government of his own country, who isn't familiar with what outstanding men have thought about the problem of the state since men began the experiment of self-government, and who hasn't a working knowledge of how modern states conduct their internal affairs and their relations with one another.'[64] Underhill does not appear to have consulted with any other political scientists in his preparations for moving into political science, but he did write to Herbert Heaton, the economic historian who served briefly as head of political science at Queen's, for assistance in drawing up a book list for the study of the constitution of each of the major countries, so that students could 'find out how far the government has diverged from the ideas of its founders.' To this query, Heaton replied: 'Why waste so much time on government? I am still wondering why it is that in this continent we give so much academic attention to politics and on this continent politics are more frankly corrupt than anywhere else. Why? Is it cause and effect, or are we trying in the universities to clean up the garage!'[65]

Two of Underhill's new courses in political science, comparative government and international relations, were launched in the fall of 1925 and final examinations in them completed by Christmas, at which time, accompanied by his wife and baby daughter, Betty, he took a six-month sabbatical leave in eastern Canada. There, dividing his time between Toronto and Ottawa, he studied the development of public opinion during the pre-Confederation period, working about six hours a day, six days a week for nine months. In Ottawa he spent mornings in the parliamentary library, afternoons in the archives. 'My opinion of the Saskatchewan faculty has gone up enormously,' he wrote to George Simpson in the history department, after attending some lecture meetings at the University of Toronto. 'I had been labouring under the delusion that we were rather commonplace compared with the supermen of the East. But if I couldn't give better stuff than some of what I have heard down here I should desert academic life for selling bonds.'[66] But Saskatoon could not compete with some of the other delights of Toronto. Underhill went to plays and concerts and, after hearing a particularly fine performance of the Toronto Mendelssohn Choir, declared it to be 'the chief feature of civilization down here on which Torontonians rely for getting themselves into heaven.'[67] Another pleasure was hunting for bargains in wallpaper and furnishings for his house in Saskatoon – 'the longer I stay here,' he related to Morton, 'the more I am convinced that the chief contributions of Toronto to Canadian civilization are not the University and the Mendelssohn Choir but the T. Eaton and the Robert Simpson Co.'[68]

Underhill's reading of the Toronto *Globe* of the 1860s led him to an unorthodox interpretation of Confederation politics. 'I am ... discovering,' he said, 'what thorough scoundrels our grandfathers, the makers of Canada, were.'[69] He came to the conclusion that George Brown, the *Globe's* feisty editor, was an admirable fellow, but not so John A. Macdonald – 'a Canadian and nothing more, and his conception of politics never rose above that of the business man on the make.'[70] Underhill thought there were many parallels to be drawn between the radical politicians of the pre-Confederation period and the western dissidents of his own time, who were fighting what appeared to be a similar battle against the domination of the financial interests and large corporations. But he was sometimes depressed about his ability to write a major work: 'I stray into so many sidepaths reading about the American Civil War and English and European politics that I don't cover the ground quickly enough to be able to look forward to writing a book about it until sometime in the 1960's.'[71] In fact, the book never did appear. The work to come directly out of his sabbatical research consisted of two articles for the Canadian Historical Association: 'Some Aspects of Upper Canadian Radical Opinion in the Decade before Confederation' (1927) and 'Canada's Relations with the Empire as Seen by the Toronto *Globe*, 1857–1867.'[72] In the earlier paper, which marked his first scholarly publication since his account of the war, he concluded with the fervent hope that the Clear Grit movement of the 1880s would find a fresh incarnation in the present through the western farmer. Later, he came to modify his interpretation of this period of Canadian history and said that he had 'rather overemphasised the agrarian aspect of Grittism.'[73]

VI

Returning to Saskatchewan in the fall of 1926, Underhill again taught the two classes in political science he had introduced before his sabbatical, but the other courses described in the *Calendar* never saw the light of day. His hopes for a position at the University of Toronto, which had been kept alive over many years by intermittent rumours from his friends in the East, were now finally to be realized. George Wrong, the head of the history department at Toronto, had often reminded Underhill to get some work published: 'As you know,' wrote Wrong in 1923, 'I have long had my eye on you in respect to University work and I have urged you to get a book with your name on the title-page ... There is no one in whose mental capacity I have greater confidence than in yours. You have the three qualities of scholarship, insight, and style, and you can produce first rate work.'[74] Now, as he neared retirement, Wrong thought of bringing Underhill to Toronto. Early in 1927, he addressed a confidential inquiry to President Murray soliciting his frank opinion: 'My doubt in respect of him is whether he is not too quiet and retiring to be an effective leader in such a community as this. By leadership I mean a person who would make his influence felt as a factor in the life of the University. I have no doubt whatever that he has the needed ability. Has he been an influential person in your own University?'[75] We do not know how Murray replied, but there is no doubt that he had a high opinion of Underhill's ability and would not have stood in the way of his advancement. In any event, Underhill was offered and, after some deliberation, accepted an appointment at Toronto, his alma mater. He became one of four senior history professors there, each receiving $4,500 a year, $200 less than his Saskatchewan salary.

'How do you feel after your escape from Siberia? Are you convinced that you have reached Heaven?' asked historian A.L. Burt, after Underhill had moved to Toronto.[76] It was true that Underhill was not sorry to leave what he called the 'pioneer atmosphere' of Saskatoon or the frustration of having to devote nearly all of his time at the university to undergraduate teaching. But he expressed one passing regret – that he would miss the new students at the university who 'are brought up in the Wheat Pool and the United Farmer circles and ... come up really interested in radical ideas.'[77]

Underhill was to say that 'it was living on the prairie in the 1920's that finally established my life-long fondness for political movements of the left.'[78] Soon after he moved to Toronto, he was drawn into a circle of intellectuals and politicians who were interested in social and political reform. Early in 1932 he and F.R. Scott of McGill University started the League for Social Reconstruction, a forerunner of the CCF party, and Underhill is generally credited with writing the first draft of the paper which became known as the Regina Manifesto. After 1929, he was a regular contributor to the *Canadian Forum*, as well as a frequent lecturer, essayist, and broadcaster. He became something of a celebrity, rare for an academic, producing what historian Kenneth McNaught has called 'by far the best-informed and most stimulating political-cultural commentary in twentieth century English-speaking Canada.'[79]

Underhill taught history at the University of Toronto from 1927 until he reached the age of retirement in 1955, in spite of some celebrated tussles with the Toronto administration over his political activities which nearly led to his leaving it against his will on several occasions. After retiring, he accepted a position as curator of Laurier House in Ottawa for four years and then taught a course in Canadian political thought at Carleton University. He was a fellow of the Royal Society of Canada and holder of a Canada Medal. Among his several honorary degrees was one from the University of Saskatchewan, where he had left a lasting influence on a number of students who later became members of faculty.

7

A New Start

Finding someone to replace Frank Underhill – in political science 'the ablest man in that field west of the Great Lakes,' according to Duncan MacGibbon of Alberta – turned out to be no easy matter.[1] Political science in 1927 was barely on its feet as an independent field of study in Canada. To recognize that a university teacher of political science should have specialized training in the subject was to narrow down the number of Canadian candidates to a very few, and in any case Murray's experience had been that a good scholar in a sister discipline could handle political science as a sideline. Underhill in history had done so, and there was the earlier precedent of MacKay in law. O.D. Skelton, who was now undersecretary of state for external affairs in Ottawa, advised President Murray 'to appoint a Canadian, or, if you bring in an outsider, to catch him young.'[2] For Skelton, the obvious choice was Norman McLeod Rogers, an able, attractive, and popular young Canadian and recent graduate in law from Queen's, who had just been appointed as secretary for privy council affairs. Without much ado, Murray offered Rogers a senior position in political science. But Rogers, after considering the proposal for several weeks, turned it down, along with a similar offer from Queen's, on the grounds that he could not so soon leave Ottawa.[3]

News travelled quickly whenever a position came open, and it would not be long before a number of applications would arrive on the president's desk. One applicant, who wrote from California, was quickly turned down when Murray heard from a correspondent of 'certain laxities in his manner of living.'[4] Another, Charles Wayland Lightbody, who twenty years later would join the history department at Saskatchewan, had been a favourite student of Underhill and a Rhodes scholar and was currently enrolled as a graduate student in history at the University of Toronto. Lightbody longed for a chance to take his mentor's place at Saskatchewan, but both Murray and Underhill regarded him as too young and inexperienced to be a serious contender.

There were two other applicants: Hugh McDowall Clokie and Robert MacGregor Dawson. Both had experience teaching political science, and both happened to be teaching in the same department at Rutgers University in New Jersey.[5] Clokie was from Saskatoon, having moved there with his family from Yorkshire when he was twelve. At the age of fifteen he completed his senior matriculation at Saskatoon Collegiate and was admitted to the University of Saskatchewan, where he received a BA in 1918 and an MA in history and political science the year after. From MacKay he took four courses in political science, three of them cross-listed in law. His master's thesis was entitled 'Federal Government in the British Empire and the United States.' When he left Saskatchewan he went on to Harvard for a year on a teaching fellowship in constitutional and international law, and then obtained a scholarship offered by the Imperial Order Daughters of the Empire which took him to Oxford where he received a BA. Afterwards he was hired as an assistant professor of political science and economics at Rutgers, but he became unhappy with the intellectual environment there. At Rutgers, as he told Murray, he found himself 'a pawn between radical groups in philosophy, history and literature and conservative groups in the business & law schools etc. There is apparently no academic place for one between the extremes of hedonism, economic determinism and of reactionary conservatism on the part of the trustees and legislature.'[6]

Clokie, who had applied to Saskatchewan for a position in 1924, quickly applied again. 'As you know,' he told Murray, 'places in Canada are very few and so rarely vacant that though most of us have a good desire to come back to the Empire we find little or no opportunity under adequate circumstances.'[7] But Clokie's plea failed to move Murray, who was not inclined to rate him highly, and a note from W.B. Munro, a Canadian who had become head of the Department of Government at Harvard, seemed to support Murray's impressions. 'In the intervening years,' wrote Munro, 'he has written nothing and assumed no part in the current activities of political science over here, nor has he made much headway at Rutgers.'[8] Clokie, who later joined the University of Manitoba, wrote *Canadian Government and Politics* (1944), which was the first of the modern textbooks on Canadian government. It was widely adopted at Canadian universities, including the University of Saskatchewan.

Of Robert MacGregor Dawson, Clokie's colleague, Murray had already heard much. Dawson had figured prominently on a list of candidates sent to Murray by the president of Dalhousie, who had just named Robert A. MacKay, author of a new work, *The Unreformed Senate of Canada*, to the chair of political science at Dalhousie. After MacKay took the position at Dalhousie, Dawson was left as the apparent heir to the next vacancy in political science in Canada. O.D. Skelton reported that Mackintosh of Queen's had found Dawson 'a very good man, the only drawback being a certain nervous noisiness, which does not in any way indicate a bumptious attitude, and which he will probably get over.'[9] Another report came from Duncan MacGibbon, who had made Dawson's acquaintance some time ago in London and was so taken with him that he had tried afterwards, but without success, to find a place for him at Alberta.[10] 'I have been told that he is somewhat eccentric. Is that your impression?' inquired Murray.[11] MacGibbon replied:

> The only thing that I noticed was that he had a head of rather long tawny hair (which, by the way, was not unkempt) and that he went around London bareheaded. He impressed me as being a very enthusiastic, interesting man with the ability to excite the interest of others in whatever he might be talking about. This I have always set down as a mark and sign of a man who would be a good teacher. In a general way, I always think that a slight touch of eccentricity that is not of an offensive type and is combined with scholarship and ability is an asset to a teacher and a department. I think that it is good for the students to come up against men who are sharply individualized ... Dawson ... impressed me as being a charming fellow and I know he was well thought of by Wallas and his fellow students whom I met.[12]

Dawson had started out as a student of economics, and it was as a possible candidate in economics that he first came to Murray's attention in 1921. Dawson, who was then a student at the London School of Economics and Political Science, was described by his supervisor, Graham Wallas, as 'a keen student who works really hard, and is capable of original thought. I ... can recommend him very strongly for a post involving the teaching of political science, one of Canadian history since Federation. I do not think it likely that you would find anyone among the younger men better than he is in that respect.'[13] George

Ling, the Saskatchewan dean of arts, who was asked to interview the overseas candidates, reported back that he liked Dawson, 'though he is, I think, rather naive and talkative. He is strong for an early transfer to Political Science.'[14] And Dawson, in his own correspondence with Murray, made it quite clear that he would be willing to teach economics only if there was some prospect of work in political science. Dawson sent applications to Murray for a position in political science in 1922, 1923, 1925, and 1927. 'A MacGregor,' he declared in one, 'is never comfortable when his foot is off his native heath, and I want to be repatriated.'[15]

It was not until mid-June of 1927, when arrangements were made for Murray to meet Dawson in Boston, that Murray's lingering reservations over Dawson's reported eccentricities were finally swept away. According to a story told later by Dawson, Murray, in the course of a long interview, showed only lukewarm interest in hiring him until it came out that Dawson was a Nova Scotian, and proud of it, at which point, Murray, whose own fondness for Nova Scotia had never diminished, was completely won over.[16] About three weeks later, when Norman Rogers decided not to come, Murray quickly dispatched a telegram to Dawson with an offer of a full professorship in political science and a salary of $3,200 a year. But Dawson, in the meantime, had elected to remain where he was and refused the offer. Apparently his wife, Sarah, who had been a student of his at Rutgers, did not relish moving; his parents in Nova Scotia were unhappy at the thought of their only son moving so far away; and the president of Rutgers had come forward with the promise of a promotion and a raise in salary. Murray received the news with equanimity: 'Should you repent ... and wish to be admitted to the true faith of the West, let me know before it is too late. Something might be done.'[17]

During the following year, no political science was taught at the university, and Murray continued to cast about for a political scientist. In February of 1928 he asked T.J. Hébert, a former member of the law faculty who had left Saskatchewan to practise law in New Brunswick, if he would return to 'fill Frankie's chair,' but Hébert said no.[18] Then, on 19 April 1928, Dawson sent word that he had changed his mind. The president of Rutgers had apparently reneged on his promise of a raise, and Mrs Dawson had become reconciled to the idea of moving to Saskatchewan. Dawson's telegram to Murray read: 'I would seriously consider full professorship thirty seven hundred stop would accept unhesitatingly four thousand stop my paternal ancestors as you may know came from Aberdeen.'[19] After several more rounds of telegrams and letters, an amount of $3,700 a year, with annual increases of $100 up to a maximum of $5,000, was finally agreed upon, and Dawson became the first full-time professor of political science at the University of Saskatchewan.

I

Robert MacGregor Dawson – he used all three names – was born on 1 March 1895 in Bridgewater, Nova Scotia, the only son of the town's leading hardware merchant. When he grew up, he chose not to enter the family business, though it was obvious that he had inherited the family's financial acumen when it came time for him to manage the considerable capital left to him. His Bluenose ancestry and freedom from financial constraints buttressed a remarkable independence of mind and spirit. 'He was honest in everything,' wrote one of his contemporaries. 'He would not say a thing behind a man's back that he would not say to his face. He never pretended to like people whom he disliked. He was never afraid to express an opinion because it was unpopular.'[20]

Dawson attended the schools of Bridgewater and then went on to Dalhousie University. His major course of study was economics, for which his professor, J.E. Todd, said he had a 'natural aptitude and a genuine enthusiasm.'[21] He graduated from Dalhousie with a BA in 1915 and stayed on for a further year to complete an MA in economics and political science. This was followed by an AM at Harvard, where he took courses in the government of England, federal government, the history of political theory, international law, and advanced economic theory. In 1919, having decided to concentrate on the study of government, he enrolled at the London School of Economics and Political Science and started on his first major research project, a study of the Canadian Civil Service, which earned him an MSc (Econ.) in 1921. His next project was a study of the boards and adjudicators in Canada that were in various ways remote from the control of Parliament. He received the DSc (Econ.) in 1922, having managed, to the surprise and satisfaction of his supervisors, to accomplish the task in one year rather than the three which usually elapsed at London between the master's degree and doctorate by negotiating to have his Harvard AM applied to part of the time requirement. The thesis was published at his own expense in London in 1922 under the title *The Principle of Official Independence*, with an introduction by his supervisor, Graham Wallas.

Adam Shortt, who reviewed Dawson's book, said it exhibited 'much honest industry in the collection of facts, and no little shrewd insight into practical affairs with which the author is not always personally familiar.'[22] 'It was to be expected,' wrote W. S. Wallace in the *Canadian Historical Review*, 'that a work sponsored by so distinguished a thinker as Professor Wallas would reach a very high level of excellence and originality; and the expectation is not disappointed. Dr. Dawson has shown himself an apt pupil of a great master.'[23]

Dawson was now resolved to make political science his life work – not an easy undertaking, as it turned out. After leaving London, the only work he could find in Canada was in economics, at Dalhousie, where he lectured for two years. In 1923, when he was twenty-eight, he was hired as a lecturer in government at the Carnegie Institute of Technology in Pittsburgh. Three years later he moved to Rutgers, where he was appointed, along with Hugh Clokie, an assistant professor in the Department of History and Political Science. His responsibilities included the teaching of American constitutional law and a section of the basic course on American government. Many years hence, when asked in the course of a newspaper interview why he left Canada, he replied: 'Tell them I went to the States because the field of Political Science in Canada was too new at that time.'[24]

II

The faculty of the University of Saskatchewan in 1928 was seventy strong, large enough to have lost some of its pioneer character, yet small enough to have retained something of its original sense of fellowship. In that year the Memorial Gates, which had been funded by subscriptions from faculty members and citizens, were officially opened, but other things had hardly changed. The campus was still virtually an open meadow, with cows and sheep sometimes grazing upon it, and the arts faculty was still cramped for room in the College Building. Many of the professors, among them Dawson, had to be accommodated with offices in the nearby residence halls.

To this small university community, Dawson added a stentorian presence. He was tall, broad-shouldered, and often noisy – 'has a voice like a fog-horn but seems a decent fellow,'[25] wrote John Eaton of his new office-mate, who by acoustical standards alone could hardly have been more opposite to his quiet-spoken predecessor, Frank Underhill. Dawson became known on campus for the figure he cut, wrapped in a great racoon coat in the winter, as well as for the eccentric performance of the ancient air-cooled car he drove. He would arrive at his lectures at exactly the appointed time and depart swiftly when the bell rang, donning his coat as he finished his last sentence.[26] When the weather was suitable, he wore tennis shoes to class so that he could proceed immediately to the tennis courts, where his abilities were well above average (he ranked second in Nova Scotia during the twenties). He would also indulge in a little bridge playing with his colleagues in his office of an afternoon, to the dismay of President Murray, who believed his professors should set better examples for the students.[27]

Dawson was a man of diverse interests and tastes. He collected stamps and Persian rugs (good investments, both, he believed). He liked chamber music and Gilbert and Sullivan.[28] But most of all he loved to garden, and his garden was half a continent away. Each year, as soon as he could decently manage it, he returned to the family homestead at Bridgewater to meet the challenges of a new planting season. As the years went on, he gradually rebuilt his grandfather's old house and developed around it one of the finest gardens in Nova Scotia.[29]

The president was not particularly pleased by Dawson's hasty exodus to his Bridgewater retreat each spring, but, in truth, Murray had a special liking for this lanky Maritimer whose laughter 'could fill a building,'[30] and whose presence helped to brighten the university halls during the bleak years of the Depression, even though Dawson would sometimes take issue with him in council.[31] Dawson was an equal with Murray where others on the staff were inclined to treat him with subservience. The two men took a special pleasure in each other's company because of their common Scots Maritime heritage. Dawson's son, Robert, remembers them together during a visit with Stephen Leacock, the McGill political economist and humorist, on the occasion of his speaking tour of western Canada: '[My father] phoned home one day, at about 4 in the afternoon, to say that he was bringing the President and Stephen Leacock home for dinner. Great rushing around on my mother's part, since we lived on Elliot St., second house down from Wiggins (now demolished), and the nearest source of food was across the river. So off, in a car-less state to the Bay and Kong Lee's (across from the Bay) for meat and vegetables to be ready in time. The rest of the evening was spent by all in helpless laughter: Mother's comment was that she thought the President was going to have a stroke – he was purple in the face and barely able to catch a breath. Leacock must have been fantastic!'[32]

Walter Murray, president, University of Saskatchewan, 1908–37. University of
Saskatchewan Archives, *Greystone*, 1936

Rev. Edmund Henry Oliver. University of Saskatchewan Archives A-2765

Ira Allan MacKay. University of Saskatchewan Archives A-8513

Lewis Cecil Gray. U.S. Department of Agriculture

William Walker Swanson. University of Saskatchewan Archives A-6481

Robert 'Pete' McQueen. University of Saskatchewan Archives A-2738

William A. Carrothers. University of Saskatchewan Archives A-3195

Frank Hawkins Underhill. University of Saskatchewan Archives A-3173

Robert MacGregor Dawson. University of Saskatchewan Archives A-3217

George Edwin Britnell. University of Saskatchewan Archives A-3270

Vernon Clifford Fowke. University of Saskatchewan Archives A-3296

Mabel Frances Timlin

Kenneth A.H. Buckley. University of Saskatchewan Archives A-3315

Norman McQueen Ward. Photo courtesy of Norah Russell

A. Edward Safarian. University of Saskatchewan Archives A-3299

Stooks in the Bowl with Saskatchewan Hall in the background, 1924. University of Saskatchewan Archives A-792

Sheep grazing on the grounds of the University of Saskatchewan campus, 1946. The Chemistry Building is on the left. Saskatchewan Archives Board

There is an amusing postscript to this Leacock story. Swanson, as head of economics, was responsible for making local arrangements for Leacock, who was to speak on the subject of 'Social Credit' at an evening dinner in Saskatoon. Swanson later related:

I had arranged that his address be broadcast in Saskatchewan and Alberta. When the evening came, I rescued him with difficulty from the McGill men who had held a reception for him. Only in the nick of time was I able to accomplish this; and after a final 'slug' in his quarters, led him to the assembled crowd in the dining room of the Bessborough, who were both impatient and voracious for food and for Leacock. After dinner, I introduced him, and as he weaved before the mike he drawled: 'Ladies and Gentlemen: I was to speak on Social Credit, but my heart melts for the farmers and their families away out on the lone prairies, who have had such a hard time these last few years in obtaining any credit at all, and have found nothing in the nature of sociability about it. Therefore, to cheer them on this dark winter night, I have decided to give them, in anticipation of their meeting the bankers in the glorious springtime when the meadow larks will sing and the flowers bloom along the trails once more, my special lecture entitled: "Murder at Two Dollars a Volume!"'[33]

To Swanson's amazement, Leacock proceeded to deliver what turned out to be a spell-binding satire on the 'whodunit' book trade.

III

Like Underhill, Dawson found in the beginning that Saskatchewan students did not take very readily to the study of politics. Interest in political science, which had just been kindled by Underhill before he left, had subsided in the intervening year. Of three classes scheduled by Dawson for 1928–9, only two were given because of low registration, an introductory course with eighteen students and one on American and European government with eight. His only other duty was a reading course for one student. Such a light load of work turned out to be a blessing for Dawson, who was beset with personal worries during the year. Soon after he arrived in Saskatoon, his mother passed away. Then he was granted a leave of absence for the following year so that he could care for his ailing father. But in May 1929, just before the leave was due to begin, his father died suddenly. Dawson offered to give up the leave and Murray was tempted to accept. 'The only thing that makes me hesitate about the matter,' he said, 'is the disordered state in which the Department has been for a number of years. It was begun as a side issue under Ira MacKay and when he left the work lapsed for a year or two then was taken up by Underhill who was ultimately transferred from History to Political Science and made it his major interest. The Department was quite nicely on its feet when he left. For a year it was a wilderness. You revived it and made it again an attractive Department. What its fate can be in new hands we can only conjecture. Naturally we would not wish to see the Department lose headway if that could be avoided.'[34] On the other hand, Dawson's plans were already well advanced and Murray knew that he could well use the year for research, so Dawson was allowed to keep his leave. Douglas Alexander Skelton, the twenty-two-year-old son of O.D. Skelton, was hired for a stipend of $300 a month and taught the three classes that would have been given by Dawson.[35] After a year during which he attended to his parents' estate and commuted from Bridgewater to Ottawa to work in the Public Archives, Dawson returned again to Saskatchewan in the autumn of 1930. He remained as head of the Department of Political Science and its only member for seven more years.

Dawson's approach to political science, which owed much to his training at the London School of Economics and Political Science and his experience in the United States, was quite different from Underhill's. Underhill was inclined to view political development through the works of the great theorists and the deeds (or misdeeds) of political leaders; Dawson's way was to construct a picture of institutional progress through statutes and official records. Underhill started from the precedents and examples of Britain and the United States; Dawson started with the machinery of Canadian government, which is where he instructed his students to begin. Dawson brought to the teaching of political science an emphasis on government and institutions rather than political thought. It was an American approach – one he had become acquainted with during his time at Rutgers – but his materials were Canadian and British rather than American. His introductory course at Saskatchewan, entitled 'General Political Science and Government of Canada,' was unique in Canada and ventured into previously unexplored territory. 'l was compelled,' he said later, 'to unearth the bulk of my material for this course from primary sources.'[36] Much of his time at Saskatchewan was devoted to amassing documentary source materials for this course and others at the advanced level in which he described and analysed the institutions of Canadian government.

    After the introductory course came five others: governments of the British Empire; governments of the United States and Europe; history of political thought (from Plato to the nineteenth century); problems of modern democracy (including such topics as public opinion, the referendum, the recall, second chambers, public administration, and proportional representation); and a seminar on Canadian government. In 1934, the seminar on Canadian government was expanded into two: one on political parties, the other on the executive branch. A course in contemporary political ideas and a seminar in imperial and foreign relations of the British Empire were added along the way. Students wishing to take political science as a major were simply instructed to take three lecture courses in political science together with, in their last two years, a special reading course or seminar; for a minor, two lecture courses were required. Until the four-year honours course was introduced in 1937, a high degree of specialization was not required of students in arts.

    Each year Dawson would teach the introductory course, one in comparative government, a seminar on a special topic (usually some aspect of Canadian government), and one other course, most often problems of democracy. Of the two theory courses listed in the calendar, one, contemporary political ideas, was seldom given, and the other, history of political thought, not at all. Dawson 'would not ... have thought Hobbes or Locke worth talking about if Bagehot or Jennings were available,' Norman Ward remarked. 'He was not ignorant of Hobbes or Locke, and occasionally surprised me by references to them; he merely found them dull, and rejoiced that after his move to Toronto he never had to teach them again.'[37]

    In the classroom, Dawson's style was commanding. J.A. Corry, his colleague in the College of Law, said that students 'were lifted out of their seats by his voice.'[38] Ward, who was a student of Dawson's at Toronto in the 1940s, remembered him as

    a brilliant rhetorical speaker in class, full of anecdotes which he told well, and occasional jokes. He loved his first-year classes, believing that freshmen – at least for a brief few weeks or months – actually can be taught, and his well-prepared lectures were great favourites with students. He used shock tactics in the first year, marking the first test or two with a rigour that would not have been out of place in a military academy, and the casualty rates at the beginning of each year were always high. He did not do this with any malice or ill-feeling, but on the contrary with the conviction that it was good for his beloved students. ('Students are the salt of the earth,' he used to say, 'and how many jobs are there where you can associate with that kind of people all your life?') He didn't really let up on the students in the second term: they either shaped up or fell by the wayside, with the result that he didn't have to treat classes in upper years the same way. They'd learned, not how to put things across Dawson, which was close to impossible, but how to work his way.[39]

V.W. Bladen, his economist colleague at Toronto, said that Dawson was that 'rare combination, a great scholar and a great teacher' who loved the company of students yet had also the 'capacity to withdraw into the privacy of his own research and writing.'[40]

Dawson's introductory course, with its unusual emphasis on Canada, became a popular arts elective at the university. By 1936 there were eighty-four students registered in his day class and sixteen others who took it by correspondence or in the evening. Enrolment in the upper-year courses in political science remained sparse. But with a lighter teaching load than was usual for a professor at a western university, Dawson was lucky enough to have time left to devote to research. From the very beginning he was never without a project of some kind, usually several at a time, and his mind was always bursting with ideas for work to be done in political science, even at Saskatchewan where he was far removed from the documentary material upon which his work depended. And from the beginning, there was never any doubt in his mind of how it was to be done. As a proud Canadian, he had watched his country's passage from colony to nationhood just at the time he had reached his maturity as a political scientist, and he now perceived it as his duty to describe the governmental institutions that were the supreme embodiment of that achievement.

Dawson's second book, *The Civil Service of Canada*, published in 1929, was an expansion of the master's project he had undertaken in London. It contained a historical account of the disentanglement of the civil service from the web of party patronage and a critical analysis of its operation. Quotations from Gilbert and Sullivan headed each chapter. Robert MacKay, the Dalhousie political scientist, expressed the hope that the work would persuade others that 'political science is an orphan worth saving ... The author of this book has placed the Canadian public in his debt. His wide reading in the field of English administration, his sound training under Professor Graham Wallas, one of the greatest masters of political science in our time, his mastery of his material, his realism, entitle him to a wide hearing. His masculine and sometimes caustic pen, his flashes of satirical humour, as well as his quotations from Gilbert and Sullivan, should serve to "sugar-coat" the pill for a subject on which no author can hope to write a "best-seller."'[41] Frank Underhill, who had become a regular contributor to the columns of the *Canadian Forum*, wrote in a review that the book was excellent, but he was puzzled by its neglect of American studies. 'Perhaps our Canadian Civil Service is only another example of how little there is in our country that is British and how much there is that is American,' said Underhill.[42] Another reader, the former prime minister, Robert Borden, wrote privately to Dawson: 'While the book is an admirable contribution to the subject, I do not consider that it is a well-balanced presentation of certain aspects with which I am more especially familiar. And you will pardon me, I am sure, if I should act as *Advocatus Diaboli* in pointing out some omissions and an occasional oversight in your statement of facts.'[43] Borden did not spell out in his letter where Dawson went astray, but the two men met later to discuss the matter in more detail.

Dawson replied to Borden that it was 'refreshing for a college professor to have the opportunity of coming into contact with those who do things in government rather than talk about them.'[44] But distressed as he was that he might have fallen into error, it was not customary for him to seek out the acquaintance of people in public life or to examine the workings of government at first hand. He preferred to work almost entirely from documentary evidence. Dawson's methods, according to Norman Ward, were 'more like those of Sir James Frazer, who allegedly wrote *The Golden Bough* without leaving England, than those of later political scientists, including Dawson's own students ... I don't think it ever occurred to Dawson that a student of the House of Commons, for example, should actually watch it a great deal.'[45]

Once he had done with his study of the civil service, Dawson turned his attention towards a more comprehensive examination of Canadian government. He had planned a textbook on the subject with Robert MacKay as early as 1930, and though the collaboration never proceeded very far, Dawson continued to work on his part of the venture, a study of the cabinet. In the meantime, he kept up a steady pace of writing on other subjects. In 1933 he contributed an article on Finance Minister W.S. Fielding to the *American Encyclopedia of the Social Sciences*, prepared in the following year a memorandum on the civil service of Nova Scotia, in which he recommended that Nova Scotia adopt the scheme of classification in use in Saskatchewan, and in 1935 wrote his oft-quoted article 'The Gerrymander of 1882' for the new *Canadian Journal of Economics and Political Science*. Thereafter, hardly a year went by without a contribution of some kind to the *Journal* from Dawson. In 1935, he was elected to the Royal Society of Canada, Section II, joining on that august body two other academic notables from Saskatchewan, President Murray and Principal Oliver.

Dawson's next two books were collections of documents for students of Canadian politics. The first, *Constitutional Issues in Canada, 1900–1931*, came out in 1933. The collection included, besides government documents and papers, unofficial opinion from contemporary newspapers and periodicals to save it from becoming, in Dawson's words, 'inadequate and stodgy.' Frank Underhill commented on the manuscript, but his many suggestions for additional items had to be mostly disregarded for lack of space. Before publication the manuscript was trimmed of nearly 350 pages, materials relating to external relations being set aside for another volume.

Four years went by before Dawson's next collection of documents, *The Development of Dominion Status, 1900–1936*, appeared in print. Although most of the materials for it had been assembled well before, Dawson laboured for some time over an extensive introductory essay to be included in the new book. As early as 1934 he had a manuscript ready. But Underhill, who read it, said that it contained 'rather too much of the pure milk of the Dafoe gospel. It seems to me that all the panegyrics of Canadian nationalism need to be reconsidered now that another war looms up and we are likely to be involved in it as automatically as we were in 1914. The Dafoe brand of nationalism was fine as long as there was no real threat of a big war, i.e. through the 1920's. Your exultant pride in it has therefore an appearance of dating.'[46] Dawson responded to this 'broadside,' as he called it, with gratitude: several others, he said, had been 'too gentle' with the manuscript.[47] But though he promised to try to cut out the more nationalistic sentiments, his 'exultant pride' in the advance of Canadian independence was too strong to be quelled. When the book came out in 1937, it was judged an important addition to Canadian political studies. W.P.M. Kennedy judged the selection of documents 'catholic and discriminating,' the introduction 'accurate and careful,' and concluded: 'We trust that Mr. Dawson will soon bring his distinguished talents, which this volume so abundantly discloses, to bear on some of the untilled fields in Canadian government.' Kennedy gently reproved Dawson for rendering some ingenuous judgments on the part taken by the United Kingdom along the road which led to Canada's statehood.[48] P.E. Corbett, writing in the *Canadian Journal of Economics and Political Science,* was less gentle. Dawson's account was 'coloured, at times highly coloured, by personal judgments ... The general impression conveyed is that the advance to Dominion status has been made by colonial statesmen battling against English politicians whose conduct and attitude have varied from gross stupidity to "mild duplicity."'[49]

It was by now virtually certain that Dawson could not be held for long at the University of Saskatchewan. The university and the community held a high place in his affections – he once reflected that its one enormous asset, 'the spirit of good-will and comradeship that pervades the entire faculty,' was not to be equalled anywhere – but there was no doubt that his remoteness from archival sources was a constant source of frustration.[50] When in 1937 Harold Innis took over the headship of the Department of Political Economy at Toronto and invited Dawson to join him, Dawson was happy to accept. It meant a smaller salary and demotion to the rank of associate professor, but he would now be able to work in a larger department, nearer to his sources of research and his beloved Bridgewater garden.

IV

After he left Saskatchewan, Dawson edited a collection of essays, *Problems of Modern Government* (1941), and wrote *Canada in World Affairs: Two Years of War, 1939–1941* (1943). In 1945 he served as president of the Canadian Political Science Association. Finally, in 1947, his long-awaited textbook, *The Government of Canada,* was published by the University of Toronto Press.[51] It immediately became the standard reference work on the subject and made Dawson's name a household word for scores of political science students in Canada. The book earned for Dawson the Governor General's Award for Non-Fiction; two years later, he again received the award, this time for *Democratic Government in Canada,* a simplified version he wrote for use in secondary schools.

For more than two decades, *The Government of Canada* was to occupy a central place in the literature and study of Canadian politics. Hugh Clokie's *Canadian Government and Politics,* published three years earlier, in 1944, enjoyed a run of popularity as an introductory text but was never a serious rival to Dawson's heftier tome. Instead of passing quietly into history as an accomplishment for its day, *The Government of*

Canada was put through several revisions and made to do duty as a contemporary textbook. Eventually, a new generation of political scientists grew restless with its virtual monopoly and subjected it to searching criticism. Dawson's style of political science had never been without its critics: C.B. Macpherson, for many years Dawson's colleague at Toronto, called it 'diagrammatic.' Yet Macpherson could understand why Dawson had pursued his single-minded objective to describe the institutions of Canadian government. Dawson had been 'driven on by sheer exasperation that nobody was paying attention to the nuts and bolts. He had found a real lack in Canadian political science, and he was able to persuade his students of it. The lack was visible and was seen. But no persvasive relation between the operation of the political system and the economic realities was seen.'[52]

In 1951, Dawson took leave from the University of Toronto to become the official biographer of William Lyon Mackenzie King. The task was not to be completed in his lifetime. The first volume of Dawson's biography, *William Lyon Mackenzie King: A Political Biography, 1874–1932*, was published posthumously in 1958, the year Dawson died, and the writing of the second volume assigned to historian Blair Neatby. *The Conscription Crisis of 1944*, a study Dawson had undertaken at the beginning of his project, was published separately in 1961. Responsibility for revisions of *The Government of Canada* was given over to Norman Ward, who had been Dawson's student at the University of Toronto. It was, in fact, Dawson who first recommended the University of Saskatchewan to Ward, and Ward to the university, which led to his coming to Saskatchewan to teach political science in 1945. Ward came to a department which, because of Dawson's association with it, was of some standing in the political science community in Canada.

8

Three Colleagues

A sharp decline in provincial revenues during the 1930s left the university a poor bidder in the academic market-place and forced a change in the composition of its faculty. 'The enforced economies of the last few years have entailed serious losses. Because of reduced salaries the University has been unable to retain or attract the best men,' reported President Murray in 1935.[1] There had been a time when the president's attempts to get the best scholars for his faculty had met with some success. In its first two decades, the university had had available to it some fine young scholars who, for the sake of adventure and experience, were willing to work in the West, hoping at some later time to move on to better positions at the more prestigious eastern universities. But now that good people were not so easily persuaded to come to such a depressed part of the country, this source of talent appeared to be dwindling. As an alternative, the university turned to its own graduates, many of whom were willing and even eager, as others often were not, to make their careers at the University of Saskatchewan. An unusually large number of these graduates, after taking further studies elsewhere, returned to the university as members of faculty. Among them were Mabel Timlin, Vernon Fowke, and George Britnell, who were to be colleagues for thirty years.

The first of the three to appear at the university, Mabel Frances Timlin, was born in Forest Junction, Wisconsin, on 6 December 1891, into a household which was anything but peaceful. 'Pappa and Mamma,' she wrote when she was eighty-two, 'were about as mismated a pair as one could find "in a month of Sundays." ' Her father, James Timlin, was irascible and capricious, a weaver of fantasies devoted to impractical schemes for improving the family's fortunes, all of which turned to naught. His wife, Sarah, on the other hand, was possessed of a strong will and a good deal of common sense, which enabled her to guide her brood through the many domestic crises brought on by her husband's improvidence. Mabel, the eldest of four children, was implanted with an early and concentrated interest in politics and economics by her father, who lectured her when she was six on bimetallism and the law of comparative advantage ('by the time I was ten,' she said, 'I suspect that if called upon I could have produced myself a fairly lucid lecture on both'), but it was her courageous mother who left the deepest impression on her.[2] As a child Mabel – or May, as she was known – was free-spirited, turning as she reached adolescence into a pertinacious, studious young woman fond of reading books and writing poetry. She attended the Wisconsin Rapids High School and the Milwaukee State Normal College, where she received sound instruction in English and the classics, and thereafter taught for four years in Wisconsin elementary schools. During this time her mother and father both became invalids. In 1916, when she was twenty-four, they died within a few months of each other.

Following the advice of her mother, who before she died had urged her eldest to move away and make a fresh start for herself, Mabel Timlin struck out for Canada in 1917. Her resources were meagre. She had decided to make her destination Saskatchewan, where there was said to be a shortage of teachers in the rural areas, but she bought a railway ticket only as far as Winnipeg so that she would have the twenty-five dollars cash in her purse that she needed as a landed immigrant. On arrival in Winnipeg she chanced to see, in a newspaper dropped by a traveller in a hotel lobby, an advertisement for summer teachers in Saskatchewan, to which she responded. She later related: 'I landed in Bounty, Saskatchewan, with ten dollars in my pocket, borrowed ten dollars from a brother during my first month, paid it back at the end of the month and have been on my own ever since.'[3] She spent a year teaching grade school in Bounty and Wilkie (according to the report of the inspector of schools, she was 'a good average teacher'[4]) and then in June 1918 set out for the city of Saskatoon with the hope of becoming a secretary. She had reckoned that her prospects as a teacher were not good. 'No matter how long I stayed at the business, I'd make only a mediocre teacher and I think ... that a year's experience will make me a more than average stenographer,' she wrote to her brother Cyril, who had been posted overseas.[5] But Cyril, who was dear to her above all others, never received her letter; she heard soon after that he had been killed in action.

After taking a six-week course at the Saskatoon Business College, she worked at various Saskatoon offices, supplementing her income by teaching remedial English to new Canadians in the evenings, and in 1920 took employment at the business college as a teacher of shorthand and typing. In the following year she moved over to the University of Saskatchewan to become secretary to John G. Rayner, the director of agricultural extension, where she was paid a salary of $90 a month, even though she had been making $125 a month at her other jobs. 'I came to the University,' she recalled, 'with the idea that I might by this action be able to complete the work for the Bachelor's degree and, if possible, an honours course in economics.' However, after taking four courses in economics of which, she said, 'only one, the first, held anything that could be called a respectable intellectual content,' she gave up on economics and concentrated instead on languages and literature.[6] Through evening classes, sacrifice of her lunch hour, and other arrangements, she worked her way in seven years through eleven courses. Along with credits obtained from her work at the Milwaukee State Normal College, this allowed her to qualify for a BA, which she received with great distinction in 1929.

In the year of her graduation, correspondence courses were established at the university, and Mabel Timlin was asked to take over their administration. In this position she remained, first as secretary and later as director, from 1929 to 1943. She herself conducted the two correspondence courses in economics, reading assignments, setting and grading examination papers, and preparing course outlines.[7] For many in the financially bereft province, particularly those living in rural areas, correspondence courses, supplemented by books from the travelling library of the Saskatchewan Wheat Pool, were the only way to start on a university education. Clarence Barber and John Deutsch were two students who were introduced to the discipline in which they were to have distinguished careers by taking Mabel Timlin's economics course by correspondence.[8] The program was run on a minuscule budget. At first Timlin handled all the clerical work for the courses as well as the administrative side. It was her job to send dunning notes to students in arrears on their fees and discreet reminders to members of faculty who neglected the marking of correspondence assignments.

In 1932, in her fortieth year, she enrolled at the University of Washington with the intention of spending several summers there working towards a master's degree in economics and business administration.

Two years later, now advanced to the PhD program, she took a leave of absence for six months to fulfil the residence requirement for the degree. Her leave was without pay, but, to keep peace at her own university, she continued to grade the assignments, set an examination, and mark the final papers for the correspondence courses in economics, all of which had to be mailed to her in Seattle. When she returned to Saskatchewan, the year that Pete McQueen was on leave of absence at Queen's, she was asked to help out in the Department of Economics by conducting tutorials for students having difficulty with the introductory course. In the following year, when the department found itself desperately short of staff, she was asked, in addition, to become an instructor in the department. She now had an excellent secretary for the correspondence work, but a rapid increase in registrations for correspondence courses combined with classroom teaching of six to seven hours a week taxed her energies to the limit. Even so, she was determined that, one way or another, she would find the time to achieve her goal of a doctorate in economics.

I

Mabel Timlin's fellow instructor in the department, Vernon Clifford Fowke, was also struggling towards a postgraduate degree. He was born on 5 May 1907 in Parry Sound, Ontario, the third of five children, and was nine when his family moved to Neville, Saskatchewan, where a group of Fowke relatives, known in the district as the 'Forty Friends' because of their warm and helping support of one another, had already settled. His first memory of his new surroundings was 'staying in a relative's "mud hut" ... and all four boys sleeping crosswise in one bed.' His father began to farm and his mother went out to teach school: 'She taught all week [and] went home for the weekends, where she washed and ironed, cleaned and baked, and taught Sunday School. On Mondays she gathered up her brood and went back to the teacherage.' At age eleven, Vernon was taken by an attack of what was first thought to be influenza but which turned out to be a severe case of poliomyelitis. For several months he was without the use of his legs. An aunt who was a nurse in Ontario came for the winter to help bring him back to health. During the summer, when the Saskatoon berries were ripe, the 'Forty Friends' would gather to picnic, play games, and pick berries. 'Nobody wanted Vern to miss a thing, and he was taken everywhere,' reports a family friend. 'There was always an uncle to hoist him to his shoulders so he could see everything that was going on ... He grew up strong in spirit because of this family solidarity.' He recovered sufficiently to be able to walk with the use of a cane and to lead a normal life, but any physical activities of a strenuous sort had to be curtailed. Having been denied the usual activities of teenage boyhood, he was taught by his mother how to amuse himself – to make quilts, to knit, to make toys of wood, and to play music. He continued to knit when he was older and made for all his children thick woollen sweaters in the traditional Indian designs known locally as siwashes.[9]

Since a life in farming was now out of the question for Vernon, his schooling became a matter of special importance in the family. After his illness, he was sent to school in Swift Current, and then to Regina College, before entering the University of Saskatchewan. He chose economics as his major, taking eleven courses in the subject over four years. In 1928 he was awarded the BA with great distinction, and the next year, after completing a thesis under the supervision of Professor Swanson entitled 'The Economic Realities of the Coal Situation,' he received an MA in economics. Swanson regarded Fowke as his protégé in the economics department: he lent him books, helped him to get what stipends were available, and generally encouraged him along the path of his career. Early in 1930, he asked Fowke to help out in the department as a reader and, in the following autumn after Carrothers resigned, supported his appointment as an instructor, which gave him a salary of $1,800. The appointment was renewed five more times. During this period he was assigned to teach courses in introductory economics, cooperative marketing, and rural economics.

Fowke had intended to apply for graduate admission to the University of Chicago, where he had once attended a summer session, but he was persuaded by Mabel Timlin to try instead at the University of Washington, where the fees were lower and he was likely to find it easier to get about. Washington was happy to have him. 'We like his personality and his courage and cheerfulness,' Howard H. Preston, later dean of the College of Economics and Business, wrote to Murray. 'If you have more people like Miss Timlin and Mr. Fowke we will be pleased if they select the University of Washington for graduate study.'[10] But there was little financial assistance to be had. For Fowke the difficulties were nearly insurmountable; he had put away eight hundred dollars towards the expenses of a year of study, but all his savings went at the last moment to help his father, who had been refused a bank loan and was in danger of losing the family farm. It is not surprising that in his later writings and teachings Fowke was always sensitive to the need for sympathetic agricultural policies on the part of government. When finally he got away to Seattle, he managed somehow to get through the year – by taking a room at the YMCA, marking papers in economics in return for a small stipend, and otherwise practising drastic economies in his living expenses. At the end of the year he married Helen Hilton, whom he had met earlier in Saskatoon. They would have five children, three by adoption.

II

George Britnell, who entered university a year after Fowke, was the flamboyant third of the triumvirate, twelve years younger than Timlin, senior to Fowke by four, and like an older brother to both. He was born in Wimbledon, England, on 9 June 1903 and was six when his family emigrated to Canada. The family settled on a homestead near Macrorie, Saskatchewan. Like Fowke, Britnell was schooled in the economics of agriculture by the vicissitudes of the prairie economy. He owned farm land in the district of Macrorie to the end of his life and kept a close watch on the progress of the crop throughout the growing season. His father served as reeve of the rural municipality of Fertile Valley for many years and was a member of the farmers' delegation which marched on Ottawa in 1942. George himself took an active part in agrarian politics in the 1920s, and some thought he was headed for a political career. But when he became a university teacher, he eschewed active involvement in politics and claimed to have 'no political stripes ... I am a detached observer.'[11]

Britnell's education began at the rural school, but for his secondary education he had to go farther afield. In 1923 he entered Outlook College where he was exposed to a free-thinker by the name of O. B. Grimley, whose lectures about economics contained frequent references to the Bible intermingled with such aphorisms as 'Competition is the law of the devil,' 'Capital should be the servant of labour,' 'Private property is the outgrowth of man's greed,' 'Socialism is co-operation.'[12] When Principal Grimley's unorthodox views led to his severance from the college in the middle of the year, Britnell and a companion left in sympathy.[13] Britnell completed his high school education in 1924 at the Prince Albert Collegiate Institute, where he was awarded the Governor General's Gold Medal. Afterwards he worked variously at the Saskatchewan Wheat Pool, the Macrorie post office, the family farm, and the *Western Producer*, the popular farm paper published in Saska-toon. He continued to work part-time at the *Western Producer* after he went to university and there first developed his skill at writing and editing. In fact, his proficiency in writing might well have led him to a career in journalism if academic work had not come along to divert his attention.

He enrolled at the university in 1926, at the age of twenty-three, where his interest was to be divided among economics, English, his-tory, and law. From Underhill he took English history but not political science. In economics he had four courses, one of which, on socialism, he took (along with Vernon Fowke) from McQueen. In his third and final year, Britnell enrolled in three courses in the College of Law and, largely through the influence of J.A. Corry, began to think seriously of a career in law. At the same time he continued to be actively involved in the farmers' movement.

In the spring of 1929 Britnell graduated with a BA and was awarded the Carswell prize in law and an Imperial Order Daughters of the Empire scholarship for overseas study. The following year he spent in leisurely study at the London School of Economics and Political Sci-ence. Since he was not going up for a degree, he could spend his time pretty much as he pleased. He attended lectures by Laski and Finer, and read voraciously in philosophy, history, politics, and economics. For the rest, he passed his time amiably savouring the delights of Lon-don – working for a time as a journalist on Fleet Street – and travelling on the continent to the extent that his purse allowed. Near the end of his stay in London, he received a message from President Murray offering him a position as a lecturer at Saskatchewan for the following year. He at first refused, intending on his return to enter law as a full-time student. But only a few days after he had replied to Murray, news reached him of the loss of his farm crop to a hailstorm. He quickly dis-patched a second telegram to Murray which read: 'Will accept econom-ics or any available instructorship I could fill crop destroyed hail no resources.'[14]

In the fall of 1930, Britnell joined Vernon Fowke in the Department of Economics as a novice instructor. He was given responsibility for the teaching of economic history, a section of introductory economics, and two other sections of economics scheduled at Regina and Moose Jaw, respectively, which involved his travelling out of the city each Thurs-day and Friday during term. At the same time, he kept his career plans alive by enrolling as a part-time student in the College of Law.

In the opinion of those who knew him, Britnell seemed headed towards a career in public life. Morton, who taught him in history, wrote in 1933: 'He has continued to be a guide, philosopher and friend to some of the more conservative of the leaders in the present Farmers' movement. He is thus not only a scholar but something of a statesman.'[15] President Murray described Britnell as 'a man of unusual individuality and ability.' In one of several recommendations on his behalf, Murray wrote: 'His record here was very good; his mind is very mature; his interests are broad and he is mentally very keen. He has been a good teacher and we would welcome him back to the staff so high is our opinion of him.'[16] He wrote to a farm leader in Britnell's locality: 'When Carrothers left we were in a difficult position. It was too late to make a permanent appointment and we had to make such arrangements as possible. Swanson's departure to Britain has added to our difficulties. We have asked Fowke and Britnell, two recent graduates, to carry on this year so it will give us time to look around for a suitable man for permanent appointment. Britnell has a lot of ability and intended to go into Law but the loss of his crop this year made it impossible for him to continue his Law work and he was willing to accept this position for the year. I fancy his ultimate destination is politics. You and your friends are probably responsible for the suggestion.'[17]

Over the next several years, with no money for the university to hire a senior member for the department, Britnell and Fowke were kept on, and Mabel Timlin added, as junior staff to meet the emergency. For Britnell's part, successive failures of his farm crop denied him the income which would have seen him through law school, and he was happy to have the job. Then, in 1933, when university members without family responsibilities were asked to take leave of absence at minimum pay, he applied to the Department of External Affairs for a secretarial position, to the University of Michigan for a scholarship, and to the University of Toronto for the Mackenzie Fellowship. Successful in the last, he went to Toronto for a year to work towards a master's degree in economics.

At Toronto, Britnell encountered the economic historian Harold Innis, who set him firmly on the path of an academic career. Not only did Innis teach his kind of economics to Britnell, he also saw to the direction of his research interests and made certain that Britnell published quickly and copiously. Britnell became Innis's favourite disciple. The two had in common a deep attachment to rural life and country folk. Carl Berger tells us that, 'according to his wife, [Innis] kept in touch with the farm all his life: with the changing seasons he would often remark on what his family would then be doing.'[18] Fowke writes that Britnell, 'whatever the season ... could tell the precise stage and state of the farming operations conducted by his brother on the home farm.'[19] Innis described Britnell as 'a Catholic but the most liberal I ever met.'[20] C.R. Fay, once asked who was closest to Innis, answered, 'the Saskatchewan chappie,' meaning Britnell.[21] Britnell himself never forgot what he later referred to as 'the Innisian tradition of helping men who find it difficult to get an academic toe-hold and who get bogged down with a heavy teaching load in a small institution.'[22]

By the end of 1934, Britnell had completed a thesis on the provincial telephone system on the prairies and was awarded a master's degree in economics from Toronto. He returned to lecture at the University of Saskatchewan, and then in the fall of 1935, during the year when the Department of Economics lost McQueen and had to make do with temporary staff, went again to Toronto to start on a doctoral program.[23] Innis had Britnell hired as a lecturer at a salary of $2,000, assigned him to teach only one class in economic history, and then set him to work on incorporating some earlier research he had done on living standards on the prairies into a more complete study of the wheat economy. Innis had in mind a large scheme in which Britnell would investigate, besides Saskatchewan, other wheat-growing regions such as Australia and Argentina. He began to campaign for funds for the project and suggested to Britnell that he should try for another year of leave in order to carry it out. 'Such a program of work,' declared Innis, 'would definitely establish the University of Saskatchewan in the study of wheat from the standpoint of standards of living and would assist enormously in restoring the morale of the province in building up faith in its own educational institution.'[24]

Innis had other plans for Britnell as well – namely a biography of A.J. McPhail based on the diary he left which told the story of the western wheat-pooling movement. 'The more I see of the work ahead of me,' he wrote to Britnell in 1935, 'the more urgent it appears that you should do the biography of McPhail. It would give you a chance to get into the whole problem of pool policy and do a piece of work of very considerable interest and value.'[25] But after reading the diary, Britnell said he was 'decidedly nervous for, though tremendously interesting, it is full of dynamite.'[26] In the end, he kept away from the work on McPhail, no doubt out of a desire to maintain the good relations he had with farm leaders in the West. Innis himself edited the diary for publication, and Britnell helped only with the final editing of proofs for the book.[27]

At first, Britnell approached the living-standards project with some diffidence. He was not, he confessed, particularly happy in this field, but he hoped by falling in line with Innis to be quickly done with his thesis so that he could go up for his degree in the spring of 1936. As it happened, the research for his thesis took longer than expected and when he returned to Saskatchewan in 1936, now as an assistant professor of economics, a heavy teaching schedule delayed him still further. At Saskatchewan, he was assigned to teach four courses: introductory economics, socialism and labour problems, the economic history of Canada and the United States, and the history of economic thought. When it was suggested that he might in addition conduct an evening class in economics, he threatened rebellion. There were fewer distractions to interrupt his work now that two of his close companions had moved to other universities, McQueen to Manitoba and Corry to Queen's to start a new career in political science. 'This seems a damnably dull place now with you gone & Alec away to Queen's,' he wrote in a letter to McQueen. 'I am sure Alec will fit into that Dept perfectly though, don't you? He thinks like they do.'[28] Corry, a Saskatchewan graduate and Rhodes scholar, was to write a textbook in political science entitled *Democratic Government and Politics*, which was widely adopted in Canada as well as at the University of Saskatchewan. He later became principal of Queen's University.[29]

Under Innis's tutelage, Britnell was kept to a rigorous schedule of publishing. Between 1934 and 1937 he wrote five articles for the *Canadian Journal of Economics and Political Science*, one for the *American Economic Review*, another for *The Canadian Economy and Its Problems* (a collection edited by Innis and A.F.W. Plumptre), a pamphlet, and a note for the *Canadian Historical Review* – all on subjects relating to agriculture and the wheat economy.[30] Then came his first diversion into government work. Late in the summer of 1937 he was asked, along with F.C. Cronkite and T.C. Davis (the dean of law and provincial attorney general, respectively) to prepare the Saskatchewan submission to the Royal Commission on Dominion-Provincial Relations (Rowell–Sirois Commission). The final brief of 434 pages took three months of intensive work. Britnell wrote the economics section, drawing on his unfinished thesis and, as he acknowledged, many of Innis's ideas, and then defended the brief before the commission during an eight-day hearing held in Regina. For his part in the affair he was highly acclaimed, and handsomely rewarded, too, with an honorarium of $600. Herbert Heaton, on reading the brief, said he was fascinated by 'this whole revival of the apparently lost art of Political Economy.'[31] One fellow economist told Britnell he did 'a hell of a lot better job than Manitoba' and that 'the eastern boys seem to be putting forth pretty feeble efforts.'[32] Harold Innis added his congratulations: 'There can be no doubt but that your name has been made on the strength of it.'[33]

Britnell was subsequently hired as a member of the commission's research staff in Ottawa, a group of about a dozen people headed by Alexander Skelton. When someone pointed out to Britnell that he was serving both sides of the dispute over dominion-provincial jurisdictions at the same time, he answered that he was 'not sure what Emily Post would say about this delicate point of political etiquette.'[34] The group that he joined in 1938 worked in close association over the summer and included the historian Donald Creighton, W.A. Mackintosh, McQueen, and Corry. Members of the group ate meals together, spent evenings together, and argued together. 'The problem each of us was working at involved, in most instances, breaking new ground. We exchanged thoughts and discoveries, and were led to face up to the central issues before the Commission,' Corry wrote in his memoirs of these historic labours. He especially remembered his two cronies from Saskatchewan: 'George Britnell, a student of McQueen at the University of Saskatchewan and an able economist, admired McQueen greatly and modelled himself on him in every particular ... They brought with them habits established in their long association. So when they discussed economics in a group, they always found room for argument and were soon reviling one another as "ignorant bastards," "stupid buggers," and more generally, in the picturesque idiom of the Saskatchewan vernacular.' Corry recalled that Creighton, who had been born into a Methodist parsonage and thereafter led a sheltered life among eastern Canadians, found the two westerners to be 'startling variations in the species, almost like creatures from another world.'[35]

In 1938 Britnell received a PhD from the University of Toronto. In the following year, *The Wheat Economy*, a revised form of his thesis, was published by the University of Toronto Press as part of a political economy series edited by Innis. Innis, who advised Britnell on the manuscript and gave it its title, declared himself pleased with the final result. 'The book will add lustre to the department of political science in Saskatchewan. I shall never have a more pleasant author to work with,' he wrote in a letter to Britnell.[36] Britnell's study, buttressed by the ample use of tables and diagrams, vividly illustrated the effects of the Depression in Saskatchewan. The Depression had reversed the movement to the land which had begun in the nineteenth century: a combination of falling prices and prolonged drought had made farming a hazardous occupation. On the other hand, exploitation of the region for the purposes of settlement and agricultural development had left the provincial economy precariously dependent on the income generated by a single agricultural product, one with high fixed costs.

Because huge capital expenditures were needed for development, the province had become essentially a debtor economy. Britnell drew a grim picture (a friend called him 'the Saskatchewan oracle of doom')[37] of declining standards of living, weakened political and social institutions, a demoralized population, a mounting burden of personal and governmental indebtedness, and little prospect of anything better. The Saskatchewan government had been forced to undertake relief programs and to supplement the private sector with public services such as telephones and support for agriculture. Britnell believed that it was not feasible under the present circumstances to expect provincial resources alone to provide for these exigencies and the costs of development. 'It should be possible,' he concluded, 'to discover a more orderly solution by making use of the broader and more stable economic base afforded by the Dominion. Furthermore, it may be argued that considerations of national well-being require that all Canadians, regardless of where they may live, be guaranteed certain minimum Canadian standards of education and health at least, and that only assumption by the Dominion government of the financial burden of a large part of the costs of education, hospitalization, mothers' allowances, etc. (in addition to old age pensions and relief expenditures), coupled with provision for a flexible system of emergency grants to meet immediate and pressing needs as they arise from year-to-year fluctuations in net income, can give this measure of security to the vulnerable and exposed sections of the Canadian economy.'[38]

In the *American Economic Review*, Joseph S. Davis of the Food Research Institute at Stanford pronounced the book a credit to the author, the editor, and its sponsors. 'The work rests upon and provides a welcome guide to an extended literature that has issued from the post-war researches of Canadians and some others; but the author has effectively sought unpublished data and other information needed to give an adequate, illuminating, up-to-date picture. It is well organized, written with clarity and conciseness of statement, and interesting rather than heavy or light ... For readers who care naught about Saskatchewan as such, or about wheat and its producers wherever they are, this volume deserves high rank as an example of a type of regional study of which many more are needed.'[39]

As Britnell's success outside the economics department grew, his position within, perhaps because of it, became more uncomfortable. During the early years of their acquintance he and the head of the department had seemed to get along well enough. Britnell's letters to Swanson show the deference one might expect of a junior addressing his superior, and Swanson's to Britnell, including the last, dated 12 June 1937, were always cordial. But just after this, about the time that Britnell was engaged to work on the Saskatchewan brief for the Rowell-Sirois commission, a rift developed between the two men. After the fall term opened, they hardly spoke to one another. The estrangement became something of a *cause célèbre* at the university, though its exact causes, if ever they were known, were soon forgotten, and the hostilities between the two men came to be looked upon as a phenomenon characteristic of academe. A reconciliation was never possible. A friend of Swanson, who made an attempt at one in 1945, when the latter was confined to a hospital bed, afterwards reported to Britnell that the mission had failed: 'I mentioned I had seen you and his whole manner changed – his only answer was "as far as George Britnell is concerned the less said soonest mended" ... All that I can say is I am very sorry. It seems stupid to carry differences to such length.'[40]

By the end of 1937, Britnell concluded that his prospects in the economics department were not bright, and he decided to look for another appointment. Two openings had come to his attention, one as secretary to the Nova Scotia Economics Council, the other the W.A. Black Chair of Commerce at Dalhousie University, and, duly giving notice to President Murray of his intentions, he made up his mind to go after them.

9

Wartime

Walter Murray had guided the university for nearly thirty years. When he stepped down in the summer of 1937, a very personal style of administration came to an end. Others of his generation of university leaders in Canada had already retired. It was a remarkable group: never again would the universities be identified to such a degree with their presidents, and never again would the presidents themselves come together in such a close circle of friendship and accord. 'In some sense,' wrote Robert Falconer to one of the circle, A.S. Mackenzie of Dalhousie, 'we have made an epoch of our own, and I doubt whether our successors will have as much real intimacy as we have enjoyed.' And what had they accomplished? 'The present,' he mused in a letter to Murray, 'so quickly becomes the past that we at our age are apt to live too much in that memory. It is so elusive and so unsatisfactory, so full of that which one did very badly. Really, I never had the courage to do what it was in me to do.' 'What I did in Toronto,' he said, 'has been neither so enduring nor so important as your work in Saskatchewan. You have built up a great university from the bottom on lines that will never change. With great self-sacrifice you have created a standard of liberal education for a new province. Those things I could never have done.'[1]

President Murray was about to leave the university by the time the troubles between Swanson and Britnell arose. Before relinquishing office, he had looked for a successor to Dawson in political science. Several candidates had declared their interest in an appointment, among them three Saskatchewan graduates, James Aitchison, S.D. Clark, and again Hugh Clokie, who was still in the United States.[2] But Murray, as usual, paid scant attention to the claims of those who applied to him directly. He had always considered that a good training in law was ample qualification for teaching political science, and the recent transfer of Corry from law at Saskatchewan to political science at Queen's, where he succeeded Norman Rogers, seemed to confirm this. Murray did his best to persuade George Curtis, another Rhodes scholar from Saskatchewan, to follow Corry's example and tried wooing him with the offer of a department of his own and a dual appointment in political science and law. Dawson's work in political science, Murray told him, had 'attracted a considerable number of some of the very best students.'[3] Curtis, who was teaching law at Dalhousie, appeared to like the idea and spent a month or so thinking it over, but then finally decided against it. Murray was fairly sure of Curtis and had not seriously pursued any others, and so the matter of a permanent appointment in political science was left unresolved when Murray's successor took over. For the session of 1937–8 a temporary appointment was made to R. Gordon Robertson, the first student to graduate from the four-year honours course in economics.[4]

The new president, James Sutherland Thomson, a minister of the Presbyterian church and formerly professor of philosophy and theology at Pine Hill Divinity Hall in Halifax, came to his office with no previous experience in administration and, as succeeding years were to show, hardly any natural aptitude for it. Nevertheless, his term, which lasted for twelve years, through the difficult period of the Second World War and its aftermath, represented a transition from the old paternalism to the newer democratic ways of university government. It meant the devolution of responsibility, more effective direction by deans, and an end to presidential involvement in the day-to-day affairs of the various colleges and departments. The faculty grew in power and influence under Thomson. Though the hiring of staff still remained the preserve of the president, J.S. Thomson, in contrast to Murray, depended far more upon the advice of his senior faculty. During the decade of the 1940s, the shift of authority away from the presidency was particularly evident in the College of Arts and Science, where the biologist Walter Palmer Thompson – called W.P. to distinguish him from J.S. – came to preside as dean.

The change to a new presidential administration, which promised to be energetic and accessible where the old had become tired and hidebound, was welcomed with enthusiasm. 'We had not realized quite how much the boat *had* rocked the past few years until we boarded the good broad-beamed Scotch ship in which we are travelling now!'

remarked Mabel Timlin early in 1938.[5] The opening move of the new president seemed to augur well, for in one stroke he solved both the schism in economics and the vacancy in political science by appointing George Britnell to the political science department. To induce him to stay on at Saskatchewan, Britnell was offered an increase in salary and promotion to the rank of full professor, a singularly swift advancement for one who had been named assistant professor less than two years before (the more usual course was that taken by Fowke, who took ten years more to become a full professor).

Britnell had kept Innis informed about his predicament in economics but was unsure how Innis would take the news. 'The "new deal" has come off here except for formal ratification by the Board of Governors at their next meeting,' wrote Britnell. 'They offered me the Pol. Science chair with an increase & promotion, and, with some misgivings I accepted. I shall have a completely free hand and can give the Pol. Sc. a definitely economic twist for the most part. I should not have considered it if my position in the Dept. of Economics had not become completely impossible since last fall. I don't regard it as more than a partial & temporary separation from Economics. I sincerely hope you don't think I've made a damned fool of myself by accepting the change.'[6] But Innis, far from thinking him a fool, had nothing but praise for the move: 'I must congratulate you on your appointment to the Political Science chair,' he wrote. 'You have deserved it and you will add distinction to it. I am more and more convinced that the separation of the social sciences is a mistake. Your approach from the economic side will greatly strengthen the subject. It would appear to be a happy solution of a great number of problems in Saskatchewan.'[7] Britnell in the meantime had withdrawn his name from the competition for the opening with the Nova Scotia Economic Council, though he still nourished the hope that he might be asked to fill the Black Chair of Commerce at Dalhousie. However, because of an administrative mix-up at Dalhousie, another man was named to the chair before Britnell's application got to receive due attention.

I

Britnell confessed in the beginning that he felt 'a trespasser' in the field of political science.[8] In fact, he had never taken a course in the subject apart from one in political philosophy offered by the philosophy department when he was an undergraduate, but he had a wide acquaintance with the literature of political science – his year in London was now to bear fruit – careful habits of preparation, and an authoritative presence in the classroom. His introductory political science course quickly became a popular elective at the university. As one student wrote to him, 'About ninety percent of the students who take Political Science 1, do so because you "make" the class.'[9] His lecture notes, complete with humorous asides, were fully typed and revised afresh each year; he would read from them in a thundering voice that could be heard well down the corridor outside the room where he lectured. He marked assignments with the same authority, leaving unremarked no grammatical deviation or logical error, and delivering his judgment on each in a gigantic backhand script, often in red crayon. He was particularly cross with students who used what he called slovenly English. He would not tolerate lack of effort – students whose work he suspected of plagiarism were warned that any further transgressions of the kind would be reported to the disciplinary committee of the university. Those who took their work seriously, on the other hand, soon found that beneath this gruff exterior was a man with a kindly, almost fatherly, regard for their academic welfare.

During what he called 'the birth-pangs of a new political scientist,' Britnell looked for advice not to an old hand like Dawson, as one might have expected, but to a fellow novitiate, J.A. Corry.[10] Corry suspected that 'Dawson would be quite derisive on the subject – the blind leading the blind!' – but evidently Corry's approach was more congenial to Britnell.[11] After consulting with Corry, Britnell decided to restore to the curriculum an emphasis on historical development and political ideas, an alteration reminiscent of Underhill's old plans for the department but with more Canadian content. 'I am treating my Political Science 1,' said Britnell, 'as an introduction to political theory purely and simply, having dropped the popular account of Canadian government which Dawson featured so strongly.'[12] As a result, a separate upper-year course on Canadian government was introduced and the first-year course given over to a general survey of the field. The first-year course was described in the university *Calendar* as 'an introductory course in political science dealing with the nature of the state; the development of political ideas; the concept of sovereignty; the reconciliation of liberty and authority; the basis of law; cabinet and responsible government; the federal principle; constitutions; the legislative, executive and judicial functions; public opinion and political parties; democracy and dictatorship; and international relations.'[13] Raymond Gettell's *Political*

Science was the prescribed textbook. The outline of the introductory course, with its distinct division into political thought in the first term and political institutions in the second, was to remain virtually unchanged, except for the updating of subject matter and textbooks, until 1994.

Britnell departed from Dawson's schedule in other respects as well: where Dawson had two courses on comparative government, there was now only one; Dawson's course on problems of modern democracy was dropped, international relations was reinstated as a lecture course, and for several years a course in international law was on offer. The two courses in political theory, one on classical and medieval thinking and the other on the modern period, both neglected by Dawson, were now actually given and assiduously promoted. For advanced students there was also a seminar on the problems of Canadian federalism in which the abundant materials provided by the researches of the Royal Commission on Dominion-Provincial Relations were examined. In fact, Britnell would insert aspects of dominion-provincial relations into any class he taught; when later he went back to teaching introductory economics, his students were always made to read W.A. Mackintosh's *The Economic Background to Dominion-Provincial Relations*, which Britnell had helped to prepare.

With a department all to himself and his numerous appearances before the public eye, Britnell was now well launched on his career. He was in constant demand as a speaker at public meetings and on radio. In 1938, David Lewis, on behalf of the Co-operative Commonwealth Federation (CCF), invited him to help plan the party's program; Britnell replied that he could not do so because his position at the university and his relationship with the provincial government made his participation 'distinctly out of place.'[14] Two of Britnell's CBC radio talks, 'Problems of Our Rural Debt Structure' (1938) and 'Bushels to Burn' (1940), were eagerly listened to by rural folk across the province and brought him many letters from farmers who thanked him for the courage and insight he had shown. The Regina *Leader-Post* declared: 'One of Canada's younger economists and known for his vigorous and modern approach to the subject of political economy is George Edwin Britnell ... His favorite sport is English billiards, but he is also known to take a keen delight in controversy, especially in company in which no quarter is asked or given.'[15] In the House of Commons, the member for Weyburn, T.C. Douglas, referred to Britnell as 'one of the best agricultural economists, and one of whose work the people of Saskatchewan are proud.'[16] And R. MacGregor Dawson, who had traded many a witticism with Britnell during his Saskatoon days, acknowledged wryly: 'Britnell, you undoubtedly have a way with you. I don't pretend to understand it, in fact, I marvel at it every time I take a square look at you ... Whenever I mention your name – and I endeavour naturally to bring your name into the conversation frequently and to make the most of our friendship – everyone's face lights up.'[17]

In the fall of 1938, Britnell went to Australia as a delegate to the second British Commonwealth Relations Conference, though by this time the full-scale comparative study of the Australian wheat economy that Innis had planned for him had had to be called off for lack of sponsors. Britnell's trip to Australia delayed his baptism as a political scientist for several weeks, and his classes were launched instead by President Thomson and a former political science student enrolled in the College of Law, William R. Lederman. The rest of the year was crowded with activity. Britnell had to prepare for classes he had never before taught (or taken), revise his thesis for publication, and write several pieces for the *Canadian Journal of Economics and Political Science*. When spring came, he was ready to take some time off. 'I confess with some shame that I propose to take about two months holiday and go to England,' he wrote to Corry in May 1939. 'I am feeling completely exhausted after my first year in Political Science which was coupled with the harrowing ordeal of getting a book through the press. The balance of the summer I propose to utilize largely in reading in Political Science, since if I am to maintain the bluff for another year, I must at least make certain appropriate gestures.' The news of his trip, he added, was for Corry's ears alone 'as I have not broken the news to that slave-driver, Harold Innis, who probably expects me to grind out another opus on Economics.'[18] Britnell went ahead with his holiday and spent the summer touring England, Scotland, and Wales in a rented English Prefect. But world events moved quickly during the summer of 1939, and he just managed to escape back to Canada on the eve of the declaration of war by Great Britain. The boat on which he travelled, the *Empress of Britain*, sailed only hours after the passenger liner *Athenia* bound for America went down off the coast of Scotland, the first victim of the U-boat attacks that signalled the start of hostilities.

In 1940, when he was thirty-seven, and after seven years of courtship, Britnell married Pauline May Paulson, daughter of W.H. Paulson, a former member of the legislature from Wynyard, and, much to the surprise of his friends, moved with apparent ease from bachelorhood to family life.[19] By this time, the pace he was to follow the rest of his life, with hardly a full day devoted to relaxation and never a substantial holiday that did not also include some plans for work, was already evident. Even his honeymoon was combined with a working visit to eastern Canada. At the time of his marriage he was chairman of the Dominion commission on the cost of living in the coal industry in Alberta and British Columbia, and following this served as chairman of a similar commission for Saskatchewan. Then in the fall of 1941, just as he was finishing a project of several weeks for the Canadian Wheat Board, he was summoned hurriedly to Ottawa – 'the holy city,' he once called it – to become an economic adviser to the Wartime Prices and Trade Board.[20] His appointment to the board was warmly greeted in the West, especially in farming circles. Frank Eliason, Saskatchewan secretary for the United Farmers of Canada, wrote to say he was 'the right man for the job particularly in view of the fact that you have the western farm viewpoint ... [and] will do what is right on behalf of the western farmer.'[21] In Ottawa, he continued to take part in radio programs on public affairs. One Sunday afternoon broadcast in particular would not be forgotten: it was 7 December 1941, during a Round Table discussion, with Britnell and law professor F.R. Scott taking part, when half-way through came the news of the bombing of the U.S. naval base at Pearl Harbor.[22]

Britnell remained in Ottawa for the duration of the war, wrestling with the setting of prices for primary foodstuffs, a task he approached with some distaste, having been well schooled by Harold Innis to view all things connected with a centralized bureaucracy with suspicion. 'I understand Innis' point of view much more clearly after 4 months in Ottawa. It has recalled some of Frank Knight's lectures on the implications of a controlled economy,' he wrote to Mabel Timlin.[23] If ever he had harboured yearnings for a more peaceable or fulfilling occupation outside the walls of academe, after his experience in Ottawa he was certain at least of one thing – the university was the place where he belonged.

II

The removal of George Britnell from the economics department in 1938 had helped to defuse a developing crisis, but other problems were left unsolved. Low morale in the department had become a chronic condition. Heavy class loads, low salaries, slow promotions, and frequent disagreements with the head of the department led to strong feelings of discontent. Vernon Fowke and Mabel Timlin had suspicions that their department head, W.W. Swanson, did not really have their interests at heart in his dealings with them or with the administration. All three were annoyed at his claims to have helped them in their achievements – 'the implication only too often being,' said Timlin, 'that without his interest we wouldn't amount to a hill of beans apiece.'[24] As she and Fowke became mature scholars and their accomplishments won recognition outside the university, they grew increasingly restive at the state of affairs in the department.

The first problem that arose after Britnell's transfer to political science was the selection of a replacement for him in economics. There were many persons seeking jobs in Canada at the time: S.D. Clark, H.D. Woods, Lorie Tarshis, W.T. Easterbrook, and C.R. Fay were among those interested in an economics appointment at Saskatchewan. The younger members in the department figured on Easterbrook's getting it. But President Thomson had his eye set on a political economist from Acadia University, C.P. Wright. Before his term as president had begun, Thomson had interviewed Wright in the Maritimes and apparently considered hiring him for political science. When this position was decided in favour of Britnell, Thomson asked Wright if he would come as an instructor in economics. Wright, who was then negotiating for a position at Princeton, at first objected to the rank of instructor, which he regarded as an embarrassment, but when the offer was changed to an assistant professorship he agreed to a conditional appointment for one year.[25] Both the president and Professor Swanson hoped that things would work out so that Wright would stay longer at Saskatchewan.

Wright was forty-five years old with degrees from Oxford and Harvard, personally attractive, but hopeless as a teacher of undergraduates.[26] Innis, in fact, had said as much to President Thomson before Wright was hired.[27] Only a few weeks into the term, it became clear that a mistake had indeed been made. 'There have been reverberations of a palace revolution in the Economics Department,' Britnell observed from his own department with detached amusement, 'and I shall be very surprised if Swanson's choice lingers on the scene for another year. He is apparently a pedagogical anarchist since his method with Garver and Hansen [the textbook] is to start in the middle and work both ways simultaneously. The students apparently found this procedure somewhat bewildering.'[28] Mabel Timlin, whose task it was to instruct small groups of students having difficulty with economics, was rather less amused. She was besieged in her office by delegations of students and accosted in the hallways by others, all begging to be admitted to her tutorials. This 'mad Englishman ...' she said, 'is giving the students in their *first* Economics course a course in mathematical economics built up on parabolas, equations, tangents, secants, and what-not when his students have not for the most part the foggiest idea of the concepts behind the symbols on which his mathematical relations are built up! As a result, some sixty-seven economic babies have all been trying to sit down in my lap at the same time!'[29] There were reports of discrepancies between Wright's system of grading and that of others in the department, of his 'rather improvised methods of teaching,' and his 'free and easy' style. The president, who had the unpleasant job of informing Wright of these transgressions, told him that, although his teaching beyond the elementary level had been well received, his appointment would not be renewed.[30] Thereupon another row ensued, lasting several weeks, in which the aggrieved Wright attempted to swing opinion over to his side and have the decision reversed.

It was after this episode that Mabel Timlin remarked wearily: 'There has never been peace in the Economics Department here since I have known this institution, and there has never been co-operation between the Economics Department and the other social science departments, and I do not expect that the situation will be completely solved for four or five years yet, but we certainly can get much closer to it than we have been doing this year.'[31]

When it looked as if Wright's contract would not last beyond the academic year, another man was hired to take his place, John Stuart Mill Allely, whose name had come up once before in connection with the vacancy left by McQueen. Allely was thirty-four, a graduate of Queen's in economics and history, and, as one of his contemporaries reported, 'can pilot aeroplanes,' 'is well up on his money and banking,' and 'cultivates a comprehensive ignorance of the original John Stuart Mill.'[32] Moreover, he was badly in need of a job. During the retrenchment of the 1930s, when university places were in short supply, he had taught variously at Queen's, McMaster, Harvard, British Columbia, Manitoba, Alberta, and the Carnegie Institute of Technology, at each place for no longer than a year, except for McMaster where he stayed for two and then left owing to a falling out with the chancellor over a religious issue.[33] Mackintosh of Queen's, who knew him well, first as a student and later as a research assistant with the Royal Commission on

Dominion-Provincial Relations, said there was no one better among his generation in Canada and that he was especially strong in teaching: 'For a young man he was unusually clear in his exposition, and sparing of his words.'[34] Good reports about Allely also came from Professors Taussig and Gay of Harvard where he had taken an AM degree.

At the same time, Archibald N. Reid, another Queen's man, was brought into the department to replace Mabel Timlin, who was away for a year. Reid and Allely had both taken their bachelor's and master's degrees at Queen's but at different times, Reid arriving as a freshman just before Allely received his second degree in 1930. Allely was hired at Saskatchewan as an instructor at a salary of $2,000 with the expectation that the appointment would be made permanent. Reid, also named as an instructor, was paid at the rate of $200 a month for eight months, and his appointment was regarded as temporary. But, as it happened, Fowke took a leave of absence the year after Mabel Timlin returned and Reid was kept on for a second year. Afterwards, other members were called away on account of the war and Reid's appointment was renewed further, until finally registrations increased to the point that he could be kept on permanently. Allely was elevated to the rank of assistant professor of economics in 1941 (at $2,000), Reid in 1944 (at $2,500).

III

At the urging of President Thomson and the promise of fifty dollars a month from the University of Saskatchewan, Mabel Timlin went in the fall of 1939 to the University of Washington to finish her doctoral studies. Her research had by this time taken a propitious turn. She had followed closely the new developments in the field of general economic theory and monetary economics. John Maynard Keynes's *General Theory of Employment, Interest and Money*, appearing in 1936, provided her with the framework she needed to work out some of her own ideas in conjunction with some of the critical refinements which had followed on Keynes. But she had been introduced to the subject even earlier through one of those curiously circuitous routes that scholars often follow. Benjamin Higgins recalls that when he was a student at London, in 1934 or thereabouts, Keynes turned up at a seminar, his fellow student Bob Bryce (later a civil servant who helped to bring Keynesian economics to Canadian policy making) took copious notes and had them mimeographed, and Higgins in his next year at Saskatchewan passed a copy on to Mabel Timlin.[35] Working largely on her own, and having no formal training in mathematics, she undertook to reformulate the General Theory in terms of a dynamic system, using the concept of the 'week' developed by J.R. Hicks and the key variables identified by Keynes and Oscar Lange, in order to examine more closely the role of interest rates in general equilibrium. The subject at the time was not much understood by economists not working in the field. At the University of Washington only one of the younger men, Ray Mikesell, could follow her argument closely enough to be of any help to her (his wife reported that he thought Timlin had 'the most theoretical mind' of any woman he had ever met).[36] Nevertheless, the year away allowed her to spend some time in Chicago with Oscar Lange and to bring her project near to completion. On the recommendation of Keynes himself, the thesis was sent for appraisal to Lange, who advocated its acceptance as follows:

> The thesis is excellent. Its outstanding features are extreme lucidity of exposition, precision of thought and competence and great facility of handling the apparatus of economic analysis. It compares very favorably with Ph.D. theses in economic theory presented at the University of Chicago; it certainly would be classified among the few of our top theses. The thesis definitely establishes its author as a person thoroughly competent in economic theory and of whom genuine contributions to the subject can be expected.[37]

In 1940, in her fiftieth year, she was awarded the PhD from the University of Washington.

Several economists, among them Harold Innis, V.W. Bladen, A.F.W. Plumptre (who had studied at Cambridge with Keynes), Ray Mikesell, and Oscar Lange, had a hand in advising Mabel Timlin on the revision of her thesis for publication. She spent two summers at the University of Toronto working on the final draft, and Innis, in particular, saw it safely through the University of Toronto Press. When it came out in 1942, under the title *Keynesian Economics*, its reception was all its author could have hoped it to be. It sold well, as such works go, was reprinted in 1948, translated into Japanese in 1951, and reissued in a paperback edition in 1977.[38] Keynes himself bought the book and in a letter to Mabel Timlin thanked her for 'your admirable effort to make some of my ideas available in another form,' and said that it looked 'an excellent piece of work,' though he was by then too harried by his involvement with the war to give it much attention.[39] Lange endorsed it enthusiastically and put it on the reading list for his seminar at Chicago. 'It makes very good reading,' he wrote, 'and I have the impression that it is the only systematic treatment of Keynesian economics available. In particular, I like the way you have succeeded in integrating all later contributions into the system. I hope that your book will become the standard introduction into the modern theory of money and employment, and will get its due recognition.'[40] The book earned for her a place among the leading Canadian economists of the day. Harry Johnson, in a 1968 review of Canadian contributions to economics, observed that *Keynesian Economics* was 'a remarkable personal achievement' and one of only two books written during the war 'that established a Canadian claim to competence in the realm of pure theory.'[41]

Those who reviewed her book offered differing opinions on where she might have elaborated further or less or not at all. Tom Wilson, in the *Economic Journal* (of which Keynes was currently the editor), called the book 'a very thorough and well-documented commentary,' but he objected to its having 'an over-elaborate method of treatment with too many diagrams.'[42] Abba P. Lerner, on the other hand, writing in the *Journal of Political Economy*, observed that the author had used 'very little mathematics ... and few diagrams.'[43] One reviewer said the book was 'a useful introduction to the Keynesian system.'[44] Another, Gottfried Haberler, held that it was 'much too difficult to serve as a text.' Writing in the *Canadian Journal of Economics and Political Science*, Haberler complained that the author 'follows too slavishly the original Keynesian position.' He was critical of her treatment of the multiplier, her disregard of recent literature on the investment function, and a lack of rigour which he said she shared with Keynes.[45] Still, the consensus was that the work was that the work was an extraordinary accomplishment. G.L.S. Shackle described it in *Economica* as 'a statement of the author's faith. She has found in the General Theory something which is both intellectually fascinating in itself, and hopeful for mankind, and she has wished to restate it in her own manner. The result is a book which makes plain on every page the high competence of the author and the very great and sustained care she has used in writing it. In its possession of clear-cut purposes and method, in its detailed thoroughness, and in consistency, good architecture, and exactness and clearness of statement it is outstanding.'[46]

Mabel Timlin's doctorate brought her a modicum of relief from some of her more tedious duties at the University of Saskatchewan. In 1941, she was promoted from instructor to assistant professor of economics, and from secretary to director of the correspondence program, now with clerical help. When Harold Innis made her an offer which would have allowed her to study at Toronto for a year, under the same terms given earlier to Britnell, she felt obliged to turn it down on the grounds that she could not with propriety ask for another year away. She doubted whether she could afford it anyway.[47] It was not until 1943, after the publication of *Keynesian Economics*, that she was freed altogether from the direction of the correspondence courses. Nevertheless, she continued to set and mark the final examination for the correspondence course in economics until her retirement a decade and a half later.

IV

After Timlin returned from Washington in 1940, it was Fowke's turn to take a year away. He had started a number of years before on a historical treatment of agricultural policy in Canada, a topic first suggested to him by Duncan MacGibbon and intended for submission to Washington towards his doctoral degree, but he had not had the time to develop it to his satisfaction. Harold Innis, hearing of his plight, invited him to Toronto and gave him a light teaching assignment, some interesting course work, and ample time to work on his project. 'If I can produce anything intelligently, or even intelligibly rounded, it will be through the Toronto facilities and influence,' he said.[48] By spring he could report real progress: 'My position now: not as close to completion – interpretation altered ... but I feel that I finally have a unity of approach to the topic which was previously lacking.'[49] Innis had him read a paper at a departmental seminar and then encouraged him to polish it up for presentation to the annual meeting of the Canadian Political Science Association the following summer. The paper, 'An Introduction to Agricultural History,' was published in the *Canadian Journal of Economics and Political Science* in 1942, following on 'Dominion Aids to Wheat Marketing, 1929–1939' (1940) and 'On Some Appendices to the Rowell–Sirois Report' (1941). In 1942 he completed his thesis and received the PhD from the University of Washington.

In the meantime, the shadow of war had settled on the university. There was much coming and going, particularly in political science and economics. The president, J.S. Thomson, who sometimes had taught one of the courses in political theory, served as head of the Canadian

Broadcasting Corporation during 1942–3 and took a leading part in national university affairs during and after the war. As president of the National Conference of Canadian Universities, Thomson was successful in negotiating federal compensation to universities for teaching veterans, which marked the beginning of federal financial support for universities.[50] John Allely, who was promoted to the rank of assistant professor in 1941, joined the Canadian army the same year and was gone for the next five years. Allely was replaced by Jacques Olivier Clerc, a young Swiss national of great personal charm, who was stranded in Toronto on a travelling scholarship when war broke out and then was invited to Saskatchewan to teach summer school in 1941. Clerc stayed on in the department for the full term, left in 1942 to enlist with the Royal Canadian Air Force, and was killed in an air raid over Germany shortly after.[51] William C. Hood came to teach economics from 1944 until 1946, when he left to resume his studies at Toronto. James R. Mallory, a graduate of New Brunswick, Edinburgh, and Dalhousie, on his first teaching assignment, came as an instructor in political science in 1941 after Britnell was called to Ottawa, and then left in 1943 to continue his studies. S. Mack Eastman, a veteran of many years' standing with international agencies and former chief of the Extra-European Studies section at the International Labour Office in Ottawa, joined the history department and filled in as a special lecturer in political science during the emergency; for many years he delivered the course in international relations to rapt audiences of students who were enthralled by his first-hand accounts of such personages as Clemenceau and de Gaulle.[52]

Meanwhile, there was a major reorganization of the arts and science curriculum, which established three areas of study: Type A, languages and literature; Type B, the social sciences; and Type C, the natural sciences. It became compulsory for students to take general courses outside their area of concentration so that they would have the benefit of a broad education. But here some heated discussions arose in the university council. The president wanted the social sciences course to be called 'Politics and Economics'; Britnell argued for 'Political Economy' and won. Swanson wanted the course to be in the hands of the economics department and proposed that Allely should teach it; Britnell pulled for Fowke.[53] It was finally decided that the course would be divided, with the political science part to be taught by Britnell and the economics side by either Allely or Fowke. But in the fall of 1941, just after Britnell began to teach the course, he was called away to Ottawa; Allely went into military service. It was left to President Thomson to continue with the inaugural lectures for the course. James Mallory, who arrived on the scene after the start of the term, took over from Thomson, and later Fowke took over from Mallory. In the following year, the whole course was handed over to Fowke.

With Britnell away for the duration, full responsibility for Political Economy A, as the course came to be called, fell to Vernon Fowke, who developed it into an integrated course and made it his own. His approach rested on his firm belief, shared by Britnell, that a political and historical framework was essential to the effective study of economic problems and in no way detracted from the rigour of the analysis. As Fowke explained, 'I envisage the class as one in Political Economy in the old-fashioned meaning of the term, rather than as a class in Political Science and Economics. Therefore I do not divide the year's work into clear-cut divisions ... It starts out with very general introductory matter which includes material with a considerable emphasis on the geographic environment ... and on population trends ... Economics and Political Science are blended.'[54] A description in the *Calendar* read as follows: 'This class is intended to introduce the student to some of the basic political and economic problems of modern society. The economic structure of society will be examined and its relation to the state carefully analyzed. A wide range of current political, economic and social questions will be discussed.'[55] With no readily available textbook for the course, two were prescribed, Clokie's *Canadian Government and Politics* and Currie's *Canadian Economic Development*. Fowke prepared, and over the years perfected, an outline for the course which was mimeographed and distributed to the students. The outline set out the structure of the course, topics to be discussed, and lists of readings, which included sections of the report of the Royal Commission on Dominion-Provincial Relations. After the introductory sections on geography and population trends were such topics as theory and its uses, Canadian economic and political development, Canadian government and politics, national income, economic systems, production, employment, money and banking, and international trade.[56] Several years later, in reply to a Manitoba colleague who inquired about the teaching of political economy, Britnell observed that, of the four introductory courses introduced because of the reorganization of the curriculum, Political Economy A became by far the most successful – the result, he said, 'of the integration achieved by having one man do the whole thing (and do it over a number of years), and ... Vern's handling of the class.'[57]

In 1941, the year Fowke began to teach Political Economy A, 270 students enrolled in it; 100 had been expected. Swanson was in favour of dividing the course into sections, but who would teach them? Fowke was not averse to going ahead with the class as it stood: 'I wouldn't have felt any relief to have 135 instead of 270.' The course was moved to a larger room, and Fowke applied to Swanson, his department head, for readers to help him with marking. At this point, he met with unexpected resistance – some people weren't suitable, the administration wouldn't approve, things were difficult because of the war, and so on, though in fact, as he was about to discover, the administration had already provided for readers. Fowke was normally serene in temper – Mabel Timlin called him 'the gentle Christian' – and those who knew him had hardly ever seen him ruffled. But, in this case, as he confessed to Britnell, he was 'damned mad,' and there was a quarrel with Swanson. Finally, W.P. Thompson, acting president in Thomson's absence, had to intervene and assign readers to Fowke.[58]

Despite these internal, or, it seemed, eternal, disagreements, a new mood prevailed at the university as a result of the excitement of wartime and the presence of so many new faces at the university. A change within her department was noticed by Mabel Timlin after her return from Washington in 1940: 'The Economics Department is a much happier place to work than it as been for many years past. I like the new members very much, and harmony seems to prevail all around.'[59] There were signs that the head of the department was withdrawing from the affairs of the university, which Britnell put down to a desire for 'peace at any reasonable price' after the battle over the course in political economy.[60] In August of 1943, Swanson was granted a year of leave on account of illness. Fowke was appointed acting head of the department and had quickly to make up a course schedule for the coming year. He took over Swanson's course in agricultural economics, Mabel Timlin claimed money and banking, and Fr Leonard Quinlan of St Thomas More College taught economic geography. As it turned out, Swanson was suffering from a skin cancer from which he would never recover. The announcement of his retirement, six months before he reached the official age, came at the beginning of May 1945. After this he had to spend long periods in hospital, but despite his terrible affliction remained strong in mind and contributed regularly under the pseudonym 'T.O.M.' to the local newspaper's book-review section, edited by his daughter. He died in 1950.

V

Mabel Timlin and Vernon Fowke confided to each other and to Britnell their worries over the future state of the economics department. Britnell, from Ottawa, did his best to console them. 'I was very interested in your University and Department news,' he wrote in reply to a distressed Mabel Timlin early in 1943: 'I can well understand your mixed feelings because I know you have a warm and sympathetic heart and that while you are by no means uncritical you can always see any good that exists in either a student or a colleague. I was very pleased to hear that Verne was standing to his guns though even at that he must have had an extremely heavy load to carry this year. Your four courses sound rather grim ... I am a firm believer in a three course load as the "ceiling" in the social sciences.'[61]

Timlin and Fowke, along with W.P. Thompson, the dean of arts, were quietly planning a new line of succession and wanted Britnell back as soon as possible, even though the event they all were waiting for – the reorganization of political science and economics – could not take place as long as Swanson was still head of economics. Furthermore, it was not at all clear how long Britnell would be kept in Ottawa. At first, it was assumed that he would return in the fall of 1943, but then he discovered that he would not likely get a release from Ottawa unless he could prove he was needed elsewhere for important work – for economics and political science, perhaps, but not for political science alone.[62] For a while it was rumoured that he might be chosen as president of the University of New Brunswick. As it turned out, work with the Wartime Prices and Trade Board kept him for another year in Ottawa, and when the year was over he was called urgently to Regina as chairman of the Saskatchewan Economic Advisory Committee to help the newly elected CCF government with its plans for reconstruction. In the autumn of 1945, just after Swanson's retirement became official, Britnell was at last able to look forward 'to returning, I hope for the rest of my days, to the university.'[63]

10

Union and the New Members

The new order began when Britnell returned to the university as professor and head of the Department of Political Science in the fall of
1945. He was immediately appointed professor and head of the
Department of Economics as well, and the process of joining the two
departments was soon under way. The case for union, which was put
before W.P. Thompson, dean of arts, and then taken for approval to the
university council, rested on the need to curb excessive specialization,
especially in economics. 'The trend in social sciences,' wrote Britnell,
'is away from intensive specialization. Modern problems are not exclusively economic or exclusively political. There has been an increased
tendency in economic writings to take more cognizance of political
problems and realities – and vice-versa.' A union of the two departments would strengthen both, 'soften any tendency to narrow specialization on either side,' and allow limited resources to go farther.
Political science, which was otherwise destined to remain 'a one-man
Department,' would be strengthened by the addition of 'a specialist in
what the Americans call government.' Britnell viewed himself 'as
straddling the fields of Political Science & Economics, so that I might
continue to make some contribution in the area where they overlap.'
And finally, there was the example of other universities in Canada:
Toronto, McGill, Queen's, McMaster, Manitoba, Alberta, and British
Columbia all had combined departments of economics and political
science. Dalhousie, which had an endowed chair in political science,
was the only important exception.[1]
   Timlin and Fowke were looking forward to having Britnell back as a
departmental colleague. 'I like the Department,' wrote Mabel Timlin to
Britnell in 1945. 'I think the Saskatchewan Department of Economics

has something as a *group* that can make us important and out-standing as an Economics Department in the Dominion. We supplement each other in a number of ways. Then too I think we have a superior *esprit de corps* – which may in part be the result of the years of adversity several of us went through together in the Department.'[2]

The alternative to union – that Britnell would remain off by himself in political science when there was no longer anything blocking his return to economics – was simply unthinkable. Nor was it reasonable to expect Britnell to turn his back on political science. He had essayed in 1938 to give political science 'a definitely economic twist'; now he resolved to infuse economics with something of political science as well by emphasizing issues of public policy.

I

In the spring of 1946 the Department of Economics and Political Science was formally brought into existence, and Britnell, as the newly appointed head, began a vigorous campaign for better conditions. He asked for a doubling of library and office space, facilities for seminars ('for the past ten years there has been no such thing as a seminar room in the University'), access to wall maps for classroom use (the current supply was apparently 'in the exclusive care of those in charge of the Field Husbandry Building'), provision for a secretary and adequate telephones (one telephone, he said, served thirty members), a decent faculty reading room (to 'assist in the development of a better *esprit de corps*'), and the restoration of sabbatical leaves ('to raise the whole academic tone of the University and help preserve the intellectual freshness and vigour of the staff').[3] He fought for, and eventually won, promotions and salary improvements for Mabel Timlin and Vernon Fowke, both of whom had suffered materially from the stringency of the Depression years, and for the establishment of an upper limit of three courses for each permanent member of the department. This last provision Britnell considered essential for the pursuit of scholarly activity and the training of future scholars. 'A university,' he reminded the dean, 'is to be distinguished by the persistent search for truth and a consequent recognition of the central position of scholarship among its interests.' Without this recognition, it was but 'a collection of trade schools.'[4] He also entered a plea for the construction of new buildings – namely, a library and one other building 'which is not an Engineering building, or an Agricultural building, or a Medical building.' But in this object he was conspicuously unsuccessful. The first buildings to be constructed after the war were the Soils and Dairy Building, the School of Agriculture Building, and the medical complex; a library was nine years distant, an arts building twelve.

Britnell was particularly anxious to raise the department from a lowly 'service' status and to fight back against the encroachment of the professional colleges. 'We are in grave danger of becoming a task force for trade schools (Commerce & Agriculture particularly) at the expense of our Honours work,' he wrote in a letter to Mabel Timlin. 'We should integrate classes leading to the Honours degree and offer something good *and* stiff in the way of honours classes to attract *good* students.' He proposed to do this by implementing a new advanced course in economic theory (to be taught by Timlin) which, added to the existing courses, would give honours students 'a definite *pattern* or *scheme of arrangement* so that one class builds definitely on – if it does not stem directly out of – a previous one.'[5] Now it became a matter of departmental policy for senior staff to teach introductory courses whenever possible, and a great deal of attention was given to strengthening their content in order to provide a firm foundation for development. No student who looked promising passed through the first-year economics course without being assiduously courted by the department for its honours program. A student who chose the honours stream would move on in second year to money and banking and intermediate economic theory, in third year to economic equilibrium and trade cycle theory, and to a selection of other courses – in public finance, labour economics, international trade, cooperatives, agricultural economics, and economic history. For a student's final year in honours, there were Mabel Timlin's seminar in the history of economic thought as well as reading courses tailored to meet the needs of individual students. Throughout, students were to be held to a higher standard in their writing; to Britnell's satisfaction, his department became known to students as one in which (unaccountably) they could expect to be 'marked on their English.'

Honours students in economics or political science, or both, would meet with Britnell in his office each year with a list of courses they wanted to take the next, only to leave an hour or so later with an entirely different list of Britnell's devising, unsure of what had transpired but secure in the knowledge that it was the right – indeed the only – way. Honours students were encouraged to stay on at Saskatchewan for a master's degree, and the majority of those who did were further persuaded to pick a topic relating to economic development in Saskatchewan, preferably one involving the use of documentary materials held by the provincial archives. Thereafter, they might be sent on to graduate school – to Toronto, to England, or perhaps to the United States. After 1946, the Sanderson Fellowship, to be awarded every two years to a male student of the University of Saskatchewan in the social sciences and tenable only at the London School of Economics and Political Science, made certain that some of the department's best students would be funnelled there and led to the development of strong links between the London graduate school and the department headed by Britnell.[6]

For the professors, whether they were engaged in research and writing or counselling governments, working with promising students was regarded as an enterprise that was rewarding in itself and complementary to their own aspirations as scholars and public servants. The relationship between the department and the students did not end when they left Saskatchewan: their progress was closely watched, encouraging letters were sent, and plans were made for their eventual employment.[7] 'I become more aware as time goes by of the benefits I have received from the personal attention I received while at Sask.,' one student wrote to Fowke from Toronto. 'None of the professors, with the exception of Innis, of course, is equal to or superior to the Sask. level.'[8] Another wrote to Mabel Timlin: 'After talking to you and Dr. Britnell I always go away with the feeling that my feet have been put back on the path I want to follow.'[9] John Floyd, who later joined the economics department at Toronto, recalls 'a lively intellectual atmosphere in which I was struggling to participate':

The message I obtained was that thinking about economic and social issues was important and that it was important for one to have his/her own opinions. I sometimes look at my old copy of Stigler's book [on price theory] and note all the marginal comments I made in it in Timmie's class on 'Economic Equilibrium and Trade Cycle Theory' (the title itself suggested we were working on the frontier of economics). These were Timmie's criticisms of Stigler. In retrospect, these comments were nonsense but, as I look back on it, that didn't really matter. The important thing is that she was encouraging us to think critically about the things Stigler was talking about rather than simply acquire a memorized understanding of them, it being understood that we would eventually have our own ideas and criticisms.[10]

Another student, Gordon Thiessen, who was to be governor of the Bank of Canada, remembered the department's dedication to public service:

> there was something special about the Department, but I am not sure I know why. I suspect that for me it was the relevance of the work that Fowke and Britnell in particular had done in explaining the western economy ... I remember being aware of all the commissions and enquiries they had contributed to as well as Timmie's long service in the extension department. I suppose it was that commitment to public policy and to public service that impressed and influenced me.[11]

During the reorganization of the department's curriculum, no changes were made in the political science offerings, which were left as Britnell had designed them in 1938. But the directing of students towards double honours in economics and political science now became a matter of deliberate policy in the department and served to expand the enrolment in political science courses. Students interested in economics were encouraged to study government and political theory for the sake of a broader education; students interested in political science were encouraged to study economics as well, for the sake of their job opportunities. Between 1948 and 1957 there were thirteen students enrolled in the double honours program in economics and political science, while in the decade before there had been only one; on the other hand, the number of students enrolled in single honours in economics was almost the same for the two periods: thirteen from 1938 to 1947; and fifteen from 1948 to 1957.

The growth of interest in political science was, to Britnell, a measure of the success of the united department: 'It is precisely in those universities in Canada where Political Science is combined with Economics in a strong department, that the study of Political Science has flourished and an impressive record of publication and scholarship has been established.'[12] He hardly expected a time would come when specialization in political science alone would make a student employable, except as a teacher of the subject. In 1956, when a single honours program in political science was about to be introduced, Britnell had doubts about it: 'the much narrower job opportunities open to specialists in Political Science as against Economics would make it unlikely that we could expect to attract many candidates.'[13] Not until then was the list of political science courses expanded (through the addition of courses in public administration and political institutions), and not until then was a second full-time political scientist added to the department.

II

The return of war veterans following the Second World War unleashed such numbers of people wanting to attend university that scholarship in Canada was practically brought to a standstill for the duration. Yet by the accounts of those who survived the episode, it was a rewarding time to be a university teacher, especially in the social sciences. The veterans were found to be mature, eager to learn, and keenly interested in the world around them they had helped to save. At the University of Saskatchewan all available space on campus was put into service, temporary buildings were erected (some of which, predictably, became permanent), and overflow classrooms and dormitories were opened in quarters of the Royal Canadian Air Force at the Saskatoon airport. Shuttle buses were used to transport students and faculty between the airport and the main campus. In 1945–6, the number of full-time registrants at the university was 2,780, nearly double the year before. Enrolment in economics and political science, which stood at 700 in 1944–5, rose to a peak of 2,042 in 1947–8, and then subsided to a low of 766 in 1952–3, whereupon it proceeded to climb slowly but steadily until the 1960s when the first crowd of postwar babies began to arrive at the university.

To cope with the wartime influx of students, several new instructors were brought into the department: Kenneth Buckley, Norman Ward, W.F. Doucet, Norman Penlington, and Murray S. Donnelly. After the wave of registrations subsided, the department was left with the seven members who formed the core of the department for the first decade of the Britnell years. Aside from the senior triumvirate of Britnell, Fowke, and Timlin, there were Reid, Allely, and the two postwar recruits raised to permanent status, Buckley and Ward. Until the office wing of the Arts Building was opened in 1960, these seven members were quartered in various offices on campus, at one time in as many as five different buildings. These awkward arrangements were the subject of many laboured memoranda from Britnell to the dean's office and made communication among the members of the department more cumbersome (five could not be reached by telephone during the day). Almost all offices (until after the 1960s) were shared by members from different departments (Mabel Timlin, until she retired, was paired with Jean Murray in history in Saskatchewan Hall, the women's residence), most were inaccessible by telephone, and some were hardly accessible at all. For instance, Norman Ward's, hidden away in the Administration Building behind the stage of Convocation Hall, was a disused dressing-room reachable only from the stage itself, which was often in use for theatrical and musical performances. Ward loved his splendid, if noisy, isolation and after many years gave it up for a spanking new office – 'fit for a vice president' was his damning first impression of it – only because he was obliged to.

Archie Reid, an unflappable man, had been on staff since 1939. Before coming to Saskatchewan, he had spent one year on the research staff of the Rowell-Sirois Commission on Dominion-Provincial Relations and two years as a PhD student at the London School of Economics and Political Science. In his relations with colleagues he was cordial but by no means confiding, and towards his students he was correct yet distant. He taught courses in local government, public finance, labour economics, and intermediate economic theory. Intermediate economic theory, introduced by him in 1941, became a major cause of examination anxiety for students in economics and commerce. Seated, and reading without evident interest from a script, he made a thorough and clear presentation of the basic principles of Marshallian economics; student folklore had it that he would sometimes turn over two pages of his script rather than one and not notice the difference.

While he was in London, Reid had undertaken special studies under Lionel Robbins on international aspects of Canadian business fluctuations with the intention of writing a doctoral thesis on the subject. But the work was never completed: 'My teaching and research,' he explained later, 'have been almost entirely in unrelated fields.'[14] During the war years, he was drawn into the field of labour problems and social security policy. He spent several summers in the International Labour Office (ILO) as a research assistant and worked for a while as a technical adviser to a provincial commission on labour. When his stint with the ILO came to an end, he turned once more to a doctoral project, this time a study of local government institutions and policy in western Canada. Encouraged by both Britnell and Innis, he took a year of leave from Saskatchewan in 1949–50 to become a teaching assistant at the University of Toronto and complete the course and residency requirements for the PhD. Innis assigned him to teach a course in economic theory. In the following summers, accompanied by

Lewis Thomas of Regina College, Reid made many visits to municipal offices in Saskatchewan to further his project. In 1956 he wrote 'Urban Local Government in the North-West Territories: Their Development and Machinery of Government' for *Saskatchewan History,* which turned out to be the only scholarly paper to come out of his research. He had always said that he would retire when he was fifty. In 1958, much to the surprise of his colleagues – especially Britnell, who never believed he would – Reid resigned from the university and from academic life and settled in a small cottage on an island in Ontario.

John Allely, who had arrived on staff with Reid, was a kindly man of fastidious taste, devoted to the army, the church, his teaching, and his collection of fine antiques and rugs, for which he developed over the years the discriminating eye of a connoisseur. When he returned from the war, he became commanding officer of the University of Saskatchewan Contingent Canadian Officers' Training Corps and among his students was known affectionately as 'the Colonel.' For most of his career at Saskatchewan he was the department's representative in the College of Commerce, where he taught courses in marketing, finance, and money and banking. In the department itself, he taught international economics and European economic history. As a member of a generation coming to maturity between the two world wars, Allely had the misfortune of trying to enter upon an academic career when there were virtually no new permanent appointments to be had in Canada.

For seven years, Allely taught at a succession of one- or two-year appointments ('I covered a good part of Canada and taught just about every course offered in Economics') before being hired at Saskatchewan and then was two years at Saskatchewan before being elevated to permanent status.[15] He had two articles in print, 'Federal Public Finances III: South Africa' (1937) and 'Some Aspects of Currency Depreciation' (1939), both in the *Canadian Journal of Economics and Political Science,* and had started on a doctoral thesis on currency depreciation for presentation to Harvard University. When war broke out, he joined up for service and rose quickly through the ranks. He became in turn a bush pilot, a lieutenant colonel, and then, in his final two years, senior finance officer of the Control Commission for Germany (British Element). This last position allowed him, as he explained, 'the opportunity to function as Head of the Central Bank, Treasury and Department of National Revenue, as well as custodian of confiscated and safe-guarded property.'[16] After the harsh realities of war and its aftermath, which kept him overseas for five years (and would have kept him longer if President Thomson had not insisted upon his return), he had to face the realities of the academic merit system. Returning to the department, now infused under Britnell's direction with a new commitment to research and scholarship, he found himself 'seriously behind my colleagues in understanding and valuing the revolutionary changes that had in the War years come about in the thinking of people in my field following Keynes' later writings. I had to study out these developments carefully, especially in view of a strongly-acquired classical mode of thought which many of the new developments tended to upset. The pressure of the huge classes immediately after the War and the problems of readjustment to civil life slowed this up.' He was aware, as he put it, 'that my failure since the War to resume publication ... and especially to complete my thesis requirements for the Ph.D. has weighed against me.'[17] He became an associate professor in 1947 but afterwards was held in rank; a recommendation from Britnell that he be promoted was turned down in committee in 1957. Not until 1969, three years before his retirement, was he finally promoted to the level of full professor in recognition of his devotion to teaching and long service to the university. He died in 1986.

Courses in economics and political science were also given by the Basilian Fathers of St Thomas More College. The college was founded in 1936, the year before President Murray retired, and was the culmination of his efforts over many years to establish a Catholic presence at the university and preserve the university as the sole degree-granting institution in the province. By a unique arrangement, St Thomas More became a federated college with a position similar to that of St Michael's at the University of Toronto; it offered work in arts courses leading to a degree but no theological instruction, unlike the affiliated colleges at the university, such as St Andrew's, Emmanuel, St Chad's, and the Lutheran seminary, which provided theological instruction but no arts courses. The arrangement, as it developed, worked very well, with St Thomas More assuming financial responsibility for its teaching and the university retaining academic control. The federated relationship was made official in 1953, and a permanent college building and chapel were established on the campus at College Drive and Wiggins Avenue in 1956. The first courses in economics were taught by Fr Gerald F. Anglin. Fr Eugene A. Cullinane, who came in 1939 and taught both economics and political science, left during the war to join the military effort. During his absence, the work was carried on by Fr Leonard C. Quinlan. Cullinane returned in 1945 and continued to teach until 1950, when his political activities in support of the Co-operative Commonwealth Federation (CCF) led to his dismissal from the college. He was succeeded by Fr Francis L. Burns in 1948, who remained with the college until 1979, with the exception of a five-year period from 1958 to 1963 when Fr John F. Callaghan took over the teaching duties. Fr Robin F. Neill, author of two studies on Canadian economic thought, joined the college in 1960 and served for a ten-year period, before moving on to the economics faculty at Carleton University.[18]

III

The first holder of the Sanderson Fellowship was Kenneth Arthur Haig Buckley, who was born 16 July 1918 in Aberdeen, Saskatchewan. Buckley spent his boyhood in Saskatoon and attended City Park Collegiate. In 1936, in Buckley's final year there, Charles McCool, the chairman of the board of high school trustees, wrote to President Murray about Buckley and one of his classmates, Douglas Cherry: 'One or the other will win the University scholarship, but they are both boys who should attend University, and both of them will have great difficulty doing so ... I think Cherry will be first, but Buckley is a very deserving boy. His parents are on relief. Should Buckley gain first place, Cherry also would find it very hard to pay his fees.'[19] Such hard-luck stories were hardly uncommon. Many who attended university during the Depression years had to make special arrangements with the president to pay their fees as they were able, and a few needy ones who had to live on their own were helped out of Murray's own pocket. As it turned out, the university scholarship went to Cherry, Buckley managed to find a part-time job writing for the Saskatoon *Star-Phoenix*, and both entered university in the fall of 1936.

Buckley registered in pre-law and majored, like Cherry, in English literature. But while Cherry continued on with the study of English (he was later head of the English department and then dean of arts and science at Saskatchewan), Buckley turned in his fourth year to economics. After receiving a BA with distinction from Saskatchewan in 1942, Buckley joined the Royal Canadian Air Force but was discharged the following year because of poor health. He spent the next two years as a teaching fellow at the University of Toronto, where he took an MA in economics and came under the influence of Harold Innis. He returned to Saskatchewan in 1945 as an instructor, and then two years later went to the London School of Economics and Political Science as the first

Sanderson fellow. His Saskatchewan professors, who regarded him as their favourite son, kept a close watch on his academic progress. When Mabel Timlin heard of his 'magnificent work in London,' it was decided to get him back to Saskatchewan to shore up the department's offerings in economic theory – 'assuming, of course,' Britnell wrote to him in London, 'that you do not succumb to the blandishments of [Lionel] Robbins or any other Englishman or of some other Canadian institution.'[20] He was appointed a special lecturer at Saskatchewan in 1949, an assistant professor when he received a PhD from London the year following, and full professor in 1958.

Buckley was an engaging, eclectic, and perceptive scholar. His wide-ranging interests found a focal point in the theory and measurement of Canadian economic development; on the theory side, he was inspired by the work of Harold Innis at Toronto. He regarded academics (including himself) and academic life with an air of irreverent scepticism. A young colleague, anxious about meeting his first class, was reassured with: 'You know, university teaching is a lot like digging a ditch. Just go in and dig the first few feet.' 'He had such a trenchant way of looking at things and I find myself quoting things he said to me ... years after the event,'[21] said political scientist Hugh Thorburn, who once shared an office with him. As Britnell and Fowke grew busy with other things, Buckley fell heir to much of the department's work of dispensing advice to groups outside the university. 'He is our front man on all matters agricultural since Vern and I have lapsed into the roles of elder statesmen,' Britnell wrote in 1959. 'I have heard Buckley take apart many fallacies and fictions in the farmers' movement most effectively and yet without antagonizing any but the most stubborn and recalcitrant.'[22] Buckley worked on the University of Saskatchewan Faculty Association and the Canadian Association of University Teachers for the improvement of university salaries and pensions, and served many other groups and agencies, among them farm and labour groups, cooperative organizations, the Restrictive Trade Practices Commission, the Department of Justice in Ottawa, and the Royal Commission on the South Saskatchewan River Project. His most important works were *Capital Formation in Canada, 1896–1930* (1955) and, with M.C. Urquhart as co-editor, *Historical Statistics of Canada* (1965).[23] The latter, a massive undertaking lasting seven years, became a standard reference work in the social sciences.

In the department, Buckley taught courses in introductory economics, political economy, agricultural economics, cooperatives, the history of economic thought, and both the intermediate and advanced courses in economic theory. 'It was in one of these classes, listed as being on the economics of agriculture or cooperatives, that the big ideas in economics came together for me,' recalls one former student. Another observed that, no matter what the title, Buckley 'more or less taught the same thing in every class ... He went over and over, at a higher level of generality, the main principles of economics.'[24]

To his students, who soon gathered a circulating fund of Buckley stories, he became something of a legend, for it seemed as if he could expound with considerable wit and candour on practically any topic, not excluding the failings of the university administration. But in his last years he took to heavy drinking, his attendance at lectures became erratic, and his health, which had never been robust, grew steadily weaker. He died in 1970, at the age of fifty-one.

IV

Norman McQueen Ward was twenty-seven, the same age as Buckley, when he joined the university as an instructor in 1945. He soon became the department's specialist in government and, in time, successor to Dawson as the leading scholar of Canadian political institutions. In a 1967 survey which asked political scientists in Canada to name those of their colleagues who had made the most significant contributions to their discipline, Dawson was ranked first for the period before 1945 and Norman Ward came second to political theorist C.B. Macpherson of the University of Toronto for the period after 1945.[25] Ward's forty-year term in the department coincided almost exactly with the life-span of the Department of Economics and Political Science, which divided again in 1985, the year he retired.

Ward was born on 10 May 1918 in Hamilton, Ontario, and, as luck would have it, McMaster University moved there from Toronto in time for him to enter it. 'I don't think I could have gone to university at all,' he later recalled, 'but the university was in town, and I could live at home and go to University, so I did.'[26] He took economics, he said, because the boy next door had taken it; and he was introduced to political science when a visiting instructor, James Aitchison, an admirer of Dawson's and aspiring political scientist himself, began to talk about it in lectures that were supposed to be devoted to economics. But becoming a political scientist was never, in the beginning, a deliberate goal; one thing just led to another. 'The only consuming ambition I ever had,' he later confessed, 'was to be an opera singer.'[27] He kept a scrap-book in which he pasted photographs of opera stars, reviews, and sou-venir programs, exchanged opera news with relatives and friends, and went to the opera whenever he could, which was fairly often since the Toronto–Hamilton area then boasted an opera season of considerable length and variety. His other amusement was writing. He liked writing about politics, though he more than once found himself out of favour with the university authorities because of editorials he wrote for the *Silhouette,* McMaster's student weekly, while he was its editor-in-chief. He recalled being called in by Chancellor Whidden for having pro-voked some local worthies by his isolationist writings just before the war. In addition, there were minor tensions with some members of fac-ulty and other students because of 'my own persistence in unreasoning pacifism.'[28] Years later, he wrote of 'the traumatic experience of mov-ing from a part of Ontario where to be a Liberal was to be a dangerous radical ... to Saskatchewan, where to be the same Liberal was to be an oaf obliged to associate with other oafs. I quickly gave up active poli-tics after coming west!'[29] In his final year at McMaster, Ward was elected president of the Political Economy Club and in this capacity first encountered R. MacGregor Dawson, who was a guest of the club. During the summers he worked at whatever employment he could get, once at a steel mill in Hamilton and, after receiving his bachelor's degree from McMaster in 1942, at the Wartime Prices and Trade Board, where his former professor, Kenneth W. Taylor, and his later colleague, George Britnell, had been called into service. Then, in the fall of 1942, he entered the University of Toronto as a master's student in political economy, which led to his next job, working for the Nova Scotia Com-mission on Provincial Development and Rehabilitation headed by Dawson. This kept him in Halifax for more than a year. Before leaving for Halifax, he married Betty Davis from Stratford, Ontario.

Ward up to this time had studied both economics and political sci-ence and showed no particular preference for either. When he returned to Toronto in 1944 with the intention of starting a PhD thesis on the growth of government activity in Nova Scotia, a suggestion of his pro-fessor, Alexander Brady, he continued to work as a teaching assistant in economics. But about this time an encounter with J.R. Hicks's *Value and Capital,* the very treatise that had helped to attract his colleague Ken Buckley to the study of economics, served to turn Ward away from it for good. 'If this is economics, I want no part of it' was his response. Then becoming a political scientist became a goal. 'But it was all pretty accidental to begin with,' he admitted later, 'which is true with a lot of scholars. They start out doing something else and end up doing what they find is really what they want to do.'[30] Dawson was a considerable influence, both as friend and adviser: he helped Ward get started on a new thesis project, a study of the Canadian House of Commons, and in 1945, when academics across the country were being recruited to help teach the huge wave of veterans returning from the war, directed him to Saskatchewan, where he was at first engaged to teach for two years. His first writings in political science appeared then: 'The Bristol Papers: A Note on Patronage' (1946) and 'Parliamentary Representation in Canada' (1947) in the *Canadian Journal of Economics and Political Science*, 'The Problem of Leadership' in *Sociology and Social Research* (1946), and 'Voting in Canadian Two-Member Constituencies' in *Public Affairs* (1947). Thereafter, except for an interval devoted to the preparation of his thesis, article followed article and book followed book; by the year of his retirement these amounted to more than 200 items, not counting the scores more which were printed in newspapers or were the product of his sideline as a gag-writer for comic strips and for cartoons which appeared in the *New Yorker* and other magazines.[31] He did his writing in longhand, in examination booklets and Jumbo scribblers, usually at home, where he had a board which he set on the arms of his easy chair to fashion a makeshift desk. He said he got started writing for pay because he needed to provide for a growing family, having been forewarned by his professors, Dawson and Brady, that to undertake the life of an academic was to commit oneself to a lifetime of penury.

In 1947, Ward returned to the University of Toronto as Maurice Cody Fellow. In the course of one year he completed most of the writing of his thesis and the reading in sociology which constituted the minor subject required for his degree. He received a PhD in 1949 after an oral examination in which Dawson vigorously defended him against any of the examiners' criticisms – 'his attitude seemed to be that he, not I, was the one being examined,' recalled Ward.[32] When George Britnell heard of Ward's achievements in Toronto, he made haste to recommend him for permanent appointment at Saskatchewan. In a confidential report to the dean, he wrote: 'Ward has ability, industry and assurance. He gets on well with both his students and his colleagues; I believe him to be a competent and stimulating teacher. In the field of scholarship there is every reason to believe that Ward will give a good account of himself ... He writes with equal facility at both academic and popular levels ... he has shown considerable zeal in publication.'[33]

And so Norman Ward came back to Saskatchewan in 1948. He was named assistant professor of political science at a salary of $3,200, promoted in 1951 to associate professor, and in 1955 to full professor. In 1948 another of Dawson's students, Murray Donnelly, was taken on as a sessional instructor, with a loose understanding that he might be kept on if things were mutually satisfactory. But when the departmental budget was cut back at the end of the year, Donnelly was released from the university. Donnelly was very upset to hear of it, and Dawson, on his behalf, responded with characteristic fulmination: 'You had better let the University of Saskatchewan know,' he wrote to Ward, 'that if that is the kind of treatment they give our people they had better try to get people somewhere else.'[34] Ward's response to the budget tightening was more philosophical: 'As between a large staff and feeding the permanent members, Sask appears to have chosen the latter alternative.'[35] As for Ward himself, he was satisfied that he had come to the right place. Growing up in south-western Ontario, he said, he had hardly known the rest of the country existed, but when he and his wife learned about the other parts they decided not to return to Ontario to stay if they could help it. Though his main area of scholarly interest was Canada, he found in Saskatchewan a political scene of considerable fascination. The CCF government that had come to power in 1944 was the first of its kind in North America: 'this was the political laboratory in the whole world, as far as English-speaking people were concerned,' thought Ward. 'It was the place for me to just stay and watch what was going on.'[36]

Ward was soon settled comfortably into the department and the university, where gophers scampered about the Bowl and sheep still grazed on the lawns as they had in Dawson's day. He liked the campus, which struck him as one of the most attractive in the country, and the foresight of the university's early planners became more evident to him as he and the university grew older: 'Geography,' he observed in 1984, 'will prevent the city from ever encircling it. No main thoroughfares pass city traffic through it on the way to somewhere else. For the calculable future, the University will not have to buy up surrounding blocks of houses in order to knock them down for academic structures.'[37] As for Saskatoon – 'the pearl of the prairies' – he found much to commend it, especially the countryside around.[38] He bought a lakefront property at Wakaw Lake, forty miles out of the city, where the Fowke family was already established, and there repaired for the summer holidays with his entire domestic entourage – wife, pets, and, in

172 No Ordinary Academics

due course, six children. In the city he settled within easy walking distance of the campus in a rambling frame house at 412 Albert Avenue, which he and his wife, Betty, gradually made over, its rooms decorated with landscapes by prairie artists and the orchids he loved to cultivate during the long winter months.

There were some early frictions with Britnell over class loads, occasioned by Britnell's frequent absences from the university, but these were eventually ironed out, and the department became for Ward as ideal a place to work and write as he could wish. Though his interests (as well as the location of his office) placed him off to one side in the department, and he was temperamentally disinclined to take much part in its running in any case, he remained close and supportive towards his colleagues in economics. The union of political science with economics he regarded as both desirable and convenient, once describing the joint department as 'a subtle device of the political scientists to get the economists to do the administrative chores.'[39] Ward never minded admitting that he was inept at such chores. Inevitably, as his reputation grew, he had several invitations from other universities. To one, from British Columbia, he answered: 'I do not think that you should consider me as a possible candidate for the chairmanship of Economics and Political Science. I have no desire to be anything else than a journeyman scholar, with considerable free time to do my own research and writing, and I have already avoided two avenues that might have led me to chairmanship.'[40] He considered studies in the humanities important to a student in the social sciences, and liked to advise his students in government to read a half-dozen novels set in the country they were studying. 'George always considered heretical [my notion] that a first class novelist is worth ten social scientists any old day of the week,' he said.[41] Neither did he take to government contracts as readily as his senior colleagues did. Though Ward prepared several notable reports for government commissions, on election boundaries and election expenses, respectively, and one, with David Hoffman, on bilingualism and biculturalism in the House of Commons, he was particular about the kind of work he did. 'I have a deep-rooted and ancient horror, as a practising student of government of getting involved with any government,' he once wrote to a senior civil servant. 'I learned from Harold Innis to disapprove profoundly of any academic who teaches anything at all connected with government, working for a government at the same time; I don't see how he can possibly remain an independent observer.'[42]

Ward's first book, *The Canadian House of Commons: Representation*, came out in 1950 to both popular and academic acclaim. In academic journals the study was welcomed as a valuable addition to a growing literature on Canadian government, and in newspapers and magazines across the country readers were assured that this was a book that could be read with profit by ordinary folk as well as, and especially, the legislators themselves. An American reviewer said the book was an indication that 'the study of political science has come of age in Canada.'[43] J.R. Mallory called it a 'high-spirited account of parliamentary representation' and said it recalled a 'time when Canada's national sport was not ice-hockey, but politics.'[44] There was but one negative, which had to do with a section on theory Ward had inserted at the behest of one of his thesis advisers: 'Edmund Burke would certainly disapprove of some of the loose deductions here drawn from his stated ideas,' Alexander Brady remarked in the *University of Toronto Quarterly*, but then added, 'if theoretical analysis is not Professor Ward's forte, a cool and sensible spirit characterizes his examination of operating institutions, and his writing is clear and easy.'[45]

Ward next wrote *Government in Canada*, a textbook for use in Canadian high schools which came out in 1961. This took him seven years from start to finish because of the difficulty of putting together a narrative that would be accessible to young readers. He wrote 30,000 words of text and scrapped them all before he found a formula that pleased him. He spent at least a day or two a month writing small pieces for magazines, and added to gag-writing a second sideline, mediating in labour disputes. He wrote frequently on parliamentary affairs for the Sifton press and provided regular commentary on radio and later on television. He had plans to bring out a second volume on the House of Commons, but this undertaking evolved into a separate and major study of the parliamentary control of finance, entitled *The Public Purse: A Study in Canadian Democracy* and published in 1962, the year he was made a member of the Royal Society of Canada. Following this, he edited *A Party Politician: The Memoirs of Chubby Power* in 1966, *Politics in Saskatchewan*, with his colleague Duff Spafford in 1968, and *The Politician: Or The Treason of Democracy* by James G. Gardiner, the prairie politician whose biography Ward had undertaken, in 1976. Ward had gone to Queen's University as Skelton-Clark Fellow in 1958–9 but never took a sabbatical or any other leave of absence until 1974, when he took one of each, the second as a Killam Fellow, to work on his study of Gardiner. When in 1984 he became ill and had to undergo heart surgery, the task of completing the work on Gardiner was passed over to his colleague in political science, David E. Smith.

Ward's revision of Dawson's *Government of Canada*, a fourth edition, came out in 1963, and a fifth followed in 1970. Making the Dawson into a Dawson and Ward, acceptable to modern readers yet satisfying the wishes of Dawson's executors, presented Ward with a nearly insurmountable task. As he confided to Frank Underhill in 1962:

> I am finding myself in trouble section after section because the whole book is written without a context. One could, in fact, read the whole thing carefully without even becoming aware of the French Canadians, let alone less obvious aspects. I still don't know what to do about all this, and for its first revision I can't do more than update the present one with a few minor additions ... In my darkest days with the Dawson, I go home on occasion and tell my wife that this is the last dam' political science book I will ever write, that my most important work is what I began in *Mice in the Beer,* and that after the Dawson I am going to take up woodcarving or some other wholly non-academic enterprise.[46]

A more complete overhaul was undertaken in Ward's last revision, which was renamed *Dawson's Government of Canada* and issued in 1987, forty years after Dawson's original work had appeared.

Ward was not serious about the woodcarving (though he later took up painting), but he meant what he said about *Mice in the Beer,* a collection of his whimsical short pieces, which came out in 1960. A reviewer in the *Globe and Mail* described it as 'brilliant, wildly funny and wholly sane ... the funniest book to have been written since Leacock laid down his pen.'[47] *Mice in the Beer* won for Ward the Leacock Medal for Humour in 1961 and outsold all his academic works put together. Two other collections of humour followed: *The Fully Processed Cheese* in 1964 and *Her Majesty's Mice* in 1977, the year after he was inducted as an officer in the Order of Canada. He received an honorary degree from McMaster in 1974 and another from Queen's in 1977. His academic achievements were recognized in 1985 in a *festschrift* edited by his colleague John C. Courtney, *The Canadian House of Commons: Essays in Honour of Norman Ward,* which followed a conference held at the University of Saskatchewan at which political scientists from across Canada came to honour him. One in attendance was Eugene Forsey, the venerable senator and watchdog of the Canadian parliament, who said: 'There is nobody comparable with him for a moment ... he has a special distinction which makes him unique among Canadian political scientists of all time – he is tops not only in his academic field but also as a humourist.'[48]

Ward has been described as 'the laughing wise man,'[49] and so he seemed in the classroom. He especially liked undergraduates and treasured their gaffes as much as their youthful wit. In a collection of reminiscences about the University of Saskatchewan, he is remembered by one of them as 'a very funny guy ... just incredibly funny.'[50] He loved politics and politicians just as he found them, warts and all. In his lectures and writings he had much to say about the 'scamps,' 'rascals,' 'scalawags,' and 'rapscallions' who had figured in Canadian politics. But he was exacting, too, and those who might have taken it for granted that his easy manner bespoke easy marks were soon disappointed. As a student and later colleague explained, 'Norman's students found that there were two Professor Wards, one serious and one very funny, and that they took turns. Some learned, alas too late, that the midterm was set and graded by the serious member of the team.'[51]

V

In 1947, sociology was added to the list of subjects offered by the Saskatchewan Department of Economics and Political Science. To launch the addition, a graduate student from Toronto, Harold E. Roseborough, was hired on a temporary basis as an instructor to teach introductory courses in sociology and political economy. For the following academic year, Britnell was granted permission to make a full-time appointment in sociology, and his description of the kind of candidate he wanted – 'a clear-headed, competent, realistic Sociologist who is ready, willing and equipped to tackle some of the problems of social change in the prairie economy' – was remarkably reminiscent of the qualities mentioned in President Murray's earlier searches for an economist. Britnell assembled a lengthy list of candidates but was disappointed that hardly any seemed suitable: 'My experience with prospects,' he remarked to the dean, 'suggests that a curiously large proportion of North American Sociologists are absorbed in criminal statistics, alcoholism, prostitution or suicide.'[52]

Britnell finally found the man he was looking for in a sociologist from New York, Henry C. Cooperstock. Cooperstock came to Saskatchewan with a PhD from Columbia, an excellent academic record, and a keen interest in undertaking studies relating to Saskatchewan. He immediately became a popular member of the department. But during his third year at Saskatchewan, in the fall of 1957, he was ordered deported by the Canadian Department of Citizenship and Immigration on grounds that he had been a card-carrying member of the Communist Party in his youth. At a hearing in Saskatoon, Walter P. Thompson, by then president of the university, Francis Leddy, the dean of arts and science, and several faculty members, among them Britnell and Fowke, spoke on his behalf. The matter was appealed directly to the Hon. Ellen Fairclough, minister for citizenship and immigration in the Diefenbaker cabinet, who intervened to have the order rescinded, and Cooperstock was allowed to remain in Canada.[53] By then, however, pressures from outside the university had led to the creation of a separate department of sociology, and in due course a new man was hired to lead it.

The separation of sociology from economics and political science effectively quashed Britnell's ambitions for a single department devoted to the social sciences, which would have added anthropology and geography to economics, political science, and sociology. Even so, it is highly unlikely that Britnell's academic imperialism would have been met with a kindly eye by the rest of the arts and science faculty.

In 1956, he put forward a suggestion for the introduction of courses and appointment of new staff members in the areas of anthropology and geography – arguing that both were 'closely allied to the work at present conducted by the members of the Department'[54] – but both areas were later developed as separate administrative units outside the Department of Economics and Political Science. In 1957, during a university council review of departmental organization, the question of whether or not economics and political science should continue as a single department was revived. Britnell once again defended the notion of the inseparability of the two disciplines, and once again it received strong support from members of his own department, notably from Norman Ward in political science. As before, Britnell was able to name other universities where economics and political science still shared a single department – namely, Toronto, Alberta, British Columbia, Queen's, McGill, McMaster, and Western Ontario – and he could point with satisfaction to the success of the department's program of double honours. On this occasion, however, the response of members of faculty from outside the department was decidedly lukewarm, their enthusiasm for the union perhaps tempered by a growing disquiet at the formidable position Britnell's department had come to occupy in the College of Arts and Science. No doubt the movement throughout the country towards greater independence of the disciplines also played a part. Though council decided to leave things as they were, it was noted in the minutes 'that there was sufficient doubt ... about the fundamental soundness of the union of the two disciplines to suggest that the matter be reviewed in the future.'[55]

11

The Britnell Years

The Britnell years lasted from 1945, when Britnell returned from the Wartime Prices and Trade Board, until his death in 1961. During these sixteen years, the department became known as one of the best in the country. At a jubilee lecture delivered at the University of Saskatchewan on 28 September 1959, Kenneth W. Taylor, the deputy minister of finance, declared that Saskatchewan had established itself in Canada as 'a third vital centre of economic training and research' – next to Toronto and Queen's. Of the twelve to fifteen economists who were leading a new resurgence in Canadian writing in economics, he found that 'four are either graduates or members of this Department.'[1] 'I ... think that you have built up at Saskatchewan just about the best economic team in Canada, and one that any really good university economist could be happy to be a member of,' Taylor wrote afterwards to Britnell. 'There are bigger teams, and there may be more brilliant individuals elsewhere, but for average quality and good balance I think Saskatoon is hard to beat.' Queen's was about the only university he put ahead of Saskatchewan in this respect, 'and that primarily for geographic reasons.'[2]

The year 1945, which marked the beginning of a new era in the economics department, was no less eventful for Mabel Timlin, whose popularity as an interpreter of Keynesian economics was at its crest. In the autumn of that year she won a Guggenheim award and went to New York, where she had the use of the Columbia University library. From New York, she travelled to other universities to meet other economists and speak at seminars. She was pleased to hear from economists who were conducting graduate classes in economic theory that they had adopted her *Keynesian Economics* as a text or reference. At Harvard, where she spoke to Alvin Hansen's seminar on 'Dr. Lange's Price Flexibility and Employment,' the lecture hall filled to overflowing with people who came to hear her, among them economists Gottfried Haberler and Wassily Leontieff. News of her triumphal tour was relayed to President Thomson by John Bartlet Brebner, the historian, who wrote: 'I thought you might like to know that your Professor Timlin is cutting quite a swathe down here ... Folk at Columbia like her and think she's having a wonderful year.'[3] During her year away she carried out research for a paper entitled 'The British Economy in the World Today,' which was presented in May to the annual conference of the Canadian Institute of International Affairs in Toronto and published afterwards in the institute's *International Journal*.

But there were few compensations for hard-working scholars, even fewer if they were female. After ten years with the Department of Economics (twenty-four in the employ of the university), she was discouraged to find that some men at the university with fewer years of service were paid more than she was, that newcomers got just as much, and that $2,500 was regarded by many as a minimum. In 1944, her net salary as an assistant professor was $1,791.92, only about four hundred dollars more than she had earned as an instructor in 1935. Since the onset of the Depression, she had lived in Saskatoon in one room, mostly in houses full of students. In order to have the use of good libraries and attend professional meetings, she would travel each summer to eastern Canada and stay at rooming-houses or the YWCA. Her Guggenheim year left her out of pocket by more than five hundred dollars, diminishing her already meagre savings for retirement. 'After many years of climbing up-hill against the wind, I am afraid I am growing a little tired!' she wrote from New York in a long letter to Britnell, who had just been named head of her department: 'don't you think that it would be both degrading to me as a scholar and derogatory to the University of Saskatchewan that I should go about the United States *looking* for another position because I am unable to survive effectively as a scholar at my own University? I had much rather let it be understood very clearly that my own University looked after me so well that any one who wanted me would have to produce rather persuasive inducements to get me to leave Saskatchewan. I have, I find, a strong predilection for remaining in Canada, and a rather strong one for remaining in Saskatchewan, where I have associations of such long standing and such great liking and deep respect for my colleagues.'[4] An offer of $3,300, she reckoned, would keep her from actively looking for another place, and $3,600 would put it out of mind completely. Her calculations, committed to paper and estimated practically to the last penny, included the cost of a small apartment and a sum for hiring someone to clean – 'an economist,' she said, 'should probably spend her time in economics rather than in waxing floors.'[5] She also hoped to save enough to buy some sets of journals.

Before writing to Britnell, she had had an interview with Harold Innis who, in an effort to bring the new teaching in economics to Toronto, had tried to lure her there with an offer of a permanent appointment and her own choice of courses. But she was not anxious to leave Saskatchewan now that Britnell was head, and she suspected that Toronto was not likely to be as congenial. What she did not know was that a member of the Toronto department had expressed reservations about her coming several years earlier, when Innis had offered her an instructorship. There were, it seems, two problems: 'first, she talks so continuously and rapidly that it is difficult for anyone to get a word in, and secondly, she pours forth her own ideas so rapidly – that is, ideas follow each other in such quick succession that it is impossible to follow her from one to another.'[6] But after Britnell went to work on her behalf, she never again considered leaving her position at Saskatchewan. When she returned from New York in the fall of 1946, she was promoted to associate professor, her salary went to $3,600, and the journals she wanted were ordered for the library. A few years later, when she was offered $5,000 to teach at McGill for a year, in place of Benjamin Higgins on leave, she declined for fear of losing her seniority at Saskatchewan. She now thought her conditions in the department 'nearly ideal.'[7]

As pleased as she was with her new conditions, the improvements in her personal arrangements were hardly what one would call lavish.[8] Low salaries in the 1930s and slow promotions made it difficult for this cohort of scholars to provide rationally for their old age, and retirement was a worry. She moved into a small flat up two flights of stairs on the strength of her promotion to associate professor, and bought a fur coat, a long-hoped-for luxury, only after further promotion to full professor in 1950. In 1957 she moved into her own house, a small cottage overlooking the banks of the South Saskatchewan River, which was painted yellow and filled with her bright, painted furniture and colourful, red-framed Gauguin prints. In the next year, her last before retirement, she learned to drive and, accompanied by her young colleague, Kenneth Rea, for expert counsel, she picked out an automobile – a brand new Volkswagen which she called 'Bébé,' after Brigitte Bardot.

During her Guggenheim year, Mabel Timlin had set out to study welfare economics, hoping eventually to write a book on developments in economic thinking since the war. But some aspects of the subject bothered her: 'I came to the conclusion,' she remarked later, 'that the analytical devices being developed by welfare theorists were too weak for the burdens being laid upon them.'[9] She was aware, though, that theoretical economics was quickly moving beyond her grasp. Then, a memorandum she prepared in the summer of 1949 for the deputy minister of mines and resources, Hugh L. Keenleyside, brought her to the study of immigration. 'The chance came,' she said, 'just at a time when I was depressed with respect to my opportunities to do anything very valuable in a world of Econometricians and Mathematical Economists!'[10]

In 1951 she published a monograph on immigration, *Does Canada Need More People?*, to which she answered a qualified yes, and in succeeding years concentrated on probing further into the history of Canadian immigration and an analysis of its effects.[11] She wrote two articles on welfare economics for the *Canadian Journal of Economics and Political Science*, 'The Economics of Control' (1945) and 'Theories of Welfare Economics' (1949), but she was far happier exploring the relations between theory and practice in the field of public policy. To this end, she wrote a number of reviews and articles on the subject for the *Canadian Journal of Economics and Political Science*, including 'Price Flexibility and Employment' (1946), 'General Equilibrium Analysis and Public Policy' (1946), 'A Rejoinder' (1947), 'John Maynard Keynes' (1947), 'Economic Theory and Immigration Policy' (1950), and, for the *American Economic Review*, 'Recent Developments in Canadian Monetary Policy' (1953). Her great admiration for Keynes was expressed in a review she wrote for the *Canadian Liberal*, 'The Harrod Life of John Maynard Keynes' (1951). In 1954 she contributed an article on 'Monetary Policy and Keynesian Theory' for *Post-Keynesian Economics*, a collection edited by Kenneth Kurihara. She also served as consultant on two royal commissions, one on prices, the other on the South Saskatchewan River Project, and spent two summers in Ottawa working in government departments. She later looked back on the first of her interludes in Ottawa:

During the summer of 1943, I worked for Bob Bryce in the Dept. of Finance. Mitchell Sharp was a red-headed young man in his early thirties. He wrote Mr. Ilsley's [the finance minister] speeches on wheat – among other things. I liked him and still do. Mr. Ilsley was a man of the strictest conscience! (No tea in the afternoons for the Department in wartime!) The women in the Department had never seen or met a *female* economist before; they kept going by the door of the office and peering in to see the queer creature! They expected me to be a very *severe* person. But they were a fine group of women – and a number of them if they had been *men* would have travelled much higher in office than confidential secretaries to Ministers or their deputies. At the end of my months that summer, they put on a beautiful afternoon tea for me! (It must have been by special permission of Mr. Ilsley.)[12]

The subject of immigration had interested members of the department from the start. Edmund Oliver, Carrothers, McQueen, Swanson, Britnell, Fowke, and Buckley had all worked in the field at one time or another, but none of them had tried to relate the effects of immigration to the Canadian economy as extensively as did Mabel Timlin. Though she never had time to complete her voluminous researches on the subject, some of her findings were presented in 'Recent Changes in Government Attitudes towards Immigration' (*Transactions of the Royal Society of Canada*, 1956) and 'Canada's Immigration Policy, 1896–1910' (*Canadian Journal of Economics and Political Science*, 1960), her presidential address to the Canadian Political Science Association.

Timlin was the first woman president of the association, the first woman member of Section II of the Royal Society of Canada on her election in 1951, and, by a vote of the membership, was elected to serve on the executive of the American Economic Association from 1958 to 1960.[13] She was also a frequent traveller overseas, where she participated in the proceedings of the World University Service, the International Federation of University Women, and the International Economic Association. Upon her retirement from the university in 1959, she was awarded a senior fellowship of $8,000 from the Canada Council, which enabled her to make a extensive tour of immigration offices in Europe. Her final work, *The Social Sciences in Canada: Two Studies* (1968), written jointly with Albert Faucher and undertaken at a time in her life when most others would have been content to hang up their scholar's caps, was an influential document which led directly to new institutional arrangements for the funding of the social sciences.[14] Her own university gave her an honorary degree in 1969. In 1976, when she was eighty-four, she was admitted to the Order of Canada.

To 'Timmie,' as everyone called her (undergraduates only well out of her hearing), students were like members of an extended family. In the classroom, she cajoled and hectored her charges into learning something of economics. A point would be made, to be followed by a staccato: 'Did you get it, Miss King? Did you get it, Mr Rempel?' She wrote copious remarks on essays, between the lines of text and up and down the margins. One handed in an essay and got back two, as one student put it.[15]

To those on the path of serious study, she was indulgent with her time and attention, though she was sometimes as severe and demanding as a parent, especially with her women students, whom she suspected of not having sufficient drive to keep to the path of a serious career. From the beginning, she held seminars in her lodgings to escape from the 'flaccid atmosphere of a regular classroom.' Honours students, she said, regarded her small flat 'as a port of call when they have problems to work out or when they are making plans for work elsewhere.'[16] In her last years of teaching, her seminar on the history of economic thought took place at her little yellow house on the riverbank. When the business part of the seminar was over, there would be coffee and cookies of her own making from recipes cut out of the *Christian Science Monitor* and, at Christmas, glasses of sherry accompanied by her special frosted date cake, with its generous lacings of rum. Over the years she kept in touch with her students and they with her, sending her news of betrothals, babies, and goings-on in the world of economics.

I

It had occurred to Mabel Timlin that Fowke, too, was deserving of a Guggenheim, but the stipend was too low for a family man (hers had come to U.S. $2,500). After returning from her tour, she ventured to suggest to the director of the foundation, Henry Allan Moe, that the amount be increased for those with family responsibilities. She suggested that her colleague Vernon Fowke would be an excellent candidate: 'He very much needs a year away ... he has never had the opportunity to build up any sum to be devoted to securing leisure for himself. Since the salary conditions became better here costs of living have risen so heavily, particularly for food, that saving is very difficult indeed for a man with a family.'[17] No Guggenheim was forthcoming, and Fowke spent many of his summers, sometimes at other universities, teaching summer school classes to augment his income. His regular teaching load was exceedingly heavy. As the primary teacher of political economy during the early years, he taught an average of 350 students each session from 1945 to 1947. And with the war and its aftermath came extra demands from government, particularly at the provincial level. Working for government, however, was not especially remunerative; nor did it leave much time for independent research. Research funds were scarce as well as insufficient, grants like the Guggenheim were few in number, and travel money was hard to get. It was not unusual for faculty members to be denied the university's transportation and per diem allowance for attending meetings of the learned societies, even if they were participating in the program. Sabbaticals were rare; at half-salary, few could afford one. Those of Fowke's generation took few absences from the regular grind of teaching. Britnell never took a sabbatical leave and neither did Timlin. Fowke himself had two, one in 1950 with the help of a senior leave fellowship from the Social Sciences Research Council of Canada and another in 1965.

Fowke's work for government informed and strengthened his academic studies. Besides the ten reports he either wrote for government or helped to write, he published two books, collaborated on another, and wrote some twenty articles. While there were a number of influences which contributed to his intellectual development – his own background on the farm and early hardships, Harold Innis's ideas, his close collaboration with George Britnell, and his old teachers, McQueen and Swanson – Fowke approached economic history in a way which was his own. A shy and sensitive man, he could not be budged once he had made up his mind. He had a searching intellect which never took any idea for granted. One example is his debunking of 'The Myth of the Self-Sufficient Canadian Pioneer,' a paper he presented to the Royal Society of Canada in 1962. Another is his objection to calling the farmers' movement an 'agrarian revolt': 'What fundamental Canadian institutions have they challenged?' he asked. 'Where have they stood on the question of private property? On the maintenance or abandonment of the free enterprise system? On law and order and the state? On the church? On marriage and the home?'[18] Throughout, Fowke argued for the application of rigorous economic analysis to the historical role of agriculture in Canadian economic development and against a romanticized view. His analysis led him to the conclusion that agriculture had been used exploitatively from the earliest days of settlement, and maintained ever since in a position of disability within the pricing system. In his words, 'The clearest and most significant uniformity regarding Canadian agriculture for more than three hundred years has been its deliberate and consistent use as a basis for commercial and political empire. Toward this end ... Canadian agriculture has been fostered and moulded, supported by legislation and public monies, advocated alike by the press and from the platform and pulpit, with all the nostalgic vigour of the ever-recurring back-to-the-land crusade.'[19]

In another place, he entered the plea 'that agricultural history be not thought to consist solely in changing censuses of rural populations and farm stock, in areas cultivated and bushels produced.'[20] Economic history, to him, was a form of literature, not the mere manipulation of statistics. But the writing did not come easily. 'Every sentence is wrung out of me,' he would often say.[21] Like his predecessor in the Department of Economics, Lewis C. Gray, whose work he admired, Fowke was a patient and thorough worker. He would turn sentences over and over in his mind, searching for the exact word or phrase he wanted. His wife, Helen, would help him with bibliographies and reference notes, sorting out endless piles of little index cards. Students who came to his house for seminars remember a warm, intellectual atmosphere and the gentle, probing way that Fowke looked at all economic phenomena.[22] 'Dr. Fowke,' recalled one of them, 'dispelled the notion that economists are just statisticians, seldom humanistic in their approaches. People in his books were never reduced to statistics; he counted them in their categories, but they never lost their identity as human beings, to be admired, respected, pitied, helped as the case might be. He was no stranger to suffering ... Perhaps this heightened his sensitivity to the problems of others. Whatever his motivation, this was the thing that shone through every lecture, and through every page of his scholarly writing.'[23]

While he worked on his first book, a revision of his doctoral thesis, Fowke wrote: 'One does worry a great deal about the flaws and shortcomings in a manuscript. If I sat down to think about those in my manuscript I should not submit it for publication for a long while.'[24] His work evolved slowly. It was not until 1946, four years after he had submitted his thesis to Washington, that *Canadian Agricultural Policy: The Historical Pattern* was finally published. 'This volume is an example of economic history at its best,' wrote W.J. Waines in the *Canadian Historical Review*. 'Written by an economist with a good sense of the use of historical materials, it combines economic analysis and the use of historical data in an interpretation of the purposes of agricultural policy in Canada. Professor Fowke condemns the "idea that agriculture is Canada's basic industry" as "a *cliché*, devoid of content" and maintains that its "ritualistic use" has befuddled the interpretation of Canadian agricultural policy and has failed to reveal the true role of agriculture in the economic and political life in Canada. He has presented a new and convincing interpretation of the historical role of agriculture and agricultural policy.'[25]

Fowke next turned to what was first intended as an examination of the farmers in politics, a project suggested to him by S.D. Clark, general editor of the Social Credit in Alberta series. The new work progressed slowly. He had to put it aside during the postwar influx of students, and his involvement in the government of Saskatchewan's reconstruction efforts delayed him still further. At first, the study was to be called 'The Economic Background of the Social Credit Movement.' By 1948, when more than half the book was in draft, its title was changed to 'Farmers' Commercial Organizations and the National Policy.' The manuscript then went through several revisions during which Fowke wrestled with the ambiguities arising out of his attempt to place the material in a suitable conceptual framework. As late as 1954 an outside reader wrote that 'the author should choose ... as to whether he is going to make a rather plain story of an era out of it or whether he is going to try and make it a study in policy and its results.'[26] The book finally came out in 1956 under the title *The National Policy and the Wheat Economy*, the seventh of ten volumes planned for the Social Credit series, and met with general approval.[27] W.L. Morton in the *Canadian Historical Review* praised its 'masterly balance of analysis and statement. Professor Fowke proves himself to be without rival in his historical grasp of Canadian agricultural policy, and anyone who reads this account cannot fail to experience the satisfaction which comes of having the crooked made straight and the rough plain.'[28]

In *The National Policy and the Wheat Economy*, Fowke described how the National Policy, the set of measures brought forward after Confederation to build a Canadian nation from sea to sea, had led to the closing of the western frontier and the creation of the wheat economy. As Fowke pointed out, it was no part of the national policy to inquire into whether or not the lands brought into cultivation by the system of free land grants would be economically viable, and agricultural policies which came later did nothing to disprove the myths of agricultural fundamentalism which began to flourish. Prairie farmers were left largely to their own devices in an economic system in which they suffered from competitive inferiority, and under such circumstances they had little alternative but to rebel against the open market system. Canadian agricultural policy, said Fowke, had been cast in a mould of economic liberalism which 'justified equality of freedom to competitive and monopolistic entrepreneurs alike,' but, because of 'its lack of theoretical or conceptual content,' tended to be inconsistent and impermanent.[29] But while Fowke was thorough in his analysis of where agricultural policy and thinking about agricultural policy had gone wrong, he showed a marked reticence at the conclusion of the book to propose new and better policy instruments. Morton took Fowke – and 'Innisian economics' – to task for this:

> Innisian economic analysis is severely pragmatic, as indeed befits the historical method. In historical analysis it has shown itself indifferent to the character, whether public or private, of the *entrepreneur*. Innisian economics are therefore in practice non-liberal economics. Its practitioners still trail some of the appurtenances of liberal economics: a classical objectivity, a cultivated detachment from men's business and bosoms, the air of one who dwells in ivory towers. This is to suffer, like Dominion agricultural policy, from a failure to develop theory completely. The Innisian economist as a pragmatic and historical economist must not only discuss policy; he must also, shedding the threadbare garment of liberalism, project and prescribe policy. This Professor Fowke has deliberately refrained from doing, and his excellent book is perceptibly less than it might have been.[30]

It may be said that Fowke's quarrel was not so much with specific instruments of agricultural policies as it was with the hazy and wrongheadedly romantic way in which scholars and politicians alike conceived of the lives of farmers and the place of agriculture in the economy. In his conclusion, he suggests the need for 'a clear recognition of the competitive disabilities of agriculture within the price system and a clear decision as to whether these disabilities are to be tolerated or removed.'[31]

Fowke did not believe in prescribing policies if it meant also prescribing the social goals and human values which the policies were supposed to serve. Social goals were established by the community – as Fowke saw things, by the Christian community. 'In general,' he wrote, 'the economist and political scientist are to be employed as technicians to secure the goals established by the public. A Christian public, thoroughly conversant with the Christian concept of the nature of man should establish the goals and define the ends of the social structure. It should say to the economist and the political scientist, these are the objectives, these are the values which we insist must be preserved.'[32]

Outside the academy, Fowke kept to a busy schedule. In the 1930s he prepared a paper on monetary theory for the Saskatchewan government's submission to the Royal Commission on Dominion-Provincial Relations. Then he served variously on the Saskatchewan Urban Assessment Committee, the Saskatchewan Reconstruction Council, the Saskatchewan Committee on Rural Municipal Boundaries, and the Saskatchewan Committee on the Tenure of Crown Lands. He was on the research staff of two Dominion royal commissions, one on cooperatives and the other on the South Saskatchewan River Project. He was also a member of the Saskatchewan Economic Advisory Committee when Britnell was chairman, and the two men worked together on the Saskatchewan Economic and Technical Committee on Transportation and Freight Rates from 1946 until 1961, when Britnell became ill. During this time the committee shaped provincial transportation policies and, through its presentations to two royal commissions and several inquiries on transportation, had a significant impact on policies at the national level.[33] At issue were proposed increases in the freight rates for eastbound shipments of grain and flour for which reduced levels had been established in 1897 by the Crow's Nest Pass Agreement between the Canadian Pacific Railway and the Canadian government. For the railway, there was the massive job of improving and expanding its deteriorating rail lines. For the farmers, who were struggling against the twin evils of increased costs of production and reduced prices for grain exports, the Crow rate became a symbolic battle cry – the '*Magna Carta* of the prairie wheat economy,' Britnell once called it.[34]

Britnell and Fowke believed that the level of freight rates should be seen in the context of national policies for regional development, rather than from the point of view of remuneration to the railways. They wrote in their final submission to the Royal Commission on Transportation in 1961:

The Province of Saskatchewan submits that it is imperative for the furtherance of the national interest that adaptations made in the national transportation policy take account, not only of changing circumstances of the present day, but also of the unequal regional burdens inherent in indi-vidual national policies. Saskatchewan strongly urges that every effort be made toward rendering these unequal burdens compensatory rather than cumulative with reference to particular regional communities. It is patently unfair and disruptive of national unity that Saskatchewan and the other Prairie Provinces, which bore the brunt of the land-grant gifts considered essential to the creation of the national railway system and which carry an undue proportion of the burden of the national policy of tariff protection, should also be called upon to shoulder the lion's share of the steadily mounting costs of the Canadian transportation industry.[35]

Fowke prepared the final report of the committee before it disbanded in 1962, but afterwards he was greatly disheartened by the New Demo-cratic government's apparent abandonment of its historic position on the Crow rates on which he and Britnell had fought so long on Saskatchewan's behalf. When Fowke was named to a new committee which had been formed in place of the old one, he declined to serve on it, setting out his reasons for doing so in a long and eloquent letter addressed to the minister in charge.[36] Thus ended one of the longest-lasting and most fruitful collaborations between the provincial govern-ment and a member of the Saskatchewan Department of Economics and Political Science.

In 1947 Fowke was asked to become the head of a two-man depart-ment at United College in Winnipeg; in 1949 he had a similar offer from the University of Manitoba; and in 1958 he was asked to fill the chair of economic history at McGill. But all these offers, as well as the prospect of a better salary, he turned down in order to remain at Saskatchewan. 'I am proud of our Department and shall do my best to see that its shadow does not dwindle,' he once declared to Britnell.[37] But towards the university itself he was considerably less indulgent. He had served as an assistant professor for nine years before he was promoted in 1946 to the level of associate; in this year, he taught 355 students and received a salary of $3,300. Britnell attempted a year later to have him promoted once more, but the university was in no hurry to make up for the losses forced on the faculty during the Depression. Because a new salary schedule had just been adopted, the administra-tion considered it too great a strain on university finances to have asso-ciate professors advanced to the floor of the next level all at once. In 1948 Fowke was made a full professor, but the experience of being held back for so long left him with some bitter feelings towards the administration. 'I sometimes think our Department is what it is in spite of rather than because of, the Board of Governors and the President,' he said to Britnell.[38] 'Frankly,' he wrote on another occasion,

> I think they are stingy, particularly with the Arts faculty ... they begrudge any increase in pay or rank. This is bad for morale, for one can hardly work cheerfully for a grudging employer. Besides begrudging salary and status changes the administration apparently regards travelling allowances as a special favour rather than as an aid to scholarship which would redound to the benefit of the institution. Unless I am mistaken the new administrative philosophy is that the educational dollar must be spread more thinly at the university level, that the whole job should be done as much 'on the cheap' as possible. It is quite possible to run a university that way, of course, but I don't think the Board of Governors want the kind of institution they are going to have if they pursue such a philosophy.[39]

When W.P. Thompson succeeded J.S. Thomson as president in 1949, Fowke was happier with the university administration, but he retained strong views on the role of a university and became a committed fighter for academic rights, particularly the right of scholars to spend time on research. In the paradoxical way in which he would look at common assumptions, he once wrote an article in which he concluded that the good teacher was one of the chief threats to modern education. 'So long ...' he declared, 'as universities can be staffed by men and women who refuse to regard their teaching duties as of sufficient importance to interfere with their work, just so long will the universities fill a vital place in the community.' The higher status of scientific departments he attributed to the fact that they did not attempt to teach and lead except as the 'inevitable by-product of absorption in creative activity,' whereas the humanities professor 'pictures himself as a sedentary cultural missionary.' In the newer field of 'social studies,' he said, professors were undecided whether to follow the scientist or the missionary, but insofar as 'they become imbued with a sense of political, social or economic mission ... they repel students completely.'[40] But, despite such disclaimers, Fowke himself left a deep impression on his students. 'He was my greatest teacher and I have never been able to approach his standard,' wrote Paul Phillips, a former student who later joined the economics faculty at Manitoba. 'He had a penchant for one word questions – why? or how? – that forced you to stop and think.

I've always wanted to create that atmosphere in my own seminars. I have not been able.'[41]

Fowke and Britnell were instrumental in the establishment in 1946 of the Faculty Association at the University of Saskatchewan, which became the accredited bargaining unit for academic staff. Members of the Department of Economics and Political Science served as chairmen of the association for nine of its first ten years, a period in which important advances were made in salary schedules and pensions.[42] Fowke went on to become an active member of the Canadian Association of University Teachers (CAUT) and president of the association from 1956 to 1958.

In 1958 Fowke served on a two-man committee of the CAUT with Bora Laskin, later chief justice of Canada, as the other member, to investigate the case of Harry Crowe, who had been dismissed from his position as professor of history at United College, Winnipeg, because of comments he had made about religion and the administration.[43] The Crowe case, which attracted national publicity, resulted in an impressive victory for academic freedom, but the whole affair was too great a strain on Fowke. Early in 1959 he suffered a severe nervous collapse and for the rest of the school year had to be absent from most of his classes. Though he returned the following autumn to his regular teaching, he never again regained his former strength.

II

In the later part of the 1950s, new staff members in political science were added, and for the first time a single honours program in political science was offered. Charles Dunlop, a graduate of Queen's University, came in 1958 as an instructor. He introduced the department's first course in public administration. Dunlop spent two years at the London School of Economics and Political Science to study for a PhD and returned to Saskatchewan in the fall of 1962 as an assistant professor of political science, but then left after only one year to join the University of Western Ontario. Terence H. Qualter of New Zealand and London taught during 1958–9 as a special lecturer in political science. Donald J. Heasman, a graduate of the London School of Economics and Political Science, came from Dalhousie in 1960–1 on a visiting appointment, and returned as a permanent member in 1963.

As jobs in political science and economics became more plentiful, finding good candidates – and keeping them – became increasingly difficult. For the candidates themselves, things were easier; they were often spared the business of formal application, yet seemed to fall almost by chance into good jobs that would last a lifetime. For example, when Alan Cairns was studying at Oxford, he received an offer 'out of the blue' from Norman Ward, acting head at Saskatchewan, followed shortly after by another unsolicited offer from British Columbia. Both were for instructor positions in Canadian politics. For advice on what to do, Cairns called on his brother, an economics teacher, who said that since Alan knew very little about either department he might as well decide on the basis of climate. Saskatchewan lost because of its cold, and in 1960 Cairns joined the department at British Columbia where he remained until the age of retirement and became one of the most respected Canadian political scientists of his generation. Cairns writes:

> I was finishing a doctoral thesis on race relations in the pre-imperial east and central Africa – the world of Stanley, Livingstone, and missionaries, etc. In other words, my doctoral program had nothing to do with political science and even less to do with Canada. There were, of course, no comprehensives for the doctoral degree at Oxford. Twenty years later, had I applied for a position as a Canadianist with this preparation my file would have been rejected in the first screening ... Clearly, I was the beneficiary of an old-boys network in which my mentor/sponsor was Alexander Brady of the U of T Pol. Sci Dept. I had done both BA and MA at U of T, and Brady had supervised my MA thesis. The 'candidate' did not have to activate the network. Indeed, did not even have to know of its existence ... In neither case was there a request for a c.v., let alone a requirement to come and deliver a paper.[44]

In 1956, the year that enrolments in economics and political science crept over 1,000 for the first time since the veterans' return, A. Edward Safarian joined the department as an associate professor of economics. Born in Hamilton, Ontario, Safarian received a BA from the University of Toronto and a PhD in economics from the University of California at Berkeley. He worked from 1950 to 1955 at the Dominion Bureau of Statistics in Ottawa in the preparation and analysis of data on Canada's international transactions, taught for a year as a lecturer in economics at the University of Toronto, and spent a summer on the research staff of the Royal Commission on Canada's Economic Prospects, where he assisted in the preparation of a study of foreign investment in Canada.

He was a member of the Saskatchewan department for ten years, except for one year spent at the University of Toronto as a visiting research professor of economics. He helped to bring the department's program into line with new developments in economics with the introduction of two courses, an undergraduate course in business cycles and a master's course in growth theory. When he arrived at Saskatchewan, Safarian was already well on his way to a productive career as a scholar, and in the next several years he received grants from the Social Science Research Council, the Canada Council, and the Ford Foundation to further his research into the effects of foreign-controlled companies on Canadian economic development. In 1959, following the publication of a revised form of his doctoral thesis, *The Canadian Economy in the Great Depression*, he turned to a major study of the effects of foreign-controlled companies on Canadian economic development.[45] For the next several years, he surveyed Canadian subsidiaries, collected extensive data, and conducted interviews with the principals of major firms owned largely by non-residents. With the publication of *Foreign Ownership of Canadian Industry* in 1966, Safarian became known, in one writer's words, as a 'high priest on the subject of investment and capital.'[46] He was named a fellow of the Royal Society of Canada in 1973 and served as president of the Canadian Economics Association in 1977–8.

Two other instructors in economics were added in the late 1950s: Kenneth J. Rea, a former student in the department, and David Winch, a graduate from the University of London. Winch stayed for two years at Saskatchewan and then went on to McMaster University. Rea received a master's degree from Saskatchewan, taught as an instructor in the department during 1955–6, and then went to the London School of Economics and Political Science on a Sanderson Fellowship. He received his PhD from London in 1959 and returned to the Saskatchewan department as a special lecturer. He was promoted to assistant professor in 1961 and to associate professor in 1964. A revised version of his doctoral thesis, *The Political Economy of the Canadian North*, was published in 1968.[47]

Rea was one of several graduates of the university who began their careers as instructors in the department and afterwards went on to work at other universities or in the public service. Gordon Thiessen was another. Thiessen taught during 1961–2 for the winter and summer sessions, completed a master's thesis entitled 'Transportation on the Mackenzie River System,' and went on to the London School of Economics and Political Science as a Sanderson Fellow. In 1963, he joined the Bank of Canada as a permanent member of staff and, with the exception of two periods, one spent at the London School of Economics where he received his PhD, and another working for the Reserve Bank of Australia, has remained with the bank ever since. He rose through the ranks to become senior deputy governor to John Crow in 1987, and in 1994 was appointed to succeed him as governor of the Bank of Canada.

Others passed through the department on their way to other places. One was Bernard Crick, who was to be professor of politics at Birkbeck College, London, biographer of George Orwell, and author of several distinguished works on politics. He came to Saskatchewan in 1955 to teach summer school and see more of Canada. He liked the campus and the 'marvellous cheese from the university farm.' 'My wife and I,' he later recalled, 'were struck by the *smallness* both of the town and the university. Many people were away in the summer, but nonetheless the peace and quietness struck one vividly, how decent, friendly and natural the people were after the intellectual pretention and awful competitiveness of Harvard and either the ethnic agonising or the complacent Englishry (often Scottish provincialism at its worst) of McGill. People talked so fully and openly, telling us all about the place ... half conversation half-lecture.' He was amazed to find that women couldn't drink in bars and noted the 'fierceness of prohibitionist sentiment' in the town. He invited all the students to his house one evening and, knowing of student ways from other places, laid in the usual stock of refreshments to find that only one would drink beer. The students were 'very earnest and straightforward and friendly' but definitely 'insular.' 'I was surprised, since they were taking Politics' courses how little they knew about the United States, still less Great Britain.' He remembered meeting Norman Ward: 'very witty, very knowledgeable about personalities and extraordinary political scandals and comic mishaps.' Vernon Fowke gave Crick introductions to some people so that he could go to CCF meetings: 'I was used to ordinary branches of the British Labour Party and was amazed to find them all farmers, looking like farmers and talking like farmers. To talk and see was to learn more than to read those books about them.'[48]

Another who passed through was Canadian political scientist Hugh Thorburn, who came to take George Britnell's place while he was on leave during 1954–5 and on two other occasions taught summer school at Saskatchewan. He shared an office with Ken Buckley: 'a most stimulating office mate whose conversation was full of stimulating and critical ideas and insights. I recall him working extremely hard for sustained periods after which he would go often go duck hunting ... through good weather and bad.' This struck Thorburn as rather hazardous, since Buckley was particularly susceptible to lung ailments: 'However, he pursued it with the kind of reckless enthusiasm that he devoted to everything else ... his slogan in life was "everything in excess."' Thorburn joined a curling team with Norman Ward and a couples' club with Vernon Fowke, who was acting department head in Britnell's absence. The club met every two weeks or so during term to hear papers from members and visitors – 'a very intellectually stimulating and broadening experience,' similar, he thought, to the Saturday Club in Kingston, except that the latter was for men only.[49]

These early experiences in academic life served to confirm Thorburn's interest in an academic career, despite the difficulty of finding a university position. When the year was up and George Britnell returned to his teaching duties, Thorburn was sorry to have to leave. 'Jobs then were very scarce everywhere,' he said, 'but I would have been particularly happy had an opportunity been available for me to stay at Saskatchewan.' Thorburn eventually became a permanent member of the Department of Political Science at Queen's University. He later reflected: 'The good spirits and stimulating companionship which I found in the Department [at Saskatchewan] were extremely attractive to me. Indeed I think I found the atmosphere of the Department in terms of intellectual stimulation and social companionship the best I have experienced in my career. Those were the days when the University of Saskatchewan had, I think, the highest calibre of Professor in Economics and Political Science, man for man, (plus Mabel Timlin) of any in the country.'[50]

III

Mabel Timlin and Vernon Fowke looked to Britnell as their leader and trusted him to work on their behalf and to support them in their enterprises. Among them, the three cultivated an ever-widening circle of contacts and associations which were invaluable to their younger colleagues and senior students. Their associations began with Harold Innis and the department at Toronto and extended out to departments at other universities, the Canadian Political Science Association, all levels of government, and all manner of other individuals and groups, from journalists to bankers and farm leaders. They kept in close touch with the London School of Economics and Political Science and the secretary of the graduate school, Anne Bohm, who took a special interest in the University of Saskatchewan and recipients of the Sanderson Fellowship. As well, there were important contacts with groups and universities in the United States, first through Timlin and Fowke, and later also by way of Ken Buckley, who knew people at the National Bureau of Economic Research in New York, where he had spent a year as a research associate.

Morale in the department was high during the Britnell years. There was a strong sense of forward direction – involving the councils of the university, the social science profession, and public affairs – which filtered down from the three senior professors to the junior members and a select group of honours students. A.E. Safarian later reflected: 'I thought I was lucky to be in the Department at the time I was there ... Quite apart from the intellectual excitement which half a dozen people in the Department sparked, and a warm social contact, there was a sense of participation in key events both inside and outside the University ... The senior trio played a formidable role in the [university] Senate, largely in terms of representing the faculty view of the University, maintaining its standards, and keeping the administration on its toes.'[51] If the younger members of the department, and those added later, did not always have as much enthusiasm for Britnell's leadership as did Timlin and Fowke, they none the less held their peace. There was never any real threat to his authority. A man of immense charm and urbanity, possessed of a large wit and quick sense of humour, Britnell was always careful to make others feel a part of the process, even though he usually made the decisions himself.

If Britnell had an Achilles' heel as head of the department, it was to be found in his attitude towards the kind of economic theory gaining in vogue, which made extensive use of mathematics. He admitted privately to knowing 'precious little about economic theory' and to 'constantly being pulled up short by the appalling weaknesses of my mathematical economics,'and he was grateful for the presence in the department of theoretically minded colleagues like Timlin, Buckley, and Safarian; but aside from these few, he tended to be dismissive of theoretical economics and most of those who practised it.[52] For instance, when William Hood, later a prominent Canadian scholar in the field of econometrics, taught at Saskatchewan near the end of the Second World War, Britnell's comment was that the major weakness of Hood's teaching, particularly in introductory classes, was his tendency 'to reduce all economic principles to terms of monetary theory, graphs and mathematical analysis.'[53] Mabel Timlin, curious as it may seem in the light of her own accomplishments in theoretical economics, seemed to share something of Britnell's bias against the use of technical apparatus in the classroom. As long as she taught, she was loath to lead her students into the more rarefied regions of economic theory and regarded even the broad outlines of the Keynesian system as beyond the capabilities of Saskatchewan undergraduates, except for seminar honours students. It was the younger members – Buckley and Safarian, in particular – who in the late 1950s led a campaign in the department to shore up its offerings in economic theory, primarily through their attempt to have tenure conferred on David Winch, who had replaced Archie Reid. However, reports of the young man's recondite methods in the classroom and a suspicion that he harboured advanced democratic notions about the running of the department reached Britnell, and he refused to budge.[54] The discussions that Britnell had with his colleagues over this matter were probably the closest the department ever came to internal strife. Britnell's victory in this matter came at some cost to the students who went on to graduate schools, where they found themselves having to scramble to catch up in statistics and mathematics.[55]

Despite the energy and attention to detail he gave to his teaching, to the department, and to affairs within the university, Britnell was involved in a staggering number of off-campus activities. He struggled to find time to write scholarly papers and books, and to keep up with developments in his field. Friends and colleagues worried about the way in which he drove himself. His close friend S.D. Clark confided to Mabel Timlin: 'George suffers a bit of feeling of being a failure even tho' he has been eminently successful. He hasn't written a great shelf of books & this I know bothers him ... Why should he go on pushing himself? I needn't tell you how great his contribution has been.'[56]

Britnell maintained a regular quota of articles for academic journals.[57] He served on the Saskatoon Public Library Board and the Saskatchewan Archives Board and fought a continuous battle for funding for the collection and preservation of public documents as a corollary to scholarly research. Besides his extensive work for the provincial government, he took on two international assignments, one as chief of an economic mission to Guatemala for the International Bank for Reconstruction and Development in 1950–1, and another as Commonwealth member of the Royal Commission of Federal-Provincial Fiscal

Relations for the Federation of Rhodesia and Nyasaland in 1957. He was active in the proceedings of the Canadian Political Science Association and the publication of its journal and served as president of the association in 1956. He was a member of the Social Science Research Council of Canada and chairman during the crucial years from 1956 to 1958 when a division of functions within the newly formed Canada Council (which was to accommodate both the social sciences and the fine and performing arts) had to be worked out. He was the initial director for its Studies in Canadian Economic Growth Project, which worked out an ambitious plan for research on the Canadian economy.

Along with Timlin, Fowke, and later Ward, Britnell was a member of the Royal Society of Canada. In 1950, he was about to take a turn as program chairman for the society when his ire was roused by a notice sent to him by the society's treasurer informing him that he needn't attend an executive meeting because of the distance he lived away. He immediately resigned from the executive and the program committee, fumed about this 'thoroughly humiliating experience,' and suggested that the society might better be named 'the Royal Society of Ontario and Quebec.'[58]

Britnell and his colleagues were no strangers to controversy. On one occasion, Britnell objected to a move by Queen's University to set up a 'Canadian Economic Research Institute' and call itself 'national' without providing adequate representation from other scholars and institutions in the country.[59] In *Workable Competition and Monopoly*, a brief presented to the Royal Commission on Canada's Economic Prospects in 1956, Britnell, Timlin, Fowke, and Buckley declared in favour of a more vigorous prosecution of combines legislation. Corporate managers, they argued, should be treated no more leniently than other offenders against the law. 'The Criminal Code of Canada is built on *social* codes and not on private morals or on private interpretations of the public interest. It is not only the thief who goes to jail,' the brief concluded, in a section contributed by Timlin. 'The Combines legislation is part of the Criminal Code of Canada and it is difficult to see why business units should be handled more tenderly under it than individuals ...' In December of 1960, Britnell, Safarian, and Buckley joined fourteen economists, among them Stefan Stykolt, Harry Eastman, and Scott Gordon, against the opinions of others in their profession, in an open letter to Donald Fleming, the minister of finance, calling for the resignation of James Coyne, governor of the Bank of Canada: 'We have lost confidence in the ability of the Bank of Canada under its present management to play its proper role.' 'As economists,' they declared, 'surely we are justified in expecting that the Bank of Canada should act as a stabilizing force in the economy and not as one whose actions tend to exacerbate our economic and financial difficulties.'[60] The *Winnipeg Free Press* ran an article entitled 'Economists Disagree over Coyne's Policies,' which quoted the Saskatchewan group as saying that the bank 'has held too tight a rein on the supply of money for far too long' and that the governor had shown 'a surprising lack of economic insight.'[61] The debate thereafter moved on to the floor of the House of Commons, and Coyne resigned the following summer.

The only hiatus in Britnell's crowded schedule was in the academic year 1954–5 when he was selected the first Harold Innis Visiting Research Professor of Political Economy at Toronto, an honour that went to Fowke three years later. After Britnell returned from Toronto, his pace was more hectic than ever. From 1957 to 1959 he served on the Dominion Royal Commission on Energy, one of the massive periodic investigations characteristic of Canadian political life and the first to look at the controversies surrounding the export of natural gas following the historic strike in 1947 at Leduc, Alberta. The commission, appointed by the Diefenbaker Progressive Conservative government immediately on its accession to power after twenty years of Liberal rule, was charged with looking into questions relating to sources of energy. However, it soon became evident that the cabinet had not yet defined what the national interest itself should be, and so the commission had to take on this task as well. Its proceedings, long and exhaustive, with hearings held in all major Canadian centres, helped to moderate some of the more volatile elements and brought the first stage of the debate to conclusion. Midway through the process, Britnell confessed in a letter to a friend overseas that the work of the commission had 'turned out to be a terrific and somewhat terrifying job' because of its broad mandate, which was to examine 'all fields of energy' including 'gas, oil, coal, water power, uranium, etc.' and to make proposals 'on the export from Canada of energy and sources of energy, on the movement of oil and gas within Canada, the prices and rates to be charged, and the structure and financial control of pipelines.'[62] The commission's recommendations led to the creation of the National Energy Board in 1959 and the adoption of the National Oil Policy in 1961, which established the principle of a regulatory market for fuels.[63]

After the intense deliberations of the commission came to a close, there was no break for Britnell. Just after handing in a memorandum of reservations to the commission's report, he travelled quickly to Europe to attend the International Economic Association meetings in Denmark, and then immediately on his return represented the Saskatchewan government at the hearings of the Royal Commission on Transportation for which he and Fowke had laboured to prepare a brief in defence of the Crow rate. He spent five gruelling days in the witness box, after which he remarked to the chief counsel of the Canadian Pacific Railway: 'It was all good clean fun like a Hitchcock murder.'[64] But when it was over, he was obviously spent. 'I need a sabbatical rather badly,' he wrote on 30 December 1960.[65] By March he was gravely ill and had to be hospitalized. He underwent abdominal surgery, returned home to rest, and at first seemed to rally. But at summer's end it became clear that he had cancer and would never recover. He died on 14 October 1961.

IV

The Britnell era was quickly over. There were already signs of the approaching deluge before Britnell died. He had just managed to see the department resettled in what he described as its 'flossy' new quarters in the Arts Building at the end of 1960, the year that six staff were added to the department because of an upsurge in enrolments.[66] Before illness had removed him from the scene of departmental affairs, Britnell had taken part in discussions with his colleagues in the College of Arts and Science on how best to accommodate the large postwar cohort which was working its way through the school system. As early as the mid-fifties, the Bureau of Statistics had forecast that university enrolment would increase as much as 80 per cent by 1964. But Britnell never foresaw, nor indeed did many others, the tremendous changes which this cohort would eventually force on the universities. Henceforth, however, there would be no more Swansons or Britnells to reproach or applaud for the state of the department. With Britnell's passing, departmental dictatorship, benevolent or otherwise, came to an end, and, with the democratization of procedures and the introduction of fixed-term appointments for heads of department, leadership in the department became more diffuse and its disparate elements less controlled. Britnell was the last to hold a lifetime appointment as head of the Department of Economics and Political Science.

Not many familiar faces were left in the department. Vernon Fowke, who was named the first Britnell Professor, was now no longer strong enough to take much part in the running of the department. He put the finishing touches to the book on which he and Britnell had collaborated for the last decade, *Canadian Agriculture in War and Peace, 1935–1960*, saw it safely through the press in 1962, and then turned to his final project, an ambitious study tentatively called 'Palliser's Triangle.' He was at work on the study at Stanford University where he had taken sabbatical leave when he died suddenly of heart failure, on 24 February 1966, after an illness of three days. In the same year, A.E. Safarian, who had inherited Britnell's mantle as head of the department and succeeded him as chairman of the Studies in Canadian Economic Growth Project of the Canada Council, left to join the Department of Political Economy at the University of Toronto, his move being motivated, the Saskatoon newspaper reported, by the chance to use 'the better research facilities at the eastern university.'[67] Rea followed Safarian to Toronto the year after. When Norman Ward, the second Britnell Professor, announced his retirement in 1985, he was the only member of the original seven left in the department; he took his leave a year before the official age because of ill health and died in 1990.

Between the old guard and the new there was hardly any overlap. Robert W. Kautz, a mathematical economist from the University of Pennsylvania who succeeded Safarian as head of the department, had arrived only in 1961. A year earlier, Leo Kristjanson, a research economist at the Centre for Community Studies on campus, was appointed a special instructor in economics. In succeeding years he received his PhD in agricultural economics from the University of Wisconsin and moved up through the ranks in the department. When Kautz left to join the civil service in Ottawa in 1969, the headship passed over to Kristjanson. In 1980, Kristjanson became the sixth president of the university. His lasting achievement, the development of a new College of Agriculture building on campus, a modern blue-glass structure, echoed the emphasis of the first president, Walter Murray, on the importance of agriculture at the university.

Mabel Timlin, the eldest of the original trio, watched in retirement from the sidelines as the process of bringing the department into line with modern practices – thereby shaking off its identification with the past – got swiftly underway. She liked meeting the new members and visiting the eighth-floor offices she had never had a chance to inhabit. In April 1969, she attended a reception held in the departmental library which bears her name and portrait and presented to the department her prized collection of journals. As the years went by, she was content in the knowledge that her life 'which looked at 30 so irretrievably impossible to climb' had turned out to be fruitful and satisfying. 'If you should hear some time that I have left this world suddenly, do not grieve for me,' she wrote in her last Christmas letter to her friends.[68] She lived on to her eighty-fifth year, active to nearly the end, until on 19 September 1976 she was finally overtaken by the infirmities of old age. She left the bulk of the proceeds from the sale of her house to a trust fund to be devoted to the furtherance of teaching and research in economics and political science at the university where she had been, first, secretary, then student, and then, by any measure, no ordinary academic.[69]

12

Conclusion

When the University of Saskatchewan was founded, in 1907, the basic structure of the state-supported university in North America, with its governing board, president, deans, departmental divisions, professorial ranks, and a budget determined in whole or part by a legislature, was well on its way to assuming its modern form.[1] For a new university, there was a template to follow – a choice of templates, in fact, for among the state-supported universities across the continent were some which were striking out on paths of their own designing. One was the University of Wisconsin, at which, as Walter Murray, the first president of the University of Saskatchewan, noted with approval after an inspection on site, 'Culture and Utility receive equal emphasis.' The University of Wisconsin had made a commitment to public service, and, in Murray's eyes, both the commitment itself and the way in which it was being discharged were altogether impressive. Service to the community – the 'utility' that went alongside 'culture' – meant professors of agriculture helping farmers solve their cultivation and harvesting problems, professors of economics providing expert advice to governments, extension services offered in a plenitude. It meant paying due attention to the applied as well as to the pure sciences, and it meant a willingness to offer programs which universities of the more traditional sort were disposed to look upon as 'purely vocational' and thus lying beyond the scope of their responsibilities. Inspired by the example of the University of Wisconsin, Murray promised to create in Saskatchewan a university 'of the people.'

Murray established the first college of agriculture at a university in Canada and made it, in substance as in symbol, the centre of the University of Saskatchewan. In the college of agriculture's curriculum, provision was made for the vocational education of practising and future farmers in a non-degree 'associate' program, which at first claimed most of the college's students. Of the ninety-one students who enrolled in the college in 1913, fifty-one were in the associate program and had an education which had stopped at the eighth grade or before. The associate program included the study of farm machinery, crop production, the management and feeding of livestock, and the control of weeds, and was supplemented by instruction in English, economics, and public speaking, all to prepare the students in the program for the leadership roles which it was supposed they would assume when they returned to their rural communities. For those who could not come to the university, the university would come to them, by means of extension services to farmers, homemakers, and other groups in the community, and, later, correspondence courses. Murray's emphasis on community service did not come to an end with the college of agriculture and the extension division. It came to rest with a weight on the shoulders of his professors of economics. Murray regarded economics as one of the useful applied subjects, an essential ingredient of the Wisconsin Idea, and a course in economics was scheduled to be given in the first year of the university's existence, when the number of courses on offer could then amount to no more than a faculty of five (the president included) could muster.

The care, time, and attention Murray devoted to recruiting the university's first full-time teacher of economics, Lewis Gray, and then once more to recruiting a replacement for Gray two years later, was extraordinary, and certainly more than can be attributed to Murray's having once taught a course in economics himself when he was in New Brunswick. His requirements were several, and each was exacting. First, the professor of economics would teach 'correct notions of economic principles' in courses whose contents took due account of the Saskatchewan setting. Second, the professor would be ready to give talks to the public, serve on commissions of inquiry, and in general offer expert advice when called upon by private groups or public agencies in the province. The third requirement called for a professor who would 'lead and mould public opinion,' particularly public opinion in the countryside. This side of the professor's work Murray once described as being 'semi-political' in nature.

Murray's professors of economics lived up to his first two requirements. Gray introduced courses combining the latest ideas in economics with topics of a practical nature relating directly to everyday problems of agriculture and rural life in Saskatchewan. One course, 'Agricultural Economics,' included, along with 'principles of farm organization and management,' a section devoted to the highly practical matter of 'farm cost accounting'; another, 'Rural Economics,' was described as a 'study of agricultural problems from the social point of view, designed to equip the student for intelligent leadership in rural life,' and encompassed 'agricultural production, prices, distribution, tenancy, credit, marketing, co-operation and community life.'[2] Other courses of local interest, such as transportation, and cooperative marketing (introduced with the advent of wheat pooling), were to be added later to the curriculum.

In the area of public service, the work done by the Saskatchewan economists must have exceeded even Murray's high expectations. No teacher in the College of Arts and Science had duties of the public service kind which were as onerous as those which fell to the teacher of economics – certainly not the teacher of political science, who, being rarely called upon for such, had few outside duties to perform. Economics was the first of the social sciences to gain public recognition, and its practitioners, in Murray's day, were expected to perform duties which, at a later time, would come to be parcelled out among sociologists, political scientists, geographers, and other specialists in the social sciences. Edmund Oliver, teaching economics part time, served on three commissions of inquiry in as many years, and in one year counted among his many off-campus activities a series of nine public lectures. This was just the start. By 1960 the public services rendered by the university's professors of economics were recorded in stack upon stack of commission reports, submissions, briefs, scripts of speeches, transcripts of testimony, and background papers. That many of the economists were able to produce scholarly work of good quality, between public service assignments either demanded of them as a part of their duties or – as was often the case – taken up voluntarily, is remarkable.

But Murray's first two full-time professors of economics were not able to perform the third, the 'semi-political,' sort of service that he hoped they might, namely, the moulding of public opinion in rural Saskatchewan. Murray firmly believed that the farmers and their organizations needed advice and direction of the kind that only a university expert in economics could provide. It seems he believed that, left to pursue a course of their own making, without guidance from the university's economist, the organized farmers were apt to take up

unsound economic doctrines and rash enterprises. That the farm organizations sought guidance from the university on the conduct of their
programs and campaigns is highly doubtful – advice, yes, when advice
was needed, but the idea of being steered in this direction or that by a
university expert would have been much less agreeable to them. When
Gray tried to provide guidance to a group of farmers, telling them of
the follies which beckoned to them from all sides, and reminding them
of the place of the middleman in the wheat economy, they gave him a
cool reception. W.W. Swanson introduced himself to the farmers with a
message they found more to their liking, but the honeymoon was
short, and the conservative cast of the economics Swanson was to urge
publicly in the 1920s and 1930s erased any prospect of his becoming
the friend and confidant of the farmer. It was not until Vernon Fowke
and George Britnell came on staff, to be joined later by Kenneth Buckley, that the university had professors in the economics department
who did enjoy the confidence of the organized farmers, and by that
time the notion that the farmers needed direction by the university
economist had passed from the scene. Murray himself had given it up.

A new university needed connections with larger and older institutions in order to thrive, and Murray made those connections. Murray
and President Falconer of the University of Toronto were close friends,
dating from their student days in Edinburgh, and carried on a regular
exchange of correspondence and visits on university matters throughout their respective terms of office. In economics and political science,
the relationship between Saskatchewan and Toronto was especially
strong in the 1940s and 1950s, when a half-dozen social scientists at
Saskatchewan had Toronto connections of some kind, in some cases by
way of their admiration for Harold Innis, but more often by way of studies undertaken at Toronto. Robin Neill writes: 'Innis was not only an
effective head at Toronto; he was the directing spirit of social science in
Canada, at least in academic circles. His influence was probably greatest
at the University of Saskatchewan where he was represented by his
former student and close friend, George Britnell ... Elsewhere, Innis'
presence would have been felt more indirectly through his position on
the Social Science Research Council.'[3] Innis and his predecessors made
a regular practice of bringing young scholars from the West to the Toronto department, where they would spend a year teaching, finishing
theses, and, as it was once put, 'absorbing its curricular attitudes.'[4] The
teaching part of the arrangement was one of mutual benefit. It helped
scholars from small universities who suffered from a lack of funds and

heavy teaching loads; at the same time, it gained teaching staff for the Toronto department with no contractual commitment beyond a year and allowed regular members of the department some relief from teaching at a time when paid sabbatical leaves or research grants were rare. Office space was found at different times for Fowke and Mable Timlin, neither of whom had been students at Toronto – Fowke to work on his doctoral thesis for the University of Washington, and Timlin to complete the manuscript of *Keynesian Economics*. Beginning in 1941, Timlin spent several summers in the Toronto department. In those days, she was later to recall, 'not only did "everybody know everybody" but Harold Innis in particular knew everybody, and was such a careful fosterer of the interests of scholars in departments other than his own that there must have been some departments at least in Canada whose members were unsure whether they were attached to their own institutions or were extra-mural outposts of the Toronto department!'[5]

For a time, the Toronto connection left its mark on curriculum at the University of Saskatchewan. In Innis's writings were intimations of a distinctly Canadian approach to the social sciences, and by offering courses at Saskatchewan in 'political economy,' itself the label which came to be attached to Innis's work, Britnell saw himself and his department as partners with Toronto in the development of an indigenous scholarly tradition. On the political science side of the department, however, this budding tradition had to contend with another, this one local and of long standing. In 1928, fresh from teaching in the United States, Robert MacGregor Dawson had established a curriculum in political science at Saskatchewan which reflected the American emphasis on the institutions and workings of government. He had also adopted the American practice of introducing students to the politics and government of their own country in the beginning course in political science. For Dawson himself, the politics and government of his own country were to be consuming interests, and upon arrival at Saskatchewan he set about immediately introducing senior courses in Canadian government – rarities at the time. Dawson's initiative and leadership in establishing Canadian government as a thriving field of study influenced the course political science was to take in Canada in years to come. At the University of Saskatchewan itself, the discipline established a strength in the field of Canadian government which was to be sustained by Norman Ward, who was to be recognized by his peers as the leading scholar in the field, just as Dawson had been. Ward, in turn, attracted young scholars to Saskatchewan who would carry the tradition on. Ward counted both Innis and Dawson among his mentors, but it was Dawson from whom he took his inspiration when he did his work.

The Saskatchewan presence in the development of the study of Canadian government is one worthy of notice. Four university text-books devoted in whole or considerable part to Canadian government were published in Canada in the 1940s, the first of their kind, and the authors of three of them had affiliations with the University of Saskatchewan: Hugh Clokie (*Canadian Government and Politics*, 1944) held bachelor's and master's degrees in history and political science from Saskatchewan; J.A. Corry (*Democratic Government and Politics*, 1946) was a graduate and then a faculty member of the College of Law at Saskatchewan; and Dawson (*The Government of Canada*, 1947) taught at Saskatchewan from 1928 to 1937.[6] After Dawson's death, Ward saw *The Government of Canada* through subsequent revisions.

Walter Murray wanted a university which would be comprehensive, but which would at the same time be specialized in agriculture, exten-sion, and public service. When Murray retired in 1937 hard questions had to be asked about whether a university in a province which had suffered seven years of economic depression could afford to be all of these things. But the university's theme of service to the community was not to reach a finale with the economic difficulties and Murray's retirement, as was made clear by Murray's successor, J.S. Thomson. Thomson wrote a memorandum to the head of the economics depart-ment, advising: 'If it is at all possible, members of the University staff should give assistance both to Government departments and to general projects calculated to help in public affairs outside of the University work.'[7] Murray's departure led to changes of other kinds, however. Decisions which had been his alone to make as president devolved rap-idly to the offices of deans, and from there to university departments and (especially) their heads, who had a great deal of power at their dis-posal to make decisions in matters of personnel and curriculum. What a discipline could make of itself at the university now depended not on the pleasure of the president, but in a critical way on the ability of its practitioners to press its claims through and within departments. Hav-ing a strong department head was a distinct advantage.

George Britnell was one who recognized and seized upon the oppor-tunities presented by the new dispensation, and it was in a department which he headed that the two social sciences of economics and political science came to a flowering in the 1940s and 1950s at the University of

Saskatchewan. The department contained several scholars of distinction: among its nine permanent members in the late 1950s were five who were, or would be, members of the Royal Society of Canada. One was Mabel Timlin, who took great pride in her department, attributing its achievments to an *esprit de corps* which had grown out of years of shared adversity in the 1930s when she, Fowke, and Britnell had been trying to make their way in the academic world, and to the opportunities that Innis had provided for Saskatchewan scholars, herself included. There was an energy in the department which reflected the conviction held by its members that the social sciences were important, and above all useful. Governments evidently found them useful, for they called upon members of the department for advice, consultation, and public service with an exhausting regularity. The catalogue of Kenneth Buckley's papers in the archives of Saskatchewan lists, as examples of the advisory and consultative appointments he held in his relatively short career, the following: 'a consultant to the Continuing Committee on Local Government in Regina, a consultant to the Restrictive Trade Practices Commission, Department of Justice in Ottawa, a consultant on Dominion-Provincial Financial Relations to the treasury board in Regina, a member of the National Conference for Research on Co-operatives, a consultant on the Royal Commission on the South Saskatchewan River Project, a member of the Advisory Committee on Census Monographs at the Dominion Bureau of Statistics in Ottawa, a member of the Canadian Council on Urban and Regional Research, and a consultant to the Saskatchewan Productivity Council.' To this could be added the considerable work he did with the farm organizations.[8] Britnell, from his university post, worked as adviser to the provincial government on a regular basis from 1944 to 1951. Afterwards he was to take on several special assignments, including a strenuous one undertaken with Fowke and others, which involved preparing, and then arguing, the government of Saskatchewan's case with respect to federal policies on transportation and freight rates, matters of keen interest to the province and its farmers. From the 1930s through to the 1950s, university scholars, acting practically as an extension of government, assumed responsibility for defining the position which Saskatchewan took on negotiations over federal-provincial financial relations. Such work inevitably found its way into the classroom, to the great interest of students.

The work for governments carried out by Buckley, Fowke, Britnell and others in the department was arduous, often frustrating, and hardly rewarding in terms of scholarly recognition, the bulk of their efforts lying buried in the anonymity of public documents. 'He undertook advisory work with governments as a public obligation and only on terms of complete political independence,' wrote Fowke of his colleague Britnell, who advised both Liberal and Co-operative Commonwealth Federation governments in Regina in the course of his career, and, to complete the political hat trick, was named to a commission by a Progressive Conservative government in Ottawa. In 1944, when Britnell was made chairman of a committee whose task was to offer advice on economic matters to the new provincial administration of T.C. Douglas, he and the other academics who sat on the committee 'made it clear to Douglas that they did not regard themselves as planners and would not act in that capacity.'[9] That they were scholars first of all, requiring a distance from the actual making of policy to preserve their independence and their ability to criticize as well as advise, was a position upon which members of the department insisted. Fowke believed that governments expected too much of the experts who were called upon to help find solutions to economic and social problems, and he did not absolve the experts themselves of all responsibility for the sometimes disappointing results. The periodic commissions of inquiry established to solve the problems of agriculture, he wrote, were regarded by the governments which appointed them as 'magicians': 'It was their job to pull the rabbit of effective agricultural policy out of the hat of a freely operating agricultural price system. The hat was always the same. Some times the magicians changed; some times they did not. In any case they were all trained in the Smith-Mill-Marshall school of frictionless politico-economic wizardry. With this training, and from the given hat, successive royal magicians drew great quantities of fluff – but no rabbit.'[10] Britnell once confided to Innis: 'There are times when I get really frightened at the things which lawyers and politicians think economists should be able to do by turning a handle and mixing a few statistics.'[11]

Britnell was a tireless worker, as scholar, adviser, consultant, and academic entrepreneur. His ambitions for the department went beyond the two subjects, economics and political science, which had been brought together to form it. When sociology was first taught at the university, the subject fell to his department, and he had his eye on geography and anthropology as well. His ambition, it seems, was to build an omnibus department which would be, in all but name, a faculty of social science. But he did not reckon on the sense of autonomy which was developing in every specialized line of study in the social sciences. At the first opportunity, sociology left Britnell's department and established one of its own. Geography obtained its own department. The idea that every discipline required a university department of its own to foster its interests had taken root, and eventually it would overtake even the combining of economics and political science in a department. With the development of disciplinary autonomy came an emphasis on peer assessment, making the discipline at large an anonymous partner of the local department in the devising of programs and the hiring of personnel. In economics, a consensus was emerging in the discipline across the continent about what courses made up an appropriate program in the subject, and about how the courses should be taught. The consensus called for more extensive use of mathematics in the economics classroom, which Britnell resisted. His successor, A.E. Safarian, had a major job of rebuilding to do. The department had been stripped of most of its senior economists by death and retirement, and the direction in which the discipline of economics was moving required a wholesale change in curriculum. The political science side of the department, with a senior scholar in Norman Ward and a specialty, Canadian government, which was still on the ascendant, was better situated to cope with the changes in the university world which came with the huge increase in student numbers in the 1960s.

Where once the department had been called upon to fill a permanent teaching position only at intervals of several years, in the 1960s appointments were being made by the twos and fours annually. 'All one needed was a heartbeat and the promise of a Ph.D. to get an academic job and a bit of praise by someone important to get a good appointment,' recalls Saskatchewan graduate John Floyd. 'It was hard for the Department at a place like Saskatchewan to compete in this market.'[12] In one year in the 1960s, Safarian conducted an extensive search for staff throughout Canada and the United States, looking both for beginning scholars willing to take tenure-track positions at Saskatchewan and for established scholars who would accept a visiting appointment for a year. Of eight vacancies in the department, only six could be filled, most at lower ranks than the budget allowed.[13]

Finding good scholars who would come to Saskatchewan had never been easy. President Murray discovered that on his list of prospects were those who 'would' come West and those who 'would not' – preferences as personal and immutable as those governing whether one would eat spinach. Of those who would and did come West, and to

Saskatchewan, some no doubt came for a job, while there were others who sensed adventure in store at a university which was trying to do something new in Canada. It was all so idiosyncratic: being at a great distance from one's extended family, for instance, was something that could be counted either for or against. The small size and remoteness of the university turned away some, perhaps a great many, but there must have been a few who saw advantage in both. Dawson, seeking a return to Canada, took up Murray's offer of a job at Saskatchewan. Murray had the only opening in Canada in Dawson's field, it is true; but being the sole political scientist on site, with no department head to answer to and few extra duties or distractions to interfere with his research, may have suited Dawson altogether. In any case, he remained long after he had gained the reputation which would have earned him a good position elsewhere. Timlin came to the province looking for work as a schoolteacher, and to the university looking for work as a secretary. Britnell became a university teacher when his crop was destroyed by hail. Ward came to Saskatchewan on Dawson's recommendation and on the strength of his own conviction that it was the part of Canada where the most exciting developments in politics and government were taking place. He never found a good reason to leave.

Frank Underhill came to Saskatchewan from Oxford on the advice of his watchful mentors at the University of Toronto, who thought he needed a year or two of seasoning in the minor leagues of the university world before he would rejoin them as a colleague. After a few months' acquaintance with his new surroundings he pronounced Saskatoon a 'back-woods settlement' and likened the university to an American factory, processing students who had little interest in ideas. When, thirteen years later, Underhill did depart for Toronto, a fellow historian wrote to ask him how it felt to 'leave Siberia.' We don't have Underhill's reply, if any, but we can be sure that it would not have been like in spirit. Underhill's view of the University of Saskatchewan had by then turned into one of respect, to which time would add affection and gratitude. On one of his visits back to the university, he spoke of his discovery in Saskatchewan of 'a live, dynamic, creative democracy, such as I had hitherto only read about in books,' of how the university itself, growing up where and how it did, was a 'miracle,' and of how, sitting in his office in Qu'Appelle Hall on summer days many years past, he could 'look out and see the wheat growing almost under my office windows.' He confessed to a 'special sentimental tie with this institution.'[14]

Notes

Preface

1 University of Saskatchewan Archives, Presidential Papers: Series I [W.C. Murray], W.C. Murray to O.D. Skelton, 11 Sept. 1915.

1 A Workman

1 The quotation is from a recollection by Jean Bayer, secretary to the first president, in Arthur S. Morton, *Saskatchewan: The Making of a University*, ed. Carlyle King (Toronto: University of Toronto Press 1959), 75. For general background on the history of the university, I have drawn extensively from Morton, as well as from Michael Hayden, *Seeking a Balance: The University of Saskatchewan, 1907–1982* (Vancouver: University of British Columbia Press 1983), and W.P. Thompson, *The University of Saskatchewan: A Personal History* (Toronto: University of Toronto Press 1970).
2 University of Saskatchewan Archives, Jean E. Murray Collection, E.H. Oliver diary, 18 Sept. 1909, typed copy (hereafter Oliver diary).
3 Ibid.
4 'Narrative of ex-mayor J.R. Wilson,' in Saskatoon Historical Association, *Narratives of Saskatoon 1882–1912, by Men of the City* ([Saskatoon}: University Book Store [1927]), 89.
5 'Narrative of ex-mayor James Clinkskill,' in Saskatoon Historical Association, *Narratives*, 67. See also Don Kerr and Stan Hanson, *Saskatoon: The First Half-Century* (Edmonton: NeWest Press 1982), 97–9 and passim.
6 Kerr and Hanson, *Saskatoon*, 105. The staff were as prone to get-rich-quick schemes as other citizens of Saskatoon, but their actual participation in the land boom, which at its height led to the opening of 267 real-estate offices

in Saskatoon, was minimal. Murray reported to Oliver on 22 March 1910: 'All your colleagues except Bateman own from one to twenty-one blocks in the city. Miss Bayer is dreaming of the thousands she is going to make. Of course all the real estate transactions are purely imaginary.' University of Saskatchewan Archives, Presidential Papers: Series I [W.C. Murray] (hereafter WMP).

7 Jean Bayer, quoted in Morton, *Saskatchewan*, 72–3.

8 Ibid., 75–6.

9 Ibid., 73–4. Academic gowns were a common sight on Canadian campuses during the early part of the century and in some cases were even required. Emmanuel students at Saskatchewan wore them on all occasions until the 1920s, even while practising football, and some were still seen wearing them in the 1950s.

10 Oliver diary, 24 and 25 Sept. 1909.

11 Quoted in Morton, *Saskatchewan*, 76.

12 Quotations in this paragraph are from Oliver diary, 15 Jan. 1912 and 19 Sept. 1909; 15 Jan. 1912; 18 Sept. 1909; 19 Sept. 1909; and 15 Jan. 1912.

13 My account of Murray's early life draws upon David R. Murray and Robert A. Murray, *The Prairie Builder: Walter Murray of Saskatchewan* (Edmonton: NeWest Press 1984). The authors, son and father, are not related to Walter Murray.

14 Ibid., 15.

15 Ibid., 19.

16 The group is described in Rev. Clarence Mackinnon, *Reminiscences* (Toronto: Ryerson Press 1938), 106; James G. Greenlee, *Sir Robert Falconer: A Biography* (Toronto: University of Toronto Press 1988), passim; and Murray and Murray, *Prairie Builder*, passim. Pine Hill in 1971 became the Atlantic School of Theology, Canada's first ecumenical theological college.

17 See E.A. Corbett, *Henry Marshall Tory: Beloved Canadian* (Toronto: Ryerson Press [1954]), and Walter H. Johns, *A History of the University of Alberta, 1908–1969* (Edmonton: University of Alberta Press 1981).

18 Quoted in Murray and Murray, *Prairie Builder*, 48.

19 Quoted in Hayden, *Seeking a Balance*, 19. Tory of Alberta also received an annual salary of $5,000; Falconer at Toronto started at $10,000.

20 The other four were: F.H. Sykes, an English professor at Columbia University in New York; A.T. DeLury, a mathematics professor at Toronto; C.G. Locke, a future librarian of the city of Toronto; and J.A. MacLean, a Toronto graduate and president of the University of Idaho, who would succeed to the next presidential vacancy in Canada, in 1913, at the University of Manitoba. W.L. Morton, *One University: A History of the University of Manitoba,*

1877–1952 ([Toronto]: McClelland and Stewart 1957), 92, 158–9, describes MacLean as an administrator as 'cold, negative, and ultra cautious,' 'a disappointment to his sponsors and his colleagues,' who 'failed to win public support for the university, as Walter Murray had so ably done in Saskatchewan.' Murray liked MacLean and corresponded frequently with him, but the University of Manitoba, with its background of denominational and language divisions, compounded by weak leadership, was altogether different from Saskatchewan, and so the relationship was never as close as with Tory of Alberta. A year before MacLean's retirement in 1934, the University of Manitoba was rocked by an embezzlement scandal which led to the imprisonment of the chairman of the board of governors, J.A. Machray.

21 For Shortt, see Carl Berger, *The Writing of Canadian History: Aspects of English-Canadian Historical Writing, 1900–1970* (Toronto: Oxford University Press 1976), 21–30; Barry Ferguson, *Remaking Liberalism: The Intellectual Legacy of Adam Shortt, O.D. Skelton, W.C. Clark and W.A. Mackintosh, 1890–1925* (Montreal: McGill-Queen's University Press 1993); and S.E.D. Shortt, *The Search for an Ideal: Six Canadian Intellectuals and Their Convictions in an Age of Transition, 1890–1930* (Toronto: University of Toronto Press 1976), 95–116.

22 Morton, *Saskatchewan*, 29.

23 Quoted in Murray and Murray, *Prairie Builder*, 53.

24 'Narrative of ex-mayor James Clinkskill,' Saskatoon Historical Association, *Narratives*, 79.

25 J. Francis Leddy, quoted in Murray and Murray, *Prairie Builder*, 237. Leddy left the University of Saskatchewan in 1964 to become president of the University of Windsor, serving in this position until his retirement in 1978.

26 Of the Murrays' three daughters, Christina, the eldest, became a nurse, Lucy taught English at Regina College, and Jean, who took a PhD at the University of Minnesota, started out teaching history at Regina College and later joined the Department of History at the University of Saskatchewan. When Lucy and Jean Murray were hired at Regina College during the 1930s, Murray paid their salaries out of his own pocket. Ibid., 236–7.

27 Oliver diary, 24 Sept. 1909.

28 See James M. Pitsula, *An Act of Faith: The Early Years of Regina College* (Regina: Canadian Plains Research Center 1988).

29 On academic standards, see Hayden, *Seeking a Balance*, 64–7. The concern of the president and his staff for the students went well beyond their academic welfare. Murray's own efforts on behalf of students were legendary: he helped many out of his own pocket, held receptions and parties at his

house, listened to their troubles, and disciplined them when necessary. In his correspondence and reports, there are frequent references to student difficulties with cost of living and accommodations. Before the opening of the university, Murray advertised for student lodgings and personally inspected each accommodation offered. Hayden, *Seeking a Balance*, 327, n32.

30 University of Saskatchewan, *President's Report*, 1908–9, 1; W.C. Murray, *Greystone*, 1936, [n.p.]; W.C. Murray, 'The University of Saskatchewan,' *Transactions of the Royal Society of Canada* 3rd ser., sec. 2, 35 (1941): 101; and 'University Act Enlarges Board of Governors, Cuts President's Powers and Affects Senate,' *Star-Phoenix*, 28 Feb. 1946.

31 Quoted in Hayden, *Seeking a Balance*, 36.

32 University of Saskatchewan, *President's Report*, 1908–9, 12, 11.

33 Ibid., 2.

34 WMP, Murray to H.M. Tory, 24 Nov. 1908.

35 Of this 'curious paradox,' E.K. Broadus, an Alberta member of faculty, remarked: 'The President of the University of Saskatchewan, who had been a Professor of Philosophy at Dalhousie, made it his first concern to establish Agriculture in the curriculum, on the principle that if the obvious thing was done first all things would be added on to it. The President of the University of Alberta, who had been a scientist at McGill, made it his first concern to establish and foster the Arts curriculum, on the principle that if he did first the thing that was hardest to do in a purely agricultural community the obvious things would come of themselves,' Quoted in Corbett, *Henry Marshall Tory*, 122. In the province of Manitoba, the agricultural college became a part of the university in 1924, following the recommendation of a royal commission on education which was chaired by Walter Murray.

A later comparison by Duncan D. Campbell in Edward Sheffield et al., *Systems of Higher Education: Canada* ([New York]: International Council for Educational Development 1978), 147, notes that both universities had the advantage of strong leadership but turned out differently: 'Though they were created during the same decade and their geographic, demographic, and social characteristics were similar, Alberta and Saskatchewan have pursued quite different courses in the development of higher education. However, Alberta's new-found wealth from oil resources in the 1950s, while not the only factor, must certainly be labeled a fundamental factor behind the quite different approaches taken by these two adjoining provinces.'

36 University folklore of the 1950s had it that the dean of agriculture was housed on campus for the convenience of farmers who wanted a weed identified. The dean's house became the faculty club in the 1960s.

37 Quotations are from Oliver diary, 15 Jan. 1912, and Murray and Murray, *Prairie Builder*, 72. See also Hayden, *Seeking a Balance*, 72; and Don Kerr, 'Building the University of Saskatchewan, 1907–1930,' *Prairie Forum* 5, no. 2 (1980): 157–81, and *Building the University of Saskatchewan*, pamphlets 1979 rev. 1983, and 1998.
38 In his diary, 22 Sept. 1909, Oliver reports what Murray told him about the two provinces: 'The Albertans regard the Saskatchewanians as slow. But for efficient legislation this province excels.' Murray thought that Alberta's government had less substance and was more 'for display,' and its premier, W.L. Rutherford, a good, honest man but not as able as Saskatchewan's premier, Walter Scott, who had gathered a more talented group around him.
39 Quoted in Johns, *History of the University of Alberta*, 41, 40.
40 WMP, Tory to Murray, 31 Mar.; Murray to Tory, 3 Apr. 1915. On fraternities and sororities, see Paul Axelrod, *Making a Middle Class: Student Life in English Canada during the Thirties* (Montreal: McGill-Queen's University Press 1990), 106.
41 Murray, 'University of Saskatchewan,' 100, says that he had a freer hand in making appointments than Tory of Alberta. The Saskatchewan legislation provided that the governors could not act until the president's recommendations had been made; at the University of Alberta, the governors could make a recommendation without first hearing from the president.
42 University of Saskatchewan, *President's Report*, 1908–9, 14.
43 WMP, Murray to Dean Howes, 12 Feb. 1937.
44 Quoted in Hayden, *Seeking a Balance*, 50–2.
45 WMP, Murray to Tory, 21 Feb.; Tory to Murray, 27 Feb. 1913.
46 WMP, Murray to Dean Gregory, 6 Nov. 1908.
47 WMP, Murray to G.E. Robinson, 12 Feb. 1912.
48 WMP, Murray to W.D. Thomas, 7 May 1919.
49 WMP, J. Brebner to Murray, 3 Mar. 1910.
50 Franek Rozwadowski, 'From Recitation Room to Research Seminar: Political Economy at Columbia University,' in William J. Barber, ed., *Breaking the Academic Mould: Economists and American Higher Learning in the Nineteenth Century* (Middletown, Conn.: Wesleyan University Press 1988), 196–7.
51 [E.H. Oliver], 'In the Land of the Turk,' *McMaster University Monthly* 18 (Feb. 1909): 193–203.
52 WMP, Oliver to Murray, 23 Apr. 1909.
53 University of Saskatchewan, St Andrew's College, Edmund Henry Oliver Papers (hereafter EOP), Murray to Oliver, 27 Apr. 1909.
54 Oliver diary, 22 Sept. 1909.

55 Saskatchewan in 1934 was the second university in Canada to raise the admission standard to Grade twelve.
56 University of Saskatchewan Archives, Minutes of Meetings of the Faculty of the College of Arts and Science of the University of Saskatchewan, 20 Sept. 1909.
57 Oliver diary, 22 Sept. 1909.
58 Oliver diary, 2 Oct. 1909.
59 Oliver diary, 17 Oct. 1909.
60 Thompson, *University of Saskatchewan*, 73.
61 Dr Wylie C. Clark, quoted in Rev. Clarence Mackinnon, *The Life of Principal Oliver* (Toronto: Ryerson Press 1936), 39.
62 WMP, Oliver to Murray, 28 Apr. 1910.
63 Oliver diary, 17 Oct. 1909.
64 E.H. Oliver, 'Saskatchewan and Alberta: General History, 1870–1912,' in Adam Shortt and Arthur G. Doughty, eds, *Canada and Its Provinces*, vol. 19 (Toronto 1914), 147–280.
65 WMP, Report of the Department of History, 24 Mar. 1914; 1912–13.
66 Oliver diary, 15 Jan. 1912.
67 *Official Synopsis of the Report of the Agricultural Credit Commission of the Province of Saskatchewan* (Regina: J.W. Reid, Government Printer 1913), 17.
68 Province of Saskatchewan, *Report of the Royal Commission Appointed to Inquire into and Report upon the System of Liquor Dispensaries Which Recently Existed in South Carolina (under State Control)* (1915), 93.
69 James H. Gray, *Booze: The Impact of Whisky on the Prairie West* (Toronto: Macmillan 1972), 81.
70 June Menzies, 'Votes for Saskatchewan's Women,' in Norman Ward and Duff Spafford, eds, *Politics in Saskatchewan* (Don Mills, Ont.: Longmans 1968), 78–92. Menzies points out that Saskatchewan was the second province to introduce voting rights for women, but the first to hold a plebiscite (one on the sale of liquor) in which women could vote.
71 Kerr and Hanson, *Saskatoon*, 182.
72 See Gordon L. Barnhardt, 'E.H. Oliver: A Study of Protestant Progressivism in Saskatchewan 1909–1935' (MA thesis, University of Regina 1977) and his 'The Prairie Pastor – E.H. Oliver,' *Saskatchewan History* 37, no. 3 (Autumn 1984): 81–94.
73 Don Kerr, a later chairman of the library board, writes of Oliver as one 'who could forcefully speak and act in defence of the library as a citadel of intellectual freedom.' Oliver's test came only six months after the library opened when it was offered a gift of forty books, including works on evolution and Christianity, from a local branch of the Rationalist Press Associa-

tion. In 'the battle of the books' which ensued, the board was sharply divided, with Oliver taking the view that 'anything that stimulated thought was not antagonistic to Christianity.' The gift was subsequently offered to the Presbyterian College and accepted by Oliver. Don Kerr, 'The Battle of the Books: Saskatoon Public Library and the Rationalist Press Association – 1913,' in Peter F. McNally, ed., *Readings in Canadian Library History* (Ottawa: Canadian Library Association 1986), 111–21.
74 E.H. Oliver, 'A Preachment by Padre,' *Sheaf* 5 (Feb. 1917): 72, quoted in Hayden, *Seeking a Balance*, 139.
75 EOP, 'The Oldest Industry – the Worst Organized,' *Saskatoon Phoenix*, 2 Jan. 1914, clipping.
76 EOP, *Saskatoon Phoenix*, 15 Jan. 1914 and undated, clippings.
77 Murray and Murray, *Prairie Builder*, 141.
78 EOP, Oliver to his wife, 15 Aug. 1916; 8 Oct. 1917.
79 Quoted in Barnhardt, 'Prairie Pastor,' 89.
80 The following articles by Oliver appeared in *Proceedings of the Royal Society of Canada*: 'The Contest between Lieutenant-Governor Royal and the Legislative Assembly of the Northwest Territories, 1888–1893' (1923); 'Beginnings of White Settlement in Northern Saskatchewan' (1925); 'Settlement of Saskatchewan to 1914' (1926); 'The Significance of the Canadian Confederation for the Church Life of the Dominion' (1928); 'The Institutionalizing of the Prairies' (1930); 'The Journal of Edward Sallows, 1844–1849' (1931); 'Peter Veregin' (1932); 'Economic Conditions in Saskatchewan, 1870–1881' (1933); 'The Beginnings of Agriculture in Saskatchewan' (1935). See also E.H. Oliver, 'The Settlement of the Prairies, 1867–1914,' in *Cambridge History of the British Empire*, vol. 6 (1930): 523–47. J.M.S. Careless refers to Oliver in 'Frontierism, Metropolitanism and Canadian History,' in *Approaches to Canadian History*, essays by W.A. Mackintosh, A.R.M. Lower, F.H. Underhill, W.L. Morton, D.G. Creighton, J.M.S. Careless, and M. Brunet ([Toronto]: University of Toronto Press 1967), 71.
81 *Winnipeg Free Press*, 13 July 1935; 'Edmund Henry Oliver,' *Proceedings of the Royal Society of Canada* 30 (1936): xxxvii.

2 Bringing the Wisconsin Idea to Saskatchewan

1 Charles McCarthy, *The Wisconsin Idea* (New York: Macmillan 1912). For more on the meaning and scope of the Wisconsin Idea, see Merle Curti and Vernon Carstensen, *The University of Wisconsin: A History, 1848–1925*, 2 vols (Madison: University of Wisconsin 1949) and 'The University of Wisconsin: to 1925' in Allan G. Bogue and Robert Taylor, eds., *The University of Wiscon-*

sin: One Hundred and Twenty-Five Years (Madison: University of Wisconsin Press 1975), 5–37; and Jack Stark, *The Wisconsin Idea: The University's Service to the State* (reprinted from the 1995–6 *Wisconsin Blue Book*, compiled by the Legislative Reference Bureau), 101–79. In its early form, the Wisconsin Idea was associated with academics' working together with political leaders such as Robert M. La Follette to produce progressive state legislation; later, it came to be defined more in terms of extension work and other services to the community.

2 University of Saskatchewan Archives, Presidential Papers: Series I [W.C. Murray] (hereafter WMP), Murray to C.R. Van Hise, 6 Nov. 1908. In letters to Murray, 24 and 28 Oct. 1908, Van Hise wrote about how to organize the university, house the students, and devise a plan for construction. Most important, he said, was the unity of the institution; combining the liberal arts and schools of applied knowledge on one campus was both economically sound and academically advantageous, allowing for a broader and more liberal training for vocational students. Curti and Carstensen, *University of Wisconsin*, vol. 2, 32, refer to the visit of the Saskatchewan committee and Van Hise's advice to them of the advantages of having the university located near the capital of the state.

3 University of Saskatchewan, *President's Report*, 1908–9, 2, 6.

4 University of Saskatchewan, *President's Report*, 1909–10, 12–13.

5 WMP, Walter Scott to Murray, 31 Dec. 1909.

6 WMP, Murray to Scott, 6 Jan. 1910.

7 Quoted in D.S. Spafford, 'The Elevator Issue, the Organized Farmers, and the Government, 1908–1911,' *Saskatchewan History* 15, no. 3 (Autumn 1962): 86, n24.

8 University of Saskatchewan, *President's Report*, 1911–12, 5.

9 WMP, Murray to J.R. Commons, 27 Feb. 1913.

10 John P. Henderson, 'Political Economy and the Service of the State: The University of Wisconsin,' in William J. Barber, ed., *Breaking the Academic Mould: Economists and American Higher Learning in the Nineteenth Century* (Middletown, Conn.: Wesleyan University Press 1988), 333.

11 WMP, Commons to Murray, 5 Mar.; Murray to A.G. Laird, 10 Mar., 22 Mar.; Laird to Murray, telegram, 25 Mar.; Murray to Laird, 17 Mar. 1913.

12 WMP, Murray to Van Hise, 24 Mar.; H.C. Taylor to Van Hise, 29 Mar.; Van Hise to Murray, 29 Mar. 1913.

13 WMP, Murray to Van Hise, 1 Apr. 1913.

14 WMP, Murray to O.D. Skelton, 24 Mar. 1913. For Skelton, see Barry Ferguson, *Remaking Liberalism: The Intellectual Legacy of Adam Shortt, O.D. Skelton, W.C. Clark and W.A. Mackintosh, 1890–1925* (Montreal: McGill-Queen's Uni-

versity Press 1993), and Carl Berger, *The Writing of Canadian History: Aspects of English-Canadian Historical Writing, 1900 to 1970* (Toronto: Oxford University Press 1976), 47–52. For the contribution of Skelton and other academics to policy making, see Doug Owram, *The Government Generation: Canadian Intellectuals and the State, 1900–1945* (Toronto: University of Toronto Press 1986) and J.L. Granatstein, *The Ottawa Men: The Civil Service Mandarins, 1935–1957* (Toronto: Oxford University Press 1982).

15 WMP, Skelton to Murray, 10 Apr.; 25 Mar.; 9 Jan.; H. MacPherson to Murray, 13 Mar.; Murray to Skelton, 24 Mar. 1913.
16 WMP, Skelton to Murray, 1 May 1913.
17 Richard S. Kirkendall, 'L.C. Gray and the Supply of Agricultural Land,' *Agricultural History* 37, no. 4 (Oct. 1963): 206–7.
18 WMP, Murray to L.C. Gray, 2 Sept. 1913.
19 L.C. Gray, 'Political Economy in Saskatchewan University,' *Sheaf*, Nov. 1913, 53, 54–5.
20 Mabel Timlin reported in 1959 that this had been confirmed by Edwin C. Witte, head of the Department of Economics, University of Wisconsin. University of Saskatchewan, Department of Economics, 'Timlin file,' 'The Teaching of Economics in the University of Saskatchewan' [1959], 2. Craufurd D.W. Goodwin, in his *Canadian Economic Thought: The Political Economy of a Developing Nation 1814–1914* (Durham, N.C.: Duke University Press 1961), 166, refers to Gray's appointment as Engen Professor at Saskatchewan and says Gray 'began what was to become one of Canada's foremost departments.'
21 University of Saskatchewan, *Calendar*, 1914–15, 34.
22 WMP, Report of the Department of Economics, 22 Apr. 1915.
23 WMP, Gray to Murray, telegram, 24 Aug. 1915.
24 L.C. Gray, 'The High Cost of Living,' *Sheaf*, Apr. 1914, 266–71; 'The Y.W.C.A.,' *Sheaf*, Apr. 1915, 245.
25 WMP, Gray to Murray, 25 Sept.; Murray to Gray, 26 Aug. 1915.
26 As related by Jean Murray in conversation with the author, 10 Mar. 1978.
27 WMP, Gray to Murray, 25 Sept. 1915.
28 'Agrarianism in the Canadian West,' *The Saturday Press and Prairie Farm*, 13 Mar. 1915, 'Co-operative Societies,' Saskatchewan Archives, Pamphlet File. I am indebted to the late Irene Spry for drawing this article to my attention. An excerpt from the article is included under the heading 'A Warning of the Risks in Co-operative Venture,' in Kevin H. Burley, ed., *The Development of Canada's Staples 1867–1939: A Documentary Collection* (Toronto: McClelland and Stewart 1972, Carleton Library no. 56), 113–16.
29 WMP, Gray to Murray, 10 Aug. 1913.
30 WMP, Gray to Murray, 9 Nov. 1915; 30 Mar. 1916; 3 Mar. 1933.

31 L.C. Gray, 'A Rural Social Survey,' *Sheaf*, Apr. 1915, 205, 207.
32 Queen's economist Marvin McInnis, who went in the early 1960s from Saskatchewan to the University of Pennsylvania graduate school, writes: 'I had gone to Pennsylvania on the advice of [Ken] Buckley to work with Richard Easterlin who in turn got me involved with the gang of "new economic historians" including Fogel, Fishlow, Gallman, Lance Davis, and others. Gray was something of a hero to them. I remember being taken with the fact that Gray was listed as having been at the University of Saskatchewan, yet in the time I was there not a word had ever been said of him ... 'he was eventually to become the most renowned economist ever to have held a faculty position at Sask.' McInnis, e-mail to the author, 7 Feb. 1999.
33 For example, see Anthony Scott, *Natural Resources: The Economics of Conservation* (Toronto: McClelland and Stewart 1973), 24, 35, 145; John McInerney, 'The Simple Analytics of Natural Resource Economics,' *Journal of Agricultural Economics* 27, no. 1 (1976): 33; Frederick M. Peterson and Anthony C. Fisher, 'The Exploitation of Extractive Resources: A Survey,' *Economic Journal* 87 (Dec. 1977): 692; and Gerald Alonzo Smith, 'National Resource Economic Theory of the First Conservation Movement (1897–1927),' *History of Political Economy* 14, no. 4 (1982): 486–9. Gray's articles are discussed in Philippe J. Crabbe and Irene M. Spry, 'Lewis Cecil Gray: Pioneer of the Economics of Exhaustible Natural Resources,' unpublished manuscript 1978.
34 See *Social Sciences Citation Index*, 1966–96.
35 Mason Gaffney, ed., *Extractive Resources and Taxation* (Madison: University of Wisconsin Press 1967), 5–6.
36 Scott, *Natural Resources*, 145.
37 Alfred H. Conrad and John R. Meyer, 'The Economics of Slavery in the Ante-Bellum South,' *Journal of Political Economy* 66 (1958): 95–130.
38 Bennett H. Wall, 'African Slavery,' in Arthur S. Link and Rembert W. Patrick, eds, *Writing Southern History: Essays in Historiography in Honor of Fletcher M. Green* (Baton Rouge: Louisiana State University Press 1965), 187.
39 Robert W. Fogel and Stanley L. Engerman, *Time on the Cross* (Toronto and Boston: Little, Brown 1974), 187–90.
40 Kirkendall, 'L.C. Gray,' 214. For more on the United States Department of Agriculture's farm policies and Gray's part in implementing them, see Richard S. Kirkendall, *Social Scientists and Farm Politics in the Age of Roosevelt* (Columbia, Miss.: University of Missouri Press 1966).
41 Henry C. Taylor, 'L.C. Gray, Agricultural Historian and Land Economist,' *Agricultural History* 26, no. 4 (Oct. 1952): 165.
42 Paul W. Gates, 'Comments,' *Agricultural History* 37, no. 4 (Oct. 1963): 214. See also E.H.W. and H.C.T., 'Lewis Cecil Gray, 1881–1952,' *Journal of Farm*

Economics 35 (1953): 157, and, 'Lewis Cecil Gray, *Agricultural Economics Research* 5, no. 1 (Jan. 1953): 11.

3 An Orthodox Economist

1 University of Saskatchewan Archives, Presidential Papers: Series I [W.C. Murray] (hereafter WMP), Murray to Skelton, 11 Sept. 1915.
2 WMP, Skelton to Murray, 28 Aug. 1915.
3 WMP, Murray to Skelton, 3 Sept. 1915.
4 K.W. Taylor, 'Economic Scholarship in Canada,' *Canadian Journal of Economics and Political Science* 26 (Feb. 1960): 7–8. For Queen's, see Barry Ferguson, *Remaking Liberalism: The Intellectual Legacy of Adam Shortt, O.D. Skelton, W.C. Clark and W.A. Mackintosh, 1890–1925* (Montreal: McGill-Queen's University Press 1993). For Toronto, see Ian M. Drummond, *Political Economy at the University of Toronto: A History of the Department, 1888–1982* (Toronto: Faculty of Arts and Science, University of Toronto 1983). I am indebted to M.C. Urquhart for passing on to me his collection of materials on the history of economics and political science at Queen's University.
5 WMP, James Mavor to Murray, 24 Jan.; Murray to Mavor, 30 Jan. 1914. For more on Mavor, see S.E.D. Shortt, *The Search for an Ideal: Six Canadian Intellectuals and Their Convictions in an Age of Transition, 1890–1930* [Toronto: University of Toronto Press 1976), 119–35, and Craufurd D.W. Goodwin, *Canadian Economic Thought: The Political Economy of a Developing Nation 1814–1914* (Durham, N.C.: Duke University Press 1961), 160, 188–90. Mavor's visit to Saskatoon is described in Don Kerr and Stan Hanson, *Saskatoon: The First Half-Century* (Edmonton: NeWest Press 1982), 53.
6 WMP, Murray to Skelton, 1 Sept. 1915; Skelton to Murray, 1 May 1913; 28 Aug. 1915; telegram, 2 Sept. 1915; 7 Sept. 1915.
7 WMP, Murray to Skelton, 11 Sept. 1915; typed copy of telegram, nd; Skelton to Murray, 28 Aug. 1915; 7 Sept. 1915. See W.A. Mackintosh, 'William Clifford Clark and Canadian Economic Policy' and 'William Clifford Clark, 1889–1952,' *Canadian Journal of Economics and Political Science* 19, no. 3 (Aug. 1953): 411–17. Michell in 1920 joined the economics faculty at McMaster.
8 WMP, R.A. Falconer to Murray, 3 Sept. 1915.
9 WMP, Murray to Skelton, 3 Sept. 1915.
10 WMP, Murray to W.W. Swanson, 17 July 1916.
11 Queen's University Archives, Lorne Pierce Papers, Swanson to Pierce, [Nov. 1947].
12 Queen's University Archives, Adam Shortt Papers, Swanson to Shortt, 11 Oct. 1905; 13 Jan. 1906.

13 Andrew McFarland Davis, review in *American Economic Review* 1, no. 1 (Mar. 1911): 119–20.
14 See Ferguson, *Remaking Liberalism*, 25–7 and passim.
15 Queen's University, *Annual Reports*, 1914–15, 12.
16 H.A. Innis, 'The Teaching of Economic History,' *Contributions to Canadian Economics* 2 (1929): 53.
17 Wesley Claire Mitchell, review of *Money and Banking* by Earl Dean Howard, *American Economic Review* 1, no. 1 (Mar. 1911): 115–17.
18 WMP, W.S. Fielding to Murray, 9 Nov. 1915.
19 W.W. Swanson, 'Studying Our New Canadians: The Ukrainians,' *Canadian Courier* 21, no. 9 (27 Jan. 1917): 12.
20 'Spirit of the West Banquet Proved Notable Occasion,' *Saskatoon Daily Star*, 13 Feb. 1917.
21 'Prof. W.W. Swanson Addresses G.G. Convention on Economic Factors,' *Saskatoon Daily Star*, 13 Feb. 1918; 'Economic Factors Affecting Western Farmers,' in Saskatchewan Archives, Minutes of Saskatchewan Grain Growers' Convention 1918.
22 University of Saskatchewan, *President's Report*, 1917–18, 8.
23 Canada, House of Commons, *Proceedings of the Select Standing Committee on Banking and Commerce* (Ottawa: King's Printer 1923), 790. Irvine was such a persistent interrogator that a fellow committee member later ribbed him about his forbearance, to which he replied: 'Well, we got hold of a lemon and I did not want to squeeze it.' Anthony Mardiros, *William Irvine: The Life of a Prairie Radical* (Toronto: James Lorimer 1979), 158.
24 Irving Brecher, *Monetary and Fiscal Thought and Policy in Canada, 1919–1939* (Toronto: University of Toronto Press 1957), 41, and 'Canadian Monetary Thought and Policy in the 1920's,' *Canadian Journal of Economics and Political Science* 21 (1955): 168. See also Milton L. Stokes, *The Bank of Canada: The Development and Present Position of Central Banking in Canada* (Toronto: Macmillan 1939), 37–44.
25 Canada, House of Commons, *Committee on Banking and Commerce*, 783–4, 807, 790, 789, 785.
26 W.W. Swanson, 'Credit and Economic Expansion,' *Saskatchewan Farmer* 14, no. 5 (May 1923): 13, 34.
27 After his work with the immigration commission was done, Swanson wrote to Murray: 'The government have granted me a sum of money to cover expenses and honorarium in connection with my duties as chairman of the Royal Commission on Immigration and Settlement. As the University was put to some expense in granting me help to carry on my duties while engaged in this work, I am immediately handing to the Bursar my

cheque for $600.00 to cover the amount in question, and assume that I may be permitted to retain the balance.' WMP, Swanson to Murray, 9 Jan. 1931.

28 WMP, Report of the Department of Economics, 6 Apr. 1920.
29 WMP, Murray to J.C. Elliott, 11 Apr. 1922.
30 WMP, James Seth, letter of recommendation, 6 Mar. 1921.
31 WMP, J.S. Nicholson to Murray, 7 Mar. 1921.
32 WMP, W.A. Carrothers to Murray, 16 Feb. 1921.
33 WMP, Murray to Carrothers, 30 May 1921.
34 See E.A. Corbett, *McQueen of Edmonton* (Toronto: Ryerson Press 1934).
35 [D.A. MacGibbon], 'Robert McQueen, 1896–1941,' *Canadian Journal of Economics and Political Science* 7 (1941): 278.
36 Innis, 'Teaching of Economic History,' 53.
37 WMP, Report of the Department of Economics, 8 May 1922.
38 University of Saskatchewan, *President's Report*, 1922–3, 9.
39 WMP, Report of the Department of Economics, 1920–1.
40 WMP, Murray to Adam Shortt, 20 Aug. 1918.
41 L.C. Paul, *Extension at the University of Saskatchewan, Saskatoon, 1910–70: A History* (Saskatoon: Extension Division, University of Saskatchewan 1979), 15; Carlyle King, *The First Fifty: Teaching, Research and Public Service at the University of Saskatchewan, 1909–1959* (Toronto: McClelland and Stewart 1959), 124.
42 University of Saskatchewan, *President's Report*, 1922–3, 4.
43 W.A. Carrothers, 'The Immigration Problem in Canada,' *Queen's Quarterly* 36 (Summer 1929): 519, 526.
44 W.A. Carrothers, *Emigration from the British Isles: With Special Reference to the Development of the Overseas Dominions* (London: King 1929; repr. 1965).
45 C.R. Fay, review in *Canadian Forum* 10 (1929–30): 291–2.
46 Helen I. Cowan, review in *Canadian Historical Review* 11, no. 1 (Mar. 1930): 69.
47 [H.F.A.], 'William Alexander Carrothers, 1889–1951,' *Canadian Journal of Economics and Political Science* 18, no. 1 (Feb. 1952): 99.

4 Retrenchment

1 University of Saskatchewan Archives, Presidential Papers: Series I [W.C. Murray] (hereafter WMP), Murray to J.W. Tait, 21 Mar. 1932.
2 WMP, Murray to Hon. Geo. F. Bryant, Minister of Public Works, memorandum, 19 June 1930.
3 W.P. Thompson, *The University of Saskatchewan: A Personal History* (Toronto: University of Toronto Press 1970), 126.

4 University of Saskatchewan, *President's Report*, 1922–3, 3.
5 W.W. Swanson and P.C. Armstrong, *Wheat* (Toronto: Macmillan 1930), 27, 25, 111, 26, 278, 34.
6 Robert England, review in *Queen's Quarterly* 37 (1930): 593–603.
7 Holbrook Working, review in *Journal of Farm Economics* 14, no. 1 (Apr. 1932): 368.
8 H.A. Innis, review in *Canadian Historical Review* 11 (1930): 270–1.
9 H.A. Innis, 'Wheat Surveys,' review in *Canadian Forum* 12, no. 141 (June 1932): 343–4. MacGibbon's book earned a more lasting place in Innis's memory than did Swanson's: ten years later, in a survey of literature in the social sciences, 'The Social Sciences,' *Canadian Geographical Journal* 25 (1942): ix, he cited only the former.
10 Robert England, review of the *Report of the Saskatchewan Royal Commission on Immigration and Settlement, 1930*, in *Queen's Quarterly* 38 (1931): 573, 579.
11 H.A. Innis, ed., *Canadian Contributions to Economics* 3 (1931): 5.
12 H.A. Innis, ed., *The Diary of Alexander James McPhail* (Toronto: University of Toronto Press 1940), 225–6. Violet McNaughton edited the 'Mainly for Women' section of the *Western Producer* from 1925 to 1950.
13 WMP, Swanson to Murray, 13 Oct. 1930.
14 Innis, *Diary of Alexander James McPhail*, 222, n11.
15 Saskatchewan Archives, 'The Wonder Worker,' *Witness and Canadian Homestead*, 3 Dec. 1930.
16 Derek Chisholm, letter to the author, 13 Feb. 1980. I am grateful to Professor Chisholm for drawing these and other references from the R.B. Bennett Papers to my attention.
17 H.A. Logan, review in *Canadian Historical Review* 13, no. 3 (Sept. 1932): 333.
18 University of Saskatchewan Archives, A.S. Morton Papers (hereafter AMP), Morton to G.W. Simpson, 23 Dec. 1931.
19 W.W. Swanson, *Depression and the Way Out* (Toronto: Ryerson 1931), 157, 158, 181, 177, 180, 148–9.
20 W.W. Swanson, 'Grain Farming in West Not Permanently Imperilled,' *Monetary Times* 90 (13 Jan. 1933): 61. See also W.W. Swanson, 'Western Economic Problems,' a series of six articles in the *Saskatoon Star-Phoenix*, Feb.–Mar. 1931; W.W. Swanson and P.C. Armstrong, 'Economic Data on the Production and Consumption of Wheat,' *Counsel Club* (Montreal), newsletter, Dec. 1931; and W.W. Swanson, 'Wheat and the Economic Recovery of the West,' *Monetary Times* 88 (8 Jan. 1932): 15–17.
21 'Swanson Offers Plan for Refunding Debts,' *Star-Phoenix*, 17 June 1931.
22 Derek Chisholm, letter to the author, 13 Feb. 1980; and Chisholm, 'How

Essential Was the Bank of Canada? The Foundation Arguments Reconsidered,' unpublished paper [n.d.], 17–18.

23 Canada, House of Commons, *Proceedings of the Royal Commission on Banking and Currency* 3 (1933): 1360–1, 1389, 1362, 1393. See also Irving Brecher, *Monetary and Fiscal Thought and Policy in Canada* (Toronto: University of Toronto Press 1957), 142–3 and passim; and Milton L. Stokes, *The Bank of Canada: The Development and Present Position of Central Banking in Canada* (Toronto: Macmillan 1939) 44, 86.

24 'Dr. Swanson's Evidence,' *Western Producer*, 31 Aug. 1933, p. 6.

25 Chisholm, letter to the author, 13 Feb. 1980.

26 V.W. Bladen, review in *Canadian Journal of Economics and Political Science* 1 (1935): 297–8.

27 George de T. Glazebrook, review in *Canadian Historical Review* 18 (1937): 337; W.R. Maxwell, review in *Dalhousie Review* 17 (1937–8): 392.

28 Review in *Queen's Quarterly* 44 (1937): 133.

29 J.L. McD., review in *Canadian Journal of Economics and Political Science* 3 (1937): 295.

30 J.A. Corry, *My Life & Work, A Happy Partnership: Memoirs of J.A. Corry* (Kingston: Queen's University 1981), 108.

31 J.A. Aitchison, conversation with the author, 9 Aug. 1982.

32 R. McQueen, 'The Approach to Economics,' review in *Canadian Journal of Economics and Political Science* 6 (Feb. 1940): 79–85.

33 WMP, McQueen to S.E. Smith, 26 Apr. 1935.

34 WMP, McQueen to Smith, 23 Mar. 1935.

35 WMP, McQueen to Murray, 23 Mar. 1935.

36 V.W. Bladen, letter to the author, 21 Dec. 1980.

37 WMP, McQueen to Murray, 23 July 1935.

38 WMP, W.A. Mackintosh to Murray, 13 May 1936; Murray to Mackintosh, 18 May 1936.

39 H.C. Pentland, *The University of Manitoba Department of Economics: A Brief History* (University of Manitoba 1977), 14. McQueen succeeded A.B. Clark, the first head of economics at Manitoba, and, after McQueen died, W.J. Waines took over.

40 Ernest Sirluck, *First Generation: An Autobiography* (Toronto: University of Toronto Press 1996), 59.

41 Jacob Viner, letter to the *Winnipeg Free Press*, 28 Feb. 1941.

42 WMP, quoted in letter of W.H. Beveridge to W.H. Thomas, Education Officer, 2 July 1935.

43 University of Saskatchewan Archives, V.C. Fowke Papers (hereafter VFP), Swanson to Fowke, 25 Oct. 1935.

44 University of Saskatchewan Archives, M.F. Timlin Papers (hereafter MTP), Timlin to H.H. Preston, 15 Dec. 1935.
45 Benjamin Higgins, *All the Difference: A Development Economist's Quest* (Montreal: McGill-Queen's University Press 1992), 9.
46 'Economics Club,' *Greystone* (University of Saskatchewan), 1936. For Lederman, see Stanley Brice Frost, *McGill University: For the Advancement of Learning*, vol. 2, *1895–1971* (Kingston: McGill-Queen's University Press 1984), 350. Robertson, who was born in Davidson, Saskatchewan, and went on to further studies at Oxford and the University of Toronto, joined the Department of External Affairs in 1941 and later became clerk of the privy council and secretary to the cabinet. He has been called 'the most influential public servant of his day.' Robert Bothwell, 'Robertson, Robert Gordon,' in *Canadian Encyclopedia*, 2nd ed., vol. 3 (Edmonton: Hurtig Publishers 1988), 1879.
47 WMP, McQueen to Murray, 26 June 1935. Deutsch became one of the most celebrated economists of his generation in Canada. He was awarded seventeen honorary degrees and held numerous academic and civil service positions, among them first chairman of the Economic Council of Canada and principal of Queen's University. See M.C. Urquhart, 'Deutsch, John James,' in *Canadian Encyclopedia*, 2nd ed., vol. 2 (1988), 589. Aitchison later joined the political science faculty at Dalhousie University. Allely, who later went to Saskatchewan, enters the story in ch. 10.
48 WTP, Murray to Preston, 9 July 1935.
49 WMP, Murray to Smith, 29 June 1935.
50 VFP, Swanson to Fowke, 25 Oct. 1935.

5 Political Science in Search of Itself

1 Albert Somit and Joseph Tanenhaus, *The Development of American Political Science: From Burgess to Behavioralism* (Boston: Allyn and Bacon 1967), 23–4, tell the story of an English historian who spent two years as a visiting lecturer at Cornell and in 1896, near the end of his stay, 'expressed puzzlement [that] he had not been able to find anyone in the United States who could tell him precisely what political science was.'
2 Quoted in Ian M. Drummond, *Political Economy at the University of Toronto: A History of the Department, 1888–1982* (Toronto: Faculty of Arts and Science, University of Toronto 1983), 18.
3 W.J. Ashley, *What Is Political Science?* (Toronto: Rowsell and Hutchison 1888), 7, 25, 9–10. See also C.B. Macpherson, 'On the Study of Politics in Canada,' in H.A. Innis, ed., *Essays in Political Economy In Honour of E.J. Urwick* (Toronto: University of Toronto Press 1938), 149; Drummond, *Political Economy*,

17–25; Craufurd D.W. Goodwin, *Canadian Economic Thought: The Political Economy of a Developing Nation 1814–1914* (Durham, N.C.: Duke University Press 1961), 176–9; and A.B. McKillop, *Matters of Mind: The University in Ontario, 1791–1951* (Toronto: University of Toronto Press 1994), 193–9.

4 Ashley, *What Is Political Science?*, 28, 22–3.

5 J.G. Bourinot, 'The Study of Political Science in Canadian Universities,' *Transactions of the Royal Society of Canada*, sec. 2 (1889): 15.

6 Adam Shortt, 'The Nature and Sphere of Political Science,' *Queen's Quarterly* 1 (1893): 97. See also Barry Ferguson, *Remaking Liberalism: The Intellectual Legacy of Adam Shortt, O.D. Skelton, W.C. Clark and W.A. Mackintosh, 1890–1925* (Montreal: McGill-Queen's University Press 1993), 3–42.

7 Macpherson, 'On the Study of Politics,' 149.

8 Drummond, *Political Economy*, 36.

9 Macpherson, 'On the Study of Politics,' 151.

10 O.D. Skelton, 'Fifty Years of Political and Economic Science in Canada,' in *Fifty Years Retrospect* (Ottawa: Royal Society of Canada 1932), 89.

11 Somit and Tanenhaus, *Development of American Political Science*, 62.

12 Macpherson, 'On the Study of Politics,' 159.

13 Canadian Political Science Association, *Papers and Proceedings*, vol. 2 (1931), frontispiece.

14 Burton S. Keirstead and Frederick M. Watkins, 'Political Science in Canada,' in UNESCO, *Contemporary Political Science: A Survey of Methods, Research and Teaching* (Paris: 1950), 171.

15 The practice of combining political science with economics for purposes of administration was not at all uncommon in the United States in the early years of the century. A survey of 263 universities and colleges at which political science was taught in the United States in 1914 showed that the discipline shared a department with economics (usually together with one or more other disciplines) in the majority of cases. There were only thirty-eight cases in which political science had a department of its own. Somit and Tanenhaus, *Development of American Political Science*, 56–7.

16 See C.B. Macpherson, 'After Strange Gods: Canadian Political Science 1973,' in T.N. Guinsburg and G.L. Reuber, eds, *Perspectives on the Social Sciences in Canada* (Toronto: University of Toronto Press 1974), 56.

17 University of Saskatchewan, *President's Report*, 1909–10, 12.

18 University of Saskatchewan Archives, Presidential Papers: Series I [W.C. Murray] (hereafter WMP), Murray to R.M. Wenley, 11 Mar. 1910.

19 WMP, H.A. Robson to Norman Mackenzie, 20 Feb. 1909.

20 Henry James Morgan, *The Canadian Men and Women of Our Time* (Toronto: William Briggs 1912), 696.

21 University of Saskatchewan Archives, Jean E. Murray Collection, E.H. Oliver diary, 15 Jan. 1912 (hereafter Oliver diary).

22 University of Saskatchewan Archives, College of Law Papers, A.S. Morton to Mrs Morgan, 8 Mar. 1919.

23 J.G. Diefenbaker, *One Canada: Memoirs of the Right Honourable John George Diefenbaker*, vol. 1, *The Crusading Years 1895–1956* (Toronto: Macmillan 1975), 79.

24 David Lewis, *The Good Fight* (Toronto: Macmillan 1981), 23–4. Paul Axelrod, *Making a Middle Class: Student Life in English Canada during the Thirties* (Montreal: McGill-Queen's University Press 1990), 33, writes that McKay, after he became dean of arts at McGill, was a major force behind the university's anti-Semitic admission policies which were in effect during the twenties and thirties.

25 Edgar Andrew Collard, ed., *The McGill You Knew: An Anthology of Memories* (Don Mills, Ont.: Longmans Canada Ltd. 1975), 26, 78, 79.

26 WMP, Murray to Oliver, 6 Jan. 1910.

27 WMP, Ira A. MacKay to Murray, 16 Apr. 1910.

28 WMP, MacKay to Murray, 18 Jan. 1910.

29 Articles by MacKay in the *Canadian Magazine* were 'Canada Not Independent,' 37, no. 4 (Aug. 1911): 297–304; 'The Original Professor Teufelsdröckh,' 43, no. 5 (Sept. 1914): 437–46; and 'Educational Preparedness,' 52, no. 1 (Feb. 1919): 807–18. His other publication was *A Study in Canadian Citizenship* (Montreal: Kiwanis Club of Montreal 1924).

30 WMP, MacKay to Murray, 18 Jan.; 13 Feb. 1910.

31 WMP, MacKay to Murray, 18 Jan. 1910.

32 Ibid.

33 WMP, Departmental Report, 1913–14.

34 Ibid.

35 WMP, Departmental Report, 1914–15.

36 *Saskatoon Daily Star*, 21 Nov. 1919.

37 Good accounts of the crisis are given in W.P. Thompson, *The University of Saskatchewan: A Personal History* (Toronto: University of Toronto Press 1970), 106–21; Michael Hayden, *Seeking a Balance: The University of Saskatchewan, 1907–1982* (Vancouver: University of British Columbia Press 1983), 78–116; Don Kerr and Stan Hanson, *Saskatoon: The First Half-Century* (Edmonton: NeWest Press 1982), 218–30; and David R. Murray and Robert A. Murray, *The Prairie Builder: Walter Murray of Saskatchewan* (Edmonton: NeWest Press 1984), 107–28. See also Bora Laskin, 'Some Cases at Law,' in George Whalley, ed., *A Place of Liberty: Essays on the Government of Canadian Universities* (Toronto: Clarke, Irwin 1964), 182–4.

38 WMP, Murray to Premier W.M. Martin, 31 Dec. 1918.

39 Jean Murray, conversation with the author, 10 Mar. 1978.
40 WMP, Murray to S.E. Smith, 17 June 1935. Murray explained: 'Hogg was very jealous of Ling's appointment as Dean and undertook to make trouble, and McLaurin was equally jealous of the public attention which Hogg and Ling received. MacKay was very anxious to become Dean and objected to Moxon being made Dean. While McLaurin and Hogg quarrelled about their place in the public eye they were willing to combine to make trouble. It was a very bitter experience for us all but results have justified the price paid for it.'
41 University of Saskatchewan Archives, College of Law Papers, A.H. Murray to A. Moxon, 21 Nov. 1919.
42 F.W. Haultain to Murray, 21 Feb. 1920, quoted in Hayden, *Seeking a Balance*, 110.
43 Stanley Brice Frost, *McGill University: For the Advancement of Learning*, vol. 2, 1895–1971 (Kingston: McGill-Queen's University Press 1984), 156.

6 A Natural Minoritarian

1 For a comprehensive study of Underhill's life and work, see R. Douglas Francis, *Frank H. Underhill: Intellectual Provocateur* (Toronto: University of Toronto Press 1986). I am indebted to Professor Francis for making available to me an early version of the portion of his manuscript relating to Underhill's career in Saskatchewan; and to Duncan Meikle for directing me towards sources of information about Underhill.
2 Frank H. Underhill, *In Search of Canadian Liberalism* (Toronto: Macmillan 1960), ix.
3 National Archives of Canada, Frank Underhill Papers, MG30 D204 (hereafter cited as FUP), Underhill to his mother, 14 Nov. 1915.
4 FUP, Charles Cochrane to Underhill, 25 Apr. [1920].
5 FUP, W.S. Milner to Underhill, 9 July 1913.
6 FUP, E.A. Kylie to Underhill, 7 Nov. 1911; 27 Jan. 1913; 10 Feb. 1912; 4 Aug. 1913.
7 FUP, George Wrong to Underhill, 14 Mar. 1912.
8 FUP, A.D. Lindsay to Underhill, 14 Sept. 1913.
9 FUP, Kylie to Underhill, 2 Aug. 1913.
10 FUP, Milner to Underhill, 9 July 1913; 20 Dec. 1913.
11 Quoted in Frank H. Underhill, 'What, Then, Is the Manitoban, This New Man? or This Almost Chosen People,' in *Canadian Historical Association Historical Papers* (1970): 33. See also Sandra Martin and Roger Hall, eds, *Rupert Brooke in Canada* (Toronto: Peter Martin Associates 1978), 85.

12 FUP, C.P. Lount to Underhill, 30 Mar. 1913; Cochrane to Underhill, 25 Jan. 1914.
13 University of Saskatchewan Archives, Presidential Papers: Series I [W.C. Murray] (hereafter WMP), Murray to J.A. MacLean, 16 Oct. 1914.
14 WMP, Murray to George Ling, 3 July 1912.
15 J.G. Rempel, 'Walter Palmer Thompson, 1889–1970,' *Transactions of the Royal Society of Canada* 9 (1971): 111.
16 FUP, Underhill to his mother, 23 Jan. 1915; 18 Oct. 1914.
17 FUP, Underhill to his mother, 5 Nov. 1914.
18 FUP, Underhill to his mother, 18 Oct. 1914.
19 Underhill, 'What, Then, Is the Manitoban,' 37. Underhill's admiration was later expressed in *James Shaver Woodsworth: Untypical Canadian: An Address Delivered at the Dinner to Inaugurate the Ontario Woodsworth Memorial Foundation* (Toronto: Ontario Woodsworth Memorial Foundation Nov. 1944).
20 FUP, Underhill to his mother, 5 Nov. 1914.
21 Paul Axelrod, *Making a Middle Class: Student Life in English Canada during the Thirties* (Montreal: McGill-Queen's University Press 1990), 91, quotes Underhill speaking at the Conference of Canadian Universities in 1930 on the subject of teaching women: 'no university teacher wants to be condemned to teaching women. He knows that that means an old age of pedantry or empty, meaningless aestheticism.' Axelrod writes that no one present challenged Underhill's views, and that no women were among those present.
22 WMP, Report of the Department of History, 1914–15.
23 FUP, Underhill to his mother, 5 Nov. 1914.
24 WMP, Reports of the Department of History, 1914–15.
25 WMP, Murray to Underhill, 5 Oct. 1915; Underhill to Murray, 15 Sept. 1915.
26 WMP, Underhill to Murray, 1 Sept. [1915].
27 *Sheaf*, Oct. 1915, 21.
28 FUP, Underhill to his mother, 4 Dec. 1915.
29 WMP, Underhill to Murray, 8 Feb. 1916.
30 Quoted in Francis, *Frank H. Underhill: Intellectual Provocateur*, 43.
31 FUP, Underhill to Mrs M.E. Angus, 22 Mar. 1918. Underhill had a good friend in Mrs Angus, the mother of his friend Henry, with whom he had shared digs at Oxford. He sent her news from the war, his socks for darning, and requests for extra clothes and supplies, including a box of chocolates for a fourteen-year-old girl at his billet in Belgium. Heny Angus became a professor of economics, and later dean of graduate studies, at the University of British Columbia.

32 FUP, Underhill to Mrs Angus, 10 Apr. 1919.

33 FUP, Underhill to Mrs Angus, 7 June 1918.

34 Quoted in R. Douglas Francis, 'Frank H. Underhill: Canadian Intellectual' (PhD diss., microfiche, York University, Toronto 1975), 46.

35 Frank H. Underhill, 'English and Canadian: A Few Unpleasant Reflections,' *Sheaf*, Jan. 1919, 27.

36 Frank H. Underhill, 'Imperial Architecture,' *Sheaf*, Mar. 1915, 155–9.

37 Frank H. Underhill, 'The Canadian Forces at War,' in Sir Charles Lucas, ed., *The Empire at War*, vol. 2 (London: H. Milford, Oxford University Press 1923), 286.

38 Underhill, *In Search of Canadian Liberalism*, x.

39 Ibid., x–xi.

40 University of Saskatchewan Archives, Frank H. Underhill, 'Convocation Address,' University of Saskatchewan, typed copy, 17 Nov. 1962.

41 FUP, Underhill to Kenneth Bell, 29 Jan. 1926.

42 FUP, Underhill to Lionel Curtis, 21 Aug. 1925.

43 University of Saskatchewan Archives, Frank H. Underhill, 'The Liberal Arts and Public Affairs,' address delivered at the official opening of the Arts Building, University of Saskatchewan, 16 Jan. 1961, 12.

44 FUP, Underhill to Bell, 29 Jan. 1926.

45 University of Saskatchewan Archives, A.S. Morton Papers (hereafter AMP), application for Carnegie grant, nd.

46 AMP, Morton to Leveson Gower, 29 June 1938. See Joan Elizabeth Champ, 'Laying the Foundations: Arthur Silver Morton and His Early Saskatchewan Heritage Activities' (MA thesis, University of Saskatchewan 1990).

47 AMP, Morton to Innis, 20 Jan. 1931.

48 AMP, C.A. Lightbody to Morton, 15 Aug. [no year given].

49 FUP, J.W. Eaton to Underhill, 21 Aug. 1941.

50 FUP, Lothian to Underhill, 6 June 1924. Lothian did eventually leave Saskatchewan to take up a position at the University of Aberdeen. There, in 1958, he came into possession, at an estate auction, of a set of manuscripts which, upon investigation, turned out to be a student's notes of lectures delivered at the University of Glasgow in 1762–3 by the celebrated economist Adam Smith. The notes were subsequently edited by Lothian under the title, *Lectures on Rhetoric and Belles Lettres* (London: T. Nelson 1963), and made Lothian's name one to be remembered. I am indebted to Peter Dooley of the Department of Economics for bringing this book to my attention.

51 FUP, Underhill to Bell, 29 Jan. 1926.

52 FUP, Underhill to Carleton Stanley, 24 July 1925.
53 FUP, Underhill to Bell, 29 Jan. 1926.
54 FUP, Minutes of meeting on 'Conservatism,' [nd], 'Lothian file.'
55 J.A. Corry, *My Life & Work, A Happy Partnership: Memoirs of J.A. Corry* (Kingston: Queen's University 1981), 60.
56 Underhill, 'Liberal Arts,' 2.
57 FUP, Underhill to Majorie Reid, 18 July 1925.
58 FUP, Underhill to Cochrane, 22 July 1925.
59 FUP, Underhill to Bell, 29 Jan. 1926.
60 FUP, Underhill to Stanley, 24 July 1925.
61 FUP, Underhill to 'Thaddeus,' 22 Mar. 1926.
62 Underhill, *In Search of Canadian Liberalism*, 180.
63 FUP, Underhill to 'Thaddeus,' 22 Mar. 1926.
64 FUP, Underhill to Alvin Thiessen, 24 May 1926.
65 FUP, Underhill to Herbert Heaton, 23 Sept. 1926; Heaton to Underhill, 13 Oct. 1926.
66 FUP, Underhill to George Simpson, 17 Mar. 1926.
67 FUP, Underhill to Lothian, 26 Mar. 1926.
68 FUP, Underhill to Morton, 2 Apr. 1926.
69 FUP, Underhill to Bell, 29 Jan. 1926.
70 FUP, Underhill to Stanley, 2 Apr. 1926.
71 FUP, Underhill to Sharrard, 2 Apr. 1926.
72 F.H. Underhill, 'Some Aspects of Upper Canadian Radical Opinion in the Decade before Confederation,' Canadian Historial Association, *Report* (1927): 46–61; and 'Canada's Relations with the Empire as Seen by the Toronto *Globe*, 1857–1867,' *Canadian Historical Review* 10 (June 1929): 106–29.
73 Underhill, *In Search of Canadian Liberalism*, 43.
74 FUP, G. Wrong to Underhill, 21 Mar. 1923.
75 WMP, Wrong to Murray, 7 Jan. 1927.
76 FUP, A.L. Burt to Underhill, 17 Dec. 1927.
77 FUP, Underhill to Bell, 15 Apr. 1927.
78 Underhill, 'Liberal Arts,' 2, 11.
79 Kenneth McNaught, 'Underhill: A Personal Interpretation,' *Queen's Quarterly* 79, no. 2 (Summer 1972): 130.

7 A New Start

1 University of Saskatchewan Archives, Presidential Papers: Series I [W.C. Murray] (hereafter WMP), MacGibbon to Murray, 23 May 1927.
2 WMP, Skelton to Murray, 19 July 1927.

3 Two years later Rogers did go to Queen's but eventually left to enter politics. Upon election to Parliament in 1935, he became a cabinet minister in the King government.

4 WMP, James A. Blaestell to Murray, 24 May 1927.

5 Dawson and Clokie taught at Rutgers, a privately run institution, during a period of upheaval which was marked by the transition from the presidency of William H.S. Demerest to that of John Martin Thomas and by intense debates about the relationship of Rutgers to the state and the development of its curriculum in the direction of vocational training. Richard P. McCormick, *Rutgers: A Bicentennial History* (New Brunswick, N.J.: Rutgers University Press 1966), 149, 214.

6 WMP, Hugh McD. Clokie to Murray, 16 Apr. 1924.

7 WMP, Clokie to Murray, 14 Nov. 1927.

8 WMP, W.B. Munro to Murray, 7 June 1927. When Clokie applied ten years later to teach political science at Saskatchewan, he was described by Dawson as having 'genuine ability' but 'too much English reserve.' University of Saskatchewan Archives, Presidential Papers: Series II [J.S. Thomson] (hereafter JTP), Dawson to J.S. Thomson, 8 Nov. 1937.

9 WMP, Skelton to Murray, 19 July 1927.

10 WMP, MacGibbon to Murray, 23 May 1927.

11 WMP, Murray to MacGibbon, 26 May 1927.

12 WMP, MacGibbon to Murray, 28 May 1927.

13 WMP, Graham Wallas to George Ling, 16 Jan. 1921.

14 WMP, Ling to Murray, 19 Mar. [1921].

15 WMP, Dawson to Murray, 14 Feb. 1925.

16 Norman Ward, 'Notes for Shirley Spafford' [1981], 5.

17 WMP, Murray to Dawson, 20 July 1927.

18 WMP, Murray to T.J. Hébert, 13 July 1927.

19 WMP, Dawson to Murray, telegram, 23 Apr. 1928.

20 G.E. Wilson, 'Robert MacGregor Dawson, 1895–1958,' *Canadian Journal of Economics and Political Science* 25, no. 2 (May 1959): 212.

21 WMP, Dawson application, copy of testimonial by J.E. Todd [1921].

22 Adam Shortt, review in *Dalhousie Review* 3 (1923–4): 127.

23 W.S. Wallace, review in *Canadian Historical Review* 4 (1923): 82.

24 Dalhousie University Archives, R. MacGregor Dawson Papers (hereafter RMDP), Jim Braden, 'White-Haired and Fiery,' 13 Jan. 1950, clipping.

25 National Archives of Canada, Frank Underhill Papers, MG30 D204 (hereafter FUP), Eaton to Underhill, 4 Dec. 1928.

26 RMDP, 'Planning Maritime Future,' 22 Apr. 1944, clipping.

27 Ward, 'Notes,' 1.

28 Ibid., 1, 5.
29 V.W. Bladen, 'Robert MacGregor Dawson, 1895–1958,' *Proceedings and Transactions of the Royal Society of Canada* 3rd ser., 54 (1960): 110–11.
30 Ward, 'Notes,' 1.
31 Michael Hayden, *Seeking a Balance: The University of Saskatchewan, 1907–1982* (Vancouver: University of British Columbia Press 1983), 219.
32 Robert Dawson, letter to the author, 23 Nov. 1980.
33 Queen's University Archives, Lorne Pierce Papers, Swanson to Lorne Pierce, [Nov. 1947].
34 WMP, Murray to Dawson, 7 Aug. 1929.
35 See W.A.M., 'Douglas Alexander Skelton, 1906–1950,' *Canadian Journal of Economics and Political Science* 17, no. 1 (Feb. 1951): 89–91.
36 RMDP, Application for Guggenheim Fellowship, 22 Oct. 1948.
37 Ward, 'Notes,' 3.
38 J.A. Corry, 'Robert MacGregor Dawson,' *Canadian Historical Review* 40 (1959): 90.
39 Ward, 'Notes,' 2.
40 Vincent Bladen, *Bladen on Bladen: Memoirs of a Political Economist* ([Scarborough, Ont.]: Scarborough College in the University of Toronto 1978), 71.
41 Robert MacKay, review in *Dalhousie Review* 10 (1930–1): 134–5.
42 Underhill, 'Our Civil Service,' *Canadian Forum* 10 (1930): 291.
43 RMDP, Robert Borden to Dawson, 2 Dec. 1930.
44 RMDP, Dawson to Borden, 6 Dec. 1930.
45 Ward, 'Notes,' 5.
46 FUP, Underhill to Dawson, 19 Dec. 1934. The reference is to John W. Dafoe, editor of the *Winnipeg Free Press* from 1901 to 1948.
47 FUP, Dawson to Underhill, 8 Jan. 1935.
48 W.P.M. Kennedy, review in *Canadian Historical Review* 19 (1938): 65.
49 P.E. Corbett, review in *Canadian Journal of Economics and Political Science* 4 (1938): 114.
50 JTP, Dawson to Thomson, 8 Nov. 1937.
51 See Eleanor Harmon, 'Founding a University Press,' in Eleanor Harmon, ed., *The University as Publisher* (Toronto: University of Toronto Press 1961), 35.
52 C.B. Macpherson, 'After Strange Gods: Canadian Political Science 1973,' in T.N. Guinsberg and G.L. Reuber, eds, *Perspectives on the Social Sciences in Canada* (Toronto: University of Toronto Press 1974), 65.

8 Three Colleagues

1 University of Saskatchewan, *President's Report*, 1934–5, 7–8.

2 University of Saskatchewan Archives, M.F. Timlin Papers (hereafter MTP), Christmas Letters, 4 Dec. 1973.
3 MTP, Christmas Letters, 8 Dec. 1969.
4 MTP, W. Chipping to Timlin, 13 June 1918.
5 MTP, Timlin to 'Cyril' [Timlin], 25 Nov. 1918.
6 MTP, Timlin to J.W.T. Spinks, 8 Apr. 1961.
7 When she retired, she was distressed to find that the administration had chosen to disregard her service to the university during these years and for the purposes of her pension had calculated her employment to have started only after she had become a regular member of the economics department. MTP, Timlin to K.A.H. Buckley, 23 Sept. 1958.
8 Barber, who was born near Wolsely, Saskatchewan, joined the Department of Economics at the University of Manitoba in 1949 and served as head of the department from 1963 to 1972. H.C. Pentland, *The University of Manitoba Department of Economics: A Brief History* (University of Manitoba 1977), 7. For Deutsch, see p. 228.
9 Betty Ward, letter to the author, enclosure re V.C. Fowke, 19 July 1978. I am indebted to Betty Ward for preparing for me a brief biography of Vernon Fowke based on her recollections and conversations with Helen Fowke.
10 University of Saskatchewan Archives, Presidential Papers: Series I [W.C. Murray] (hereafter WMP), H.H. Preston to Murray, 3 July 1935.
11 University of Saskatchewan Archives, G.E. Britnell Papers (hereafter GBP), Britnell to H.D. Woods, 20 Mar. 1940.
12 GBP, Lecture Notes.
13 V.C. Fowke, 'George Edwin Britnell, 1903–1961,' *Canadian Journal of Economics and Political Science* 28, no. 2 (May 1962): 283–4.
14 WMP, Britnell to Murray, telegram, 3 Aug. 1930.
15 University of Saskatchewan Archives, A.S. Morton Papers (hereafter AMP), Morton to Professor Brett, 22 Apr. 1933.
16 WMP, letter in support of application for IODE scholarship for G.E. Britnell, 5 Dec. 1928; Murray to G.E. Jackson, 5 Apr. 1933.
17 WMP, Murray to Geo. Douglas, 27 Sept. 1930.
18 Carl Berger, *The Writing of Canadian History: Aspects of English-Canadian Historical Writings, 1900–1970* (Toronto: Oxford University Press 1976), 85 and passim.
19 Fowke, 'George Edwin Britnell,' 283.
20 Quoted in Berger, *Writing of Canadian History*, 103.
21 Robin Neill, letter to the author, 19 Jan. 1981.
22 GBP, Britnell to N.A.M. Mackenzie, 27 Feb. 1954.
23 For more on the role of the University of Toronto in the development of

research and scholarship in the social sciences in Canada during this period, see Ian M. Drummond, *Political Economy at the University of Toronto: A History of the Department, 1888–1982* (Toronto: Faculty of Arts and Science, University of Toronto 1983), 73–80.

24 GBP, Innis to C.M. Coyne, 8 Aug. 1936.
25 GBP, Innis to Britnell, 3 Aug. 1935.
26 GBP, Britnell to Murray, 14 Jan. 1936.
27 H.A. Innis, ed., *The Diary of Alexander James McPhail* (Toronto: University of Toronto Press 1940).
28 GBP, Britnell to McQueen, 23 Sept. 1936.
29 Corry was born in rural Ontario, came to Saskatchewan to study law (an uncle was university registrar), and attended Oxford as a Rhodes scholar, afterwards returning to Saskatchewan as professor of law. Finding his interest in private law diminishing, he moved to Queen's to teach political science in 1936. Corry in his memoirs, *My Life & Work, A Happy Partnership: Memoirs of J.A. Corry* (Kingston: Queen's University 1981), 38, writes of his student days in the Saskatchewan law school and its 'extraordinary *esprit de corps*, never since equalled in my observation of student bodies.' Frederick W. Gibson, *To Serve and Yet Be Free: Queen's University, 1917–1961*, vol. 2 of Hilda Neatby, *Queen's University: To Strive, to Seek, to Find, and Not to Yield*, Frederick W. Gibson and Roger Graham, eds (Montreal: McGill-Queen's University Press 1978–83), 417 and ff, says that Corry in June 1959 was offered the presidency of the University of Saskatchewan, setting off a complicated series of events which led to Corry's appointment as principal of Queen's University. In an obituary notice, Jeffrey Simpson calls Corry 'one of the remarkable breed of citizens from that province [Saskatchewan] who so enriched the public life of Canada after the Second World War' and refers to Corry and John Deutsch, his successor to the office of principal at Queen's, as members of 'what later became known in Ottawa as the "Saskatchewan Mafia."' 'James A. Corry,' *Globe and Mail*, 28 Dec. 1985.
30 G.E. Britnell, 'Profit and Loss: The Depression in Rural Saskatchewan,' in H.A. Innis and A.F.W. Plumptre, eds, *The Canadian Economy and Its Problems* (Toronto: University of Toronto Press 1934), 97–110; *The Western Farmer*, Machine Age Series, pamphlet no. 6 (Toronto: Social Service Council of Canada 1935); 'Saskatchewan, 1930–1935,' *Canadian Journal of Economics and Political Science* 2, no. 2 (May 1936): 143–66; 'Agricultural Debt Adjustment in Canada: A Note,' *Canadian Journal of Economics and Political Science* 2, no. 3 (Aug. 1936): 402–3; 'The Prairie Frontier,' *American Economic Review* 26 (Sept. 1936): 524–32; 'Alberta, Economic and Political: The Elliott-Walker Report,' *Canadian Journal of Economics and Political Science* 2, no. 4 (Nov.

1936): 524–32; 'The Colonization of Canada: A Review Article,' *Canadian Historical Review* 27, no. 1 (Mar. 1937): 71–4; 'The Saskatchewan Debt Adjustment Programme,' *Canadian Journal of Economics and Political Science* 3, no. 3 (Aug. 1937): 370–5; 'The Rehabilitation of the Prairie Wheat Economy,' *Canadian Journal of Economics and Political Science* 3, no. 4 (Nov. 1937): 508–29.

31 GBP, H. Heaton to Britnell, 4 Mar. 1938.
32 GBP, H.D. Woods to Britnell, [1938].
33 GBP, Innis to Britnell, 3 Feb. 1938.
34 GBP, Britnell to G.M.A. Grube, 4 June 1938.
35 Corry, *My Life & Work*, 107–8.
36 GBP, Innis to Britnell, [1939].
37 GBP, Woods to Britnell, 28 Jan. 1940.
38 G.E. Britnell, *The Wheat Economy* (Toronto: University of Toronto Press 1939), 240–1.
39 Joseph S. Davis, review in *American Economic Review* 39 (1939): 837–8.
40 GBP, Colin E. Henderson to Britnell, 24 Oct. 1945.

9 Wartime

1 Quotations from James G. Greenlee, *Sir Robert Falconer: A Biography* (Toronto: University of Toronto Press 1988), 326, 331, and David R. Murray and Robert A. Murray, *The Prairie Builder: Walter Murray of Saskatchewan* (Edmonton: NeWest Press 1984), 238.

2 Aitchison took his schooling in Saskatoon and went to the university with the intention of taking medicine but was eventually diverted towards a career in political science. Aitchison remembers taking Underhill's first course in political science at Saskatchewan, and later, when he went to teach high school at Prince Albert Collegiate Institute, he took a correspondence course in political science from R. MacGregor Dawson. Afterwards, he taught economics at McMaster University, where he introduced a student named Norman Ward to Dawson. Aitchison later joined the political science faculty at Dalhousie. Conversation with the author, 9 Aug. 1982. S.D. Clark, a classmate and lifelong friend of George Britnell, took a BA and MA from the University of Saskatchewan, where he studied under A.S. Morton, R. McQueen, and Dawson. He wrote an MA thesis on 'Settlement in Saskatchewan with Special Reference to Dry Farming,' and received a PhD in economics and political science from the University of Toronto in 1938. He taught sociology at Toronto until his retirement in 1976. See Deborah Harrison, *The Limits of Liberalism: The Making of Canadian Sociology* (Montreal: Black Rose Books 1981), and Harry H. Hiller, *Society and Change:*

S.D. Clark and the Development of Canadian Sociology (Toronto: University of Toronto Press 1982).

3 University of Saskatchewan Archives, Presidential Papers: Series I [W.C. Murray] (hereafter WMP), Murray to G. Curtis, 20 Apr. 1927.

4 University of Saskatchewan, Department of Economics and Political Science, 'Timlin' file, M.F. Timlin, 'The Teaching of Economics in the University of Saskatchewan,' 4.

5 University of Saskatchewan Archives, M.F. Timlin Papers (hereafter MTP), Timlin to Preston, 29 Mar. 1938.

6 University of Saskatchewan Archives, G.E. Britnell Papers (hereafter GBP), Britnell to Innis, 20 Feb. 1938.

7 GBP, Innis to Britnell, [Mar. 1938].

8 GBP, Britnell to J.S. Davis, 7 Oct. 1939.

9 GBP, Kathleen Holtby to Britnell, 26 Oct. 1941.

10 GBP, Britnell to G.R. Elliott, 18 Jan. 1939.

11 GBP, Corry to Britnell, 10 Jan. 1939.

12 GBP, Britnell to Corry, 7 Jan. 1939.

13 University of Saskatchewan, *Calendar*, 1941–2, 92.

14 GBP, Britnell to David Lewis, 7 June 1938.

15 'Three Months on Brief,' *Leader-Post*, 14 Dec. 1937.

16 Canada, House of Commons, *Hansard*, 27 Feb. 1939, 1471.

17 GBP, Dawson to Britnell, 8 Dec. 1937.

18 GBP, Britnell to Corry, 10 May 1939.

19 V.C. Fowke, 'George Edwin Britnell, 1903–1961,' *Canadian Journal of Economics and Political Science* 28, no. 2 (May 1962): 286.

20 GBP, Britnell to F.C. Cronkite, 16 June 1938.

21 GBP, Frank Eliason to Britnell, 22 Oct. 1941.

22 Arthur R.M. Lower, *My First Seventy-Five Years* (Toronto: Macmillan 1967), 256.

23 MTP, Britnell to Timlin, 11 Feb. 1942.

24 MTP, Timlin to Britnell, 13 Dec. 1942.

25 University of Saskatchewan Archives, Presidential Papers: Series II [J.S. Thomson] (hereafter JTP), C.P. Wright to Thomson, 19 July 1938.

26 Wright had one short piece published during his year at Saskatchewan, 'Report of the Royal Grain Inquiry Commission, 1938,' *Canadian Journal of Economics and Political Science* (1939): 229–32.

27 GBP, Innis to Britnell, 12 Apr. 1939.

28 GBP, Britnell to Mackintosh, 13 Feb. 1939. The textbook referred to is Frederic B. Garver and Alvin H. Hansen, *Principles of Economics* (Minneapolis, Minn.: Perine Book 1926).

29 MTP, Timlin to Preston, 14 Dec. 1938.
30 JTP, Thomson to Wright, 29 Apr. 1939.
31 MTP, Timlin to Preston, 15 Apr. 1939.
32 GBP, Frank Burton to Britnell, 13 Sept. [1936].
33 JTP, McQueen to Thomson, 22 Apr. 1938.
34 JTP, W.A. Mackintosh to Thomson, 18 Apr. 1938.
35 Benjamin Higgins, *All the Difference: A Development Economist's Quest* (Montreal: McGill-Queen's University Press 1992), 9–10. Higgins remembered Timlin as one 'who hid a razor-sharp mind behind a rather matronly appearance and manner, and who wrote one of the very first and one of the very best books explaining and criticizing Keynes's *General Theory*.'
36 MTP, Desyl Mikesell to Timlin, 25 May 1941. Ray Mikesell went on to work for the U.S. treasury department, before returning to university teaching, first at the University of Virginia, later at the University of Oregon. Tipton R. Snavely, *The Department of Economics at the University of Virginia, 1825–1956* (Charlottesville: University Press of Virginia 1967), 171.
37 MTP, Oscar Lange, 'Appraisal of M.F. Timlin's "Keynesian Economics: A Synthesis,"' undated.
38 Mabel F. Timlin, *Keynesian Economics* (Toronto: University of Toronto Press 1942; repr. 1948). The 1977 reissue of *Keynesian Economics* (Toronto: McClelland and Stewart 1977, Carleton Library no. 107) includes a foreword by L. Tarshis and a fine biographical note by A.E. Safarian.
39 MTP, J.M. Keynes to Timlin, 7 Nov. 1943.
40 MTP, Lange to Timlin, 21 Jan. 1943.
41 Harry G. Johnson, 'Canadian Contributions to the Discipline of Economics since 1945,' *Canadian Journal of Economics* 1, no. 1 (Feb. 1968): 131. The other book mentioned by Johnson is B.S. Keirstead's *Essentials of Price Theory* (Toronto: University of Toronto Press 1942; repr. 1947).
42 Tom Wilson, review in *Economic Journal* 53 (1943): 224, 226.
43 Abba P. Lerner, review in *Journal of Political Economy* 52 (1944): 80.
44 R.M. Goodwin, review in *Review of Economic Statistics* 26 (1944): 162.
45 G. Haberler, review in *Canadian Journal of Economics and Political Science* 10 (1944): 104, 103.
46 G.L.S. Shackle, review in *Economica* 10 (1943): 260.
47 MTP, Innis to Timlin, 28 Apr. 1941; Timlin to Innis, 8 May 1941.
48 GBP, Fowke to Britnell, 24 Oct. 1940.
49 University of Saskatchewan Archives, V.C. Fowke Papers (hereafter VFP), Fowke to Preston, 20 May 1941.
50 Stanley Brice Frost, *McGill University: For the Advancement of Learning*, vol. 2, 1895–1971 (Kingston: McGill-Queen's University Press 1984), 219. J.S.

Thomson left the University of Saskatchewan in 1949 to become dean of the first Faculty of Divinity at McGill.

51 Vincent Bladen, *Bladen on Bladen: Memoirs of a Political Economist* ([Scarborough, Ont.]: Scarborough College in the University of Toronto 1978), 92. Clerc became a close friend of Mabel Timlin.

52 June and Merrill Menzies, conversation with the author, 20 May 1983. S. Mack Eastman held degrees in history from the University of Toronto and Columbia University and was head of the Department of History at the University of British Columbia from 1919 to 1925. While at Saskatchewan, he wrote *Canada at Geneva: An Historical Survey and Its Lessons* (Toronto: Ryerson Press 1946).

53 VFP, Britnell to Fowke, 26 Jan. 1941.

54 GBP, Fowke to W.J. Waines, 9 Dec. 1945.

55 University of Saskatchewan, *Calendar*, 1950–1, 128.

56 VFP, 'Political Economy A,' nd.

57 GBP, Britnell to Waines, 9 Dec. 1948.

58 GBP, Fowke to Britnell, 11 Dec. 1942; Timlin to Britnell, 13 Feb. 1943; Timlin to 'George and Mae' [Britnell], 13 Dec. 1942; Fowke to Britnell, 11 Dec. 1942.

59 MTP, Timlin to Preston, 16 Dec. 1940.

60 VFP, Britnell to Fowke, 26 Jan. 1941.

61 GBP, Britnell to Timlin, 31 Mar. 1943.

62 VFP, Timlin to Fowke, 24 June 1943.

63 GBP, Britnell to Morton, 28 Nov. 1944.

10 Union and the New Members

1 University of Saskatchewan Archives, Department of Economics and Political Science Papers, Memorandum on the union of the Departments of Economics and Political Science, 19 Feb. 1946.

2 University of Saskatchewan Archives, M.F. Timlin Papers (hereafter MTP), Timlin to Britnell, 2 Dec. 1945.

3 University of Saskatchewan, *Annual Report*, 1945–6, 72–3.

4 University of Saskatchewan, *Annual Report*, 1948–9, 54.

5 MTP, Britnell to Timlin, 12 Jan. 1946.

6 George B. Sanderson, who was killed on active service with the Royal Canadian Air Force, bequeathed the scholarship to be known as the Benjamin J. Sanderson Fellowship to the University of Saskatchewan. Originally from Saskatoon, he had studied at the University of British Columbia and had taken a PhD in economics from the London School of Economics

and Political Science. He expressed in his will the wish 'that the young men selected ... would return eventually to Western Canada to use their knowledge of Economics and Political Theory to benefit of their community.' Candidates were to have the characteristics of 'idealism rather than ambition; scholastic achievement; humanitarian views.' He also gave to the university a valuable collection of 150 books on economics and politics. University of Saskatchewan, Department of Economics and Political Science, 'Book Gift to Varsity,' *Star-Phoenix*, 26 June 1946, clipping; University of Saskatchewan, 'Report of Sub-Committee of the Committee on Scholarships and Awards,' 13 June 1946. Holders of the Sanderson Fellowship to 1962 were: Kenneth Buckley, Merrill Menzies, Harry Halliwell, John Downs, Jack McLeod, Kenneth Rea, Duff Spafford, and Gordon Thiessen.

7 In addition to the Sanderson Fellows, Saskatchewan students of this period who went on to postgraduate studies in economics included: Fred W. Anderson, June Green (later Menzies), Tanyss Bell (later Phillips), Evelyn L. Eager, G.R. Elliott, E.P. Neufeld, D.B. Climenhaga, C.M. Chesney, A.W. Wood, Thomas Powrie, Isabel Anderson, John Floyd, Marvin McInnis, and Thomas Courchene.

8 University of Saskatchewan Archives, V.C. Fowke Papers (hereafter VFP), J. Woodley to Fowke, 7 Oct., 14 Dec. 1945.

9 MTP, K.J. Rea to Timlin, 11 Jan. 1958.

10 John Floyd, e-mail to the author, 15 June 1998.

11 Gordon Thiessen, letter to the author, 5 Jan. 1999.

12 University of Saskatchewan Archives, Department of Economics and Political Science Papers, 'Should Economics and Political Science Be Separate Departments,' Memorandum to the Special Council Committee [1956].

13 Ibid.

14 Department of Economics and Political Science, Memorandum re A.N. Reid, 'Reid' file.

15 Department of Economics and Political Science, J.S.M. Allely to Britnell, 20 Feb. 1946, 'Allely' file.

16 Ibid.

17 Ibid.

18 See Margaret Sanche, *Heartwood: A History of St. Thomas More College and Newman Centre at the University of Saskatchewan* (Muenster, Sask.: St Peter's Press 1986). I am grateful to Margaret Sanche for providing me with information about the Basilian Fathers who taught economics and political science at St Thomas More College. Books by Neill are *A New Theory of Value* (see p. 250, n3) and *A History of Canadian Economic Thought* (London and New York: Routledge 1991).

19 University of Saskatchewan Archives, Presidential Papers: Series I [W.C. Murray] (hereafter WMP), Charles McCool to Murray, 7 Feb. 1936.

20 MTP, Timlin to Donald Gordon, 15 Mar. 1948; University of Saskatchewan Archives, G.E. Britnell Papers (hereafter GBP), Britnell to K.A.H. Buckley, 27 May 1948.

21 MTP, Hugh Thorburn to Timlin, 15 June 1970.

22 GBP, Britnell to R.S. Elliott, 24 Nov. 1959.

23 K.A.H Buckley, *Capital Formation in Canada, 1896–1930* ([Toronto]: University of Toronto Press 1955; repr. McClelland and Stewart, Carleton Library 1974) and M.C. Urquhart and K.A.H. Buckley, eds, *Historical Statistics of Canada* (Cambridge: Cambridge University Press 1965). Buckley also wrote, with Helen Buckley, a high-school text, *Economics for Canadians* (Toronto: Macmillan 1960; rev. 1968). Papers left by Buckley in the keeping of the Saskatchewan Archives are described by Isabel Anderson in 'Kenneth Buckley's Research Papers,' University of Saskatchewan, Department of Economics and Political Science, June 1974.

24 Gordon Thiessen, letter to the author, 5 Jan. 1999; and Duff Spafford, quoted in Michael Taft, ed., *Inside These Greystone Walls: An Anecdotal History of the University of Saskatchewan* ([Saskatoon]: University of Saskatchewan 1984), 165.

25 R.R. March and R.J. Jackson, 'Aspects of the State of Political Science in Canada,' *Midwest Journal of Political Science* 11, no. 4 (Nov. 1967): 443.

26 'A Conversation with Norman Ward,' *Green and White*, Spring 1985, 9.

27 Ibid.

28 Norman Ward to C.M. Johnston, 15 Oct. 1974. I am grateful to Richard Rempel for passing on to me correspondence with Johnston in which Ward recalls his time as a student at McMaster. About his pacifism, Ward said that he worried himself into an ulcer, which got steadily worse and finally led him to spend most of 1943–4 as a patient and convalescent, ironically allowing him 'to escape a decision about being conscripted.'

29 National Archives of Canada, Frank Underhill Papers, MG30 D204 (hereafter FUP), Ward to Underhill, 24 Mar. 1961.

30 'Conversation with Norman Ward,' 9.

31 Shirley Spafford, 'Norman Ward: A Selected Bibliography,' in John C. Courtney, ed., *The Canadian House of Commons: Essays in Honour of Norman Ward* (Calgary: University of Calgary Press 1985), 201–14.

32 Norman Ward, 'Notes for Shirley Spafford' [1981], 2.

33 University of Saskatchewan Archives, Presidential Papers: Series II [J.S. Thomson] (hereafter JTP), Report of the Department of Economics and Political Science, 30 June 1949.

34 Dalhousie University Archives, R. MacGregor Dawson Papers (hereafter RMDP), Dawson to Ward 17 Jan. 1949.
35 RMDP, Ward to Dawson, 11 Jan. 1949.
36 'Conversation with Norman Ward,' 9.
37 Norman Ward, 'Special Significance in Year for Retirees,' *Star-Phoenix*, U of S 75th Anniversary, 1984.
38 Norman Ward, 'On with the New,' in *Mice in the Beer* (Winnipeg: Longmans, Windjammer edition 1970), 94.
39 Hugh G. Thorburn, 'Political Science in Canada: Graduate Studies and Research,' typed manuscript, Mar. 1975, 11.
40 Department of Economics and Political Science, Ward to G.M. Shrum, 9 Oct. 1959, 'Ward' file.
41 FUP, Ward to Underhill, 29 Apr. 1962.
42 Department of Economics and Political Science, Ward to D.D. Tansley, 17 Feb. 1956, 'Ward' file.
43 Charles W. Shull, review in *Southwestern Social Science Quarterly* 32, no. 3 (Dec. 1951).
44 J.R. Mallory, reviews in *Canadian Journal of Economics and Political Science* 17, no. 3 (Aug. 1951): 412; and *Canadian Forum* 31 (Feb. 1951): 259.
45 Alexander Brady, review in *University of Toronto Quarterly* 20, no. 3 (Apr. 1951): 285.
46 FUP, Ward to Underhill, 11 Apr. 1962.
47 Joan Walker, 'She laughed Till She Cried,' *Globe and Mail*, 10 Dec. 1960.
48 Eugene Forsey, 'Parliamentary Reform Is More Than Mechanics,' in Courtney, ed., *The Canadian House of Commons*, 195. Ward greatly admired Forsey for his lore and acumen as the watchdog of the Canadian parliamentary system.
49 Neil M. Agnew and Sandra W. Pyke, *The Science Game: An Introduction to Research in the Behavioral Sciences* (Englewood Cliffs, N.J.: Prentice Hall 1969), viii.
50 Bobs Caldwell, quoted in Taft, ed., *Inside These Greystone Walls*, 203.
51 Duff Spafford, 'Tribute to Norman Ward, Memorial Service, Convocation Hall, February 9, 1990,' *Vox*, no. 6 (Apr. 1990), 2.
52 GBP, Memorandum re a permanent appointment in sociology, Feb. 1954.
53 Roger Carter, who acted as counsel for Cooperstock at the hearing, confirmed this account in a telephone conversation with the author, 14 May 1984.
54 Department of Economics and Political Science, Memorandum to the Committee on Forward Planning, 31 Mar. 1956, 4.
55 GBP, Memorandum re a permanent appointment in sociology, Feb. 1954.

11 The Britnell Years

1 K.W. Taylor, *Fifty Years of Canadian Economics*, Jubilee Lecture, University of Saskatchewan , 28 September 1959, 17. The lecture was afterwards published as 'Economic Scholarship in Canada,' *Canadian Journal of Economics and Political Science* 26, no. 1 (Feb. 1960): 6–18, with the specific references to the Saskatchewan department taken out.

2 University of Saskatchewan Archives, G.E. Britnell Papers (hereafter GBP), K.W. Taylor to Britnell, 20 Mar. 1960.

3 University of Saskatchewan Archives, Presidential Papers: Series II [J.S. Thomson] (hereafter JTP), J.B. Brebner to Thomson, 16 Nov. 1945.

4 University of Saskatchewan Archives, M.F. Timlin Papers (hereafter MTP), Timlin to Britnell, 14 Nov. 1945.

5 MTP, Timlin to Britnell, 2 Dec. 1945.

6 University of Saskatchewan Archives, V.C. Fowke Papers (hereafter VFP), A.F.W. Plumptre to Fowke, 4 Sept. 1941.

7 MTP, Timlin to B.S. Keirstead, 30 Apr. 1948.

8 MTP, Timlin to J.W.T. Spinks, 8 Apr. 1961.

9 University of Saskatchewan, Department of Economics and Political Science, Timlin to Britnell, memorandum, 7 June 1952, 'Timlin' file.

10 MTP, Timlin to C.C. Lingard, 2 Dec. 1949.

11 Mabel Timlin, *Does Canada Need More People?* (Toronto: Oxford University Press; published under the auspices of the Canadian Institute of International Affairs 1951).

12 MFT, handwritten notes on news release, 'The Honourable Mitchell Sharp,' Department of External Affairs, Apr. 1971.

13 The Canadian historian Hilda Neatby, also a Saskatchewan graduate who became a faculty member, was, in 1957, the second woman to be elected to Section II (the humanities and social sciences section) of the Royal Society of Canada.

14 Mabel F. Timlin and Albert Faucher, *The Social Sciences in Canada: Two Studies/Les sciences sociales au Canada: Deux études* (Ottawa: Social Science Research Council of Canada 1968). See Donald Fisher, *The Social Sciences in Canada: Fifty Years of National Activity* (Waterloo, Ont.: Wilfrid Laurier University Press 1991), esp. 52–5.

15 Duff Spafford, 'In Memoriam: Mabel F. Timlin.' *Canadian Journal of Economics* 10, no. 2 (May 1977): 279–81.

16 MTP, Timlin to Britnell, 2 Dec. 1945.

17 MTP, Timlin to Henry Allen Moe, 20 Sept. 1948.

18 V.C. Fowke, review of Paul F.. Sharp, *Agrarian Revolt in Western Canada*, in *Saskatchewan History* 11, no. 1 (Winter 1949): 33.
19 V.C. Fowke, 'An Introduction to Canadian Agricultural History,' *Canadian Journal of Economics and Political Science* 8, no. 1 (Feb. 1942): 57.
20 Ibid.
21 Betty Ward, letter to the author, 19 July 1978.
22 Paul Phillips, 'The Man of Saskatchewan' [1980], 9–20, unpublished manuscript.
23 Quoted in 'Dr. Vernon C. Fowke,' *Western Producer*, 10 Mar. 1966.
24 VFP, Fowke to Preston, 11 Sept. 1944.
25 W.J. Waines, review in *Canadian Historical Review* 28 (1947): 81–2.
26 VFP, Clark to Fowke, enclosure, 21 June 1954.
27 V.C. Fowke, *The National Policy and the Wheat Economy* (Toronto: University of Toronto Press 1957; repr. 1973).
28 W.L. Morton, review in *Canadian Historical Review* 39 (1958): 342.
29 Fowke, *National Policy*, 296.
30 Morton, review in *Canadian Historical Review*, 343
31 Fowke, *National Policy*, 296.
32 VFP, V.C. Fowke, 'Political Economy and Christianity,' typed address, Winter 1955.
33 Paul Phillips, 'Vernon Fowke: A Retrospective,' *NeWest Review*, May 1982, and 'The Hinterland Perspective: The Political Economy of Vernon C. Fowke,' *Canadian Journal of Political and Social Theory* 2, no. 2 (Spring/Summer 1978): 73–95.
34 GBP, Britnell to Robert M. Hardy, 31 Dec. 1959.
35 Quoted in Phillips, 'Man of Saskatchewan,' 19.
36 Department of Economics and Political Science, Fowke to R. Brown, 10 Oct. 1963, 'Fowke' file.
37 University of Saskatchewan Archives, Department of Economics and Political Science Papers, Fowke to Britnell, 10 June 1947.
38 Ibid.
39 VFP, 'Personal – to G.E. Britnell' [1947].
40 V.C. Fowke, 'The Function of a University,' *Sheaf*, 4 Mar. 1947.
41 Phillips, 'Vernon Fowke: A Retrospective.'
42 On the organization of university teachers in Canada, see V.C. Fowke, 'Professional Association: A History of the C.A.U.T.,' in George Whalley, ed., *A Place of Liberty: Essays on the Government of Canadian Universities* (Toronto: Clarke, Irwin 1964), app. B, 195–215.
43 See 'Report on the Crowe Case,' *C.A.U.T. Bulletin* 7, no. 3 (Jan. 1959) and

Bora Laskin, 'Some Cases at Law,' in *A Place of Liberty*, 188–94. David J. Bercuson, Robert Bothwell, and J.L. Granatstein, *The Great Brain Robbery: Canada's Universities on the Road to Ruin* (Toronto: McClelland and Stewart 1984), 93, assert that the Crowe case 'led inexorably to the establishment of tenure in Canadian universities,' a practice they judge to be detrimental to the quality of university teaching in Canada.

44 Alan Cairns, 'Memo re Hiring Practices in the "Old Days,"' 8 Dec. 1998. Britnell wrote afterwards to A. Brady: 'I am still sorry I was not able to compete with British Columbia's climate for Alan Cairns (at least I like to think it must have been the climate that was my undoing).' GBP, 6 Sept. 1960,

45 A.E. Safarian, *The Canadian Economy in the Great Depression* (Toronto: University of Toronto Press 1959; repr. McClelland and Stewart, Carleton Library 1970), and *Foreign Ownership of Canadian Industry* (Toronto: McGraw Hill 1966; repr. University of Toronto Press 1973). Later publications include: *Foreign Ownership and the Structure of Canadian Industry*, co-author, Report of the Task Force on the Structure of Canadian Industry (Ottawa: Privy Council Office 1968); *The Performance of Foreign-Owned Firms in Canada* (Montreal: Canadian-American Committee 1969); *Canadian Federalism and Economic Integration* (Ottawa: Privy Council Office 1974); *Governments and Multinationals: Policies in the Developed Countries* (Washington, D.C.: British North-American Committee 1983); *FIRA and FIRB: Canadian and Australian Policies on Foreign Direct Investment* (Toronto: Ontario Economic Council/University of Toronto Press 1985); *Multinational Enterprise and Public Policy: A Study of the Industrial Countries* (Aldershot, Hants., Eng.: Edward Elgar Publishing 1993), in addition to edited books, chapters in books, articles in refereed journals, papers presented to conferences and in refereed proceedings, and many other publications and reviews.

46 University of Saskatchewan Archives, 'A.E. Safarian' file, 'He Says Foreign Ownership Is Good for Us,' *Canadian*, 16 Apr. 1966, clipping.

47 Kenneth J. Rea, *The Political Economy of the Canadian North: An Interpretation of the Course of Development in the Northern Territories of Canada to the Early 1960's* (Toronto: University of Toronto Press 1968). Other publications include *The Political Economy of Northern Development* (Ottawa: Science Council of Canada 1976), and *The Prosperous Years: The Economic History of Ontario, 1939–1975* (Toronto: University of Toronto Press 1985); two anthologies – *Business and Government in Canada* (Toronto: Methuen 1969; rev. and repr. 1976), co-edited with J.T. McLeod; and *Government and Enterprise in Canada* (Toronto: Methuen 1985), co-edited with N. Wiseman; and a text entitled *A Guide to Canadian Economic History* (Canadian Scholars Press 1991).

48 Bernard Crick, letter to the author, 17 June 1986.

49 Hugh Thorburn, letter to the author, 29 July 1986.
50 Ibid.
51 A.E. Safarian, letter to the author, 27 Mar. 1980. Within the university, the department was held in generally high regard. McMaster historian Richard Rempel, who took double honours in economics and history at the University of Saskatchewan during the 1950s, recollects that his father, J.G. Rempel, a biology professor, spoke highly of Britnell and his colleagues and thought them 'more professional' than others in the College of Arts and Science. Conversation with the author, 15 Aug. 1998.
52 GBP, Britnell to Colin Henderson, 19 Mar. 1937; Britnell to Timlin, 31 Mar. 1943.
53 GBP, Britnell to R.C. Epstein, nd. Britnell's misgivings about mathematical economics were not so unusual at the time. Richard Lipsey, a Canadian who was to have a distinguished career as an economic theorist, recalls that in his third year as an honours student at the University of British Columbia he suggested learning some mathematics, to which his professor, Joseph Crumb, replied, 'No ... economics is based on the three pillars of history, accounting and statistical analysis; learn those as outside courses but do not waste time on mathematics.' After graduating from UBC in 1950 'still innocent of Keynesian economics,' he went on to Toronto for a master's degree where the deficiency was repaired by William Hood through 'an excellent course in micro-economic theory.' Richard Lipsey, 'Introduction: An Intellectual Autobiography,' *Macroeconomic Theory and Policy: The Selected Essays of Richard G. Lipsey,* vol. 2 (Cheltenham, Eng.: Edward Elgar Publishing 1997), xi–xii.
54 Safarian, letter to the author, 27 Mar., 1980.
55 Gordon Thiessen, letter to the author, 5 Jan. 1999, writes: 'What the department did not provide all that well to an honours course in 1960 was a firm grounding in the new mathematical and statistical tools that had been developed in the post-war period and that were required for more advanced and analytical work in both macro- and micro-economics in the 1960s.'
56 MTP, S.D. Clark to Timlin [no date given].
57 For a selected list of publications by Britnell, see V.C. Fowke, 'George Edwin Britnell, 1903–1961,' *Canadian Journal of Economics and Political Science* 28, no. 2 (May 1962): 289–91.
58 GBP, N.E. Gibbons to Britnell, 25 Sept. 1957; Britnell to Gibbons, 2 Oct. 1957; Britnell to Del Clark, 20 Oct. [1957].
59 MTP, Britnell to F.A. Knox, 16 May 1956.
60 VFP, copy of letter to D.M. Fleming, Minister of Finance, 2 Dec. 1960.

61 'Economists Disagree over Coyne Policies,' *Winnipeg Free Press*, 13 Dec. 1960.
62 GBP, Britnell to Federico Consolo, 5 Aug. 1958.
63 G. Bruce Doern and Glen Toner, *The Politics of Energy: The Development and Implementation of the NEP* (Toronto: Methuen 1985), 74.
64 GBP, Britnell to Douglas Gibson, 24 Oct. 1960.
65 GBP, Britnell to J. Percy Smith, 30 Dec. 1960.
66 Ibid.
67 University of Saskatchewan Archives, 'A.E. Safarian' file, 'Safarian, Tracy Leave U of S Posts,' *Star-Phoenix*, 22 Apr. 1966, clipping. Safarian later became dean of graduate studies at the University of Toronto.
68 MTP, Christmas Letters, 4 Dec. 1973.
69 In 1983, the trustees established an annual lecture series in her honour. The first lecture was presented by A.E. Safarian. For information on the Web devoted to Timlin, see Thomas K. Rymes, 'Timlin and Keynesian Economics' and 'Mabel Timlin's Publications,' and Marianne Gosztonyi Ainley, 'Mabel Frances Timlin, FRSC (1891–1976),' *www.yorku.ca/research/cwen/wemlife.htm*. Mabel Timlin appears as a real-life character in a work of fiction about academic life entitled *Zinger and Me*, written by her former student Jack McLeod (Toronto: McClelland and Stewart 1979).

12 Conclusion

1 Laurence R. Veysey, *The Emergence of the American University* (Chicago: University of Chicago Press 1965), 338, says that 'by 1910 the structure of the American university had assumed its stable twentieth-century form.'
2 University of Saskatchewan, *Calendar*, 1915–16.
3 Robin Neill, *A New Theory of Value: The Canadian Economics of H.A. Innis* (Toronto: University of Toronto Press 1972), 17–18.
4 Ian M. Drummond, *Political Economy at the University of Toronto: A History of the Department, 1888–1982* ([Toronto], University of Toronto Faculty of Arts and Science 1983), 64.
5 Mabel F. Timlin and Albert Faucher, *The Social Sciences in Canada: Two Studies/Les sciences sociales au Canada: Deux études* (Ottawa: Social Science Research Council of Canada 1968), 76. Timlin went on to say: 'The methods for gathering information were somewhat informal. The writer spent the summer of 1941 in an office of the Toronto department rewriting a manuscript. George Britnell was at this time attached to the Wartime Prices and Trade Board in Ottawa and "Pete" McQueen had some years before departed for Queen's University. The writer had hardly arrived on the cam-

pus before she was invited to the Innis home along with a senior member of the Toronto department. Professor Innis proceeded to question her exhaustively concerning everything that had happened on the Saskatchewan campus touching social science or social scientists during the preceding twelve months. Questions in some instances came very close to what might be called an exposure of "dirty linen" of a departmental nature and were answered evasively. A long forelinger was pointed in her direction and a firm voice said, '*You do not need to be so careful!* George Britnell and Pete McQueen have sat right where you are sitting and they have told us everything." After that the proceeding became an annual ritual. The last interview took place in mid-September of 1952, very shortly before Professor Innis's death, and was nearly as lively as the first.'

6 The fourth title was Alexander Brady, *Democracy in the Dominions: A Comparative Study in Institutions* (Toronto: University of Toronto Press 1947).

7 University of Saskatchewan Archives, Presidential Papers Series II [J.S. Thomson], J.S. Thomson to W.W. Swanson, 24 Sept. 1937.

8 Isabel Anderson, 'Kenneth Buckley's Research Papers,' Department of Economics and Political Science, University of Saskatchewan, June 1974, 2.

9 Thomas H. McLeod and Ian McLeod, *Tommy Douglas: The Road to Jerusalem* (Edmonton: Hurtig Publishers 1987), 168.

10 V.C. Fowke, 'Royal Commissions and Canadian Agricultural Policy,' *Canadian Journal of Economics and Political Science* 14, no. 2 (May 1948): 174.

11 Quoted in Doug Owram, *The Government Generation: Canadian Intellectuals and the State, 1900–1945* (Toronto: University of Toronto Press 1986), 200.

12 J. Floyd, e-mail to the author, 15 June 1998.

13 Safarian reported that thirty-one of those offered a position declined to come, five at a senior level, nineteen at the level of assistant professor, and seven at the instructor level. Saskatchewan Archives, Kenneth A.H. Buckley Papers, Department of Economics and Political Science Correspondence file, 'Appointments in Economics and Political Science, 1962–3,' 17 May 1962; University of Saskatchewan, *Annual Report*, 1961–2, 27.

14 University of Saskatchewan Archives, Frank Underhill, 'The Liberal Arts and Public Affairs,' address delivered at the official opening of the Arts Building, University of Saskatchewan, 16 Jan. 1961, 1–2.

Index

academic freedom, Crowe case, 191
Acadia University, 147
'Agricultural Cooperation in Saskatchewan' (Sherriff, thesis), 58
Agricultural Co-operative Societies Act (1913), 23
agricultural credit commission, 23, 25
Agricultural Economics (Taylor), 36
agriculture, 64, 68, 208; exploitation of, 184–5; policies, 42, 51, 132; and politics, 51, 52; romantic view of, 187. *See also* college of agriculture
Aitchison, James, 76, 140, 168
Alexander Mackenzie Fellowship, 18
Allely, John Stuart Mill, 76, 148–9, 153, 162, 164
American Economic Association, 182
American Economic Review, 49, 50, 136, 138, 181
American Encyclopedia of the Social Sciences, 123
American Political Science Review, 105
Anglin, Fr Gerald F., 165
arbitration board, milk prices, 53
architecture: Collegiate Gothic, 15–16;

University of Alberta, 16; University of Saskatchewan, 15–16
archives, provincial, 22, 102, 197
archives, Saskatchewan, 209
Armstrong, P.C., 63
Arnold, Bradley, 86
Ashley, W.J., 78, 80
Athenia, 145
athletics, curling team, 195
Australia, 145

Balliol College, Oxford University, 93
Banish-the-Bar movement, 23
Bank of Canada, 161, 194, 198, 199; board of directors, 73
banking system, 53
Barber, Clarence, 129
Basilian Fathers, 165
Bateman, Reginald, 6, 8, 20, 97
Battleford, 12
Bayer, Jean, 3, 5–6, 7–8
Bell, Kenneth, 102
Bennett, R.B., 66, 68
Berger, Carl, 134
Better Farming Trains, 59
Birkbeck College, 194
Black, W.A.: W.A. Black Chair of

Commerce, Dalhousie University, 139, 142
Bladen, Vincent W., 70, 72, 122, 150
Bohm, Anne, 196
Bole, J.F., 23
Borden, Robert, 123
Bourinot, John George, 79
Brady, Alexander, 169, 173
Brebner, James Bartlet, 18, 19
Brebner, John Bartlet, 179
Brecher, Irving, 52
Brehaut, Louis, 97, 98
Bridgewater, Nova Scotia, 118, 120
'The Bristol Papers: A Note on Patronage' (Ward in *CJEPS*), 170
Britain. *See* United Kingdom
British Columbia, 172
British Commonwealth Relations Conference, 145
'The British Economy in the World Today' (Timlin, paper), 179
Britnell, George, 127, 132–6, 142–5, 153, 161, 176, 178, 182, 184, 195–8, 206, 212; academic degrees, 137; economics and political science departments, 74, 76–7, 133, 142, 146, 157–9, 200, 208–11; Faculty Association, 191; and Harold Innis, 134–5; Harold Innis Visiting Research Professor of Political Economy, 199; international assignments, 197–8; Mackenzie Fellowship at University of Toronto, 134; notice to President Murray, 139; and organized farmers, 206; part-time student at College of Law, 133; and provincial government, 209–10; public policy, 158; Royal Society of Canada, 198; Saskatchewan Economic

Advisory Committee, 156; and sociology, 175; and Swanson, 139, 140; and Ward, 170; Wartime Prices and Trade Board, 146, 156
Brooke, Rupert, 95
Brown, George, 109
Brown and Vallance, architects, 15
Bryce, Bob, 149, 181
Buckley, Kenneth Arthur Haig, 162, 166–9, 182, 194–8, 209; and organized farmers, 206
building program, 6, 201; postwar, 158–9
Bulletin (Queen's University), 49
Burns, Fr Francis L., 166
Burt, A.L., 110
'Bushels to Burn' (Britnell, radio talk), 144

Cairns, Alan, 192
Cairns, J.F., 4–5
Cairns's department store, 96
Calendar, 57, 104, 105, 154; political science courses, 87; University of Saskatchewan economics department 1914–15, 36
Callaghan, Fr John F., 166
Cambridge History of the British Empire, 27
Cambridge tradition, 76
Cameron, Christina (wife of Murray), 9, 11
Canada and Its Provinces (ed. Shortt and Doughty), 22
Canada, Department of Citizenship and Immigration, 176
Canada Council, 182, 193; Studies in Canadian Economic Growth Project, 198, 201

Canada in World Affairs: Two Years of War, 1939–1941 (Dawson), 125

Canada medal, 111

Canada's Economic Prospects, Royal Commission on, 192, 198

'Canada's Immigration Policy' (Timlin in *CJEPS*), 182

'Canada's Relations with the Empire as Seen by the Toronto *Globe*, 1857–1867' (Underhill), 109

Canadian Agricultural Economics Society, 71

Canadian Agricultural Policy: The Historical Pattern (Fowke), 185

Canadian Agriculture in War and Peace, 1935–1960 (Britnell and Fowke), 201

Canadian army, 55, 153; life in, 98–100

Canadian Association of University Teachers (CAUT), 167, 191

Canadian Bank Inspection (Swanson), 49

Canadian Bankers' Association, 49, 69–70

Canadian Broadcasting Corporation (CBC), 152–3; radio, 144

Canadian Courier, 49, 50

Canadian Economic Development (Currie), 154

Canadian Economics Association, 193

The Canadian Economy and Its Problems (Innis and Plumptre), 136

The Canadian Economy in the Great Depression (Safarian), 193

Canadian Forum, 60, 64, 110, 123

Canadian Frontiers of Settlement (Mackintosh and Joerg), 70

Canadian Government and Politics (Clokie), 113–14, 125, 154, 208

The Canadian Grain Trade (MacGibbon), 47, 64

Canadian Historical Association, 109

Canadian Historical Review, 60, 64, 67, 70, 117, 136, 185–6

The Canadian House of Commons: Essays in Honour of Norman Ward (Courtney), 174

The Canadian House of Commons: Representation (Ward), 173

Canadian Institute of International Affairs, 179

Canadian Journal of Economics and Political Science, 70, 81, 124, 125, 145, 151, 164, 170, 181

Canadian Liberal, 181

Canadian Magazine, 49, 86

Canadian Manufacturers' Association (CMA), 101

Canadian Northern Railway, 5

The Canadian North-West, Its Early Development and Legislative Records (Oliver), 22

Canadian Pacific Railway, 3, 70, 101, 188, 200

Canadian Pioneer Problems Committee, 70, 72

Canadian Political Science Association, 47, 63, 73, 81, 125, 152, 182, 195, 198

Canadian Society of Agricultural Economics, 63, 71

Canadian Wheat Board, 146

Capital Formation in Canada, 1896–1930 (Buckley), 167

Careless, J.M.S., 27

Carleton University, 111, 166

Carnegie Institute of Technology, 117

Carr, Ruth, 104

Carrothers, William A. (Pat), 55–7,

71, 74, 131, 134, 182; economic historian, 60; immigration studies, 59; University of British Columbia, 60
Carswell prize, 133
CCF. *See* Co-operative Commonwealth Federation
Cecil, Lord Hugh, 104
census (1903), Saskatoon, 5; (1911, 1921, 1931, and 1941), Saskatchewan, 11
central bank, Canada, 51, 69, 75
Central Selling Agency, 66
Centre for Community Studies, 201
Cherry, Douglas, 166
Christian Science Monitor, 183
church union, 26
civil service, in Nova Scotia, 123
Civil Service of Canada, 10, 49, 116
The Civil Service of Canada (Dawson), 122
Clark, A.B., 72
Clark, George, 4
Clark, S.D., 140, 147, 186, 197
Clark, William Clifford, 45, 46, 69
Clear Grit movement, 109
Clerc, Jacques Olivier, 153
Clinskill, James, 5, 11
Clinskill's Café, 5
Clokie, Hugh McDowall, 113, 117, 125, 140, 154, 208
Coates, R.H., Dominion statistician, 66
Coates, W.G., 58
Cochrane, Charles, 95
Cole, G.D.H., 94
college of agriculture, 52, 57, 59; building, 201; centre of University of Saskatchewan, 203; Manitoba, 63; Oklahoma, 34; Oregon, 33
College of Arts and Science, 141

College of Commerce, 164
Columbia University, 175; library, 178; School of Political Science, 19
combines legislation, prosecution of, 198
commissions of inquiry, Oliver on, 23
Commons, John R., 30–1, 33, 34
Communist Party, 176
community consciousness, development of, 40
community service, professors of economics, 204
Congregationalist church union, 26
Conrad, Alfred H., 41
The Conscription Crisis of 1944 (Dawson), 126
Conservatism (Cecil), 104
Control Commission for Germany (British Element), 164
Co-operative Commonwealth Federation (CCF), 144, 166; government, 156, 171, 210; meetings, 194
Cooperstock, Henry C., 175–6
Copland, Margaret E., 22
Copland, Thomas, 22
Corbett, P.E., 125
Cornell University, 84
Corporation Finance (Meade), 36
Corry, J.A., 104, 121, 133, 136–7, 141, 143, 145, 208
courses (University of Saskatchewan): correspondence, 59, 129, 204; economics, 36–7, 54–9, 131, 185; finance, 57; government, 80–1, 88, 108, 207; growth theory, 193; industrial relations, 57; international relations, 108; international trade, 57; law, 87; marketing, 57, 131; money and banking, 54, 57; philosophy, 88; political sci-

ence, 80, 87–8, 105–6, 120–1, 143–4, 153–5; public finance, 55, 57; rail and water transportation, 54, 57; social sciences, 153; socialism and labour problems, 55, 57
Courtney, John C., 174
Cowan, Helen I., 60
Cowling, Stella Marguerite, 21
Coyne, James, 198–9
'Credit and Expansion' (Swanson in *Saskatchewan Farmer*), 53
credit system, 52
Creighton, Donald, 137
Creighton, Pauline, 58
Crerar, Thomas, 104
Crick, Bernard, 194
Criminal Code of Canada, 198
Cronkite, F.C., 72, 136
Crow, John, 194
Crow rates, 189, 200
Crowe, Harry, 191
Crow's Nest Pass agreement, 188
Cullinane, Fr Eugene A., 165–6
Curtis, George, 141
Curtis, Lionel, 101
Cypress Hills, 4

Dafoe, John, 72, 124
Dalhousie Review, 70
Dalhousie University, 83–4, 86, 114, 116, 140, 191
Dankert, C.E., 59–60
Davidson, Clive B., 58
Davis, Betty, 169
Davis, Joseph S., 138
Davis, T.C., 136
Dawson, Robert MacGregor, 81, 113–26, 140, 169, 171, 207, 208; on Britnell, 145; research and teaching methods, 116, 121, 123; and University of Saskatchewan, 212; and Ward, 170; writing, 123–5
Dawson, Robert (son), 118
Dawson, Sarah, 115
Dawson's Government of Canada (1987), 174
Debating Club, University of Saskatchewan, 37
debtor economy, 138
democracy, in university government, 141, 200
Democratic Government in Canada (Dawson), 125
Democratic Government and Politics (Corry), 136, 208
Denmark, 200
Department of Economics and Political Science, 30–7, 43, 47, 55, 59, 135, 155–8; facilities, 158; federal government studies, 211; political science side, 207, 211; problems in, 146–8; public policy and public service, 161; sociology, 175; and students, 160
Depression, 27, 118, 138, 208; effects on the university, 62
Depression and the Way Out (Swanson), 67
Deutsch, John J., 76, 129
The Development of Dominion Status, 1900–1936 (Dawson), 124
de Wolfe, Margaret, 84
Diefenbaker, John G., 58, 84–5, 90, 199
disciplinary autonomy, 210; and peer assessment, 211
Does Canada Need More People? (Timlin), 181
'Dominion Aids to Wheat Marketing, 1929–1939' (Fowke in *CJEPS*), 152

Dominion Bureau of Statistics, 192, 200

Dominion Commission on the Cost of Living in the Coal Industry, 146

Dominion-Provincial Relations, Royal Commission on, 60, 73, 82, 136, 139, 144, 149, 163, 188

Donnelly, Murray S., 162, 171

Doucet, W.F., 162

Doughty, Arthur G., 22

Douglas, T.C., 144, 210

Drinkle, James C., 5

Drinkle Block, 5, 7

Dunlop, Charles, 191

Dunning, Charles Avery, 23

Easterbrook, W.T., 147

Eastman, Harry, 198

Eastman, S. Mack, 153

Eaton, John, 97, 103, 117

Eaton: T. Eaton Co., 108

econometrics, 196

Economica, 151

The Economic Background to Dominion-Provincial Relations (Mackintosh), 144

'The Economic Factors Affecting Western Agriculture' (Swanson speech, SGGA 1917 convention), 51

Economic Journal, 151

'The Economic Possibilities of Conservation' (Gray in *Quarterly Journal of Economics*), 41

Economic Problems of the Prairie Provinces (Mackintosh and Joerg), 70

'The Economic Realities of the Canadian Coal Situation' (Fowke, thesis), 58, 131

'Economic Theory and Immigration Policy' (Timlin in *CJEPS*), 181

economics, 30, 52, 57, 131, 133; agricultural, 205; conservative, 206; law graduates as teachers of, 47; and mathematics, 211; and political science, 176, 208; resource, 41; rural, 131, 205; theoretical, 196–7

Economics Club, 37, 57, 74, 75

'The Economics of Control' (Timlin in *CJEPS*), 181

'The Economics of Slavery in the Ante-Bellum South' (Conrad and Meyer), 41

economists: agricultural, 144; and political scientists, 82; reform and conservative, 51

'Economists Disagree over Coyne's Policies' (*Winnipeg Free Press*), 199

Edmonton, 56

education, of Canadian soldiers, 99

Elements of Political Science (Leacock), 105

Elements of Statistical Methods (King), 36

Eliason, Frank, 68, 146

Elliott, J. Courtland, 54, 55

Ely, Richard T., 22, 31, 34, 36, 54

Emigration from the British Isles (Carrothers), 60–1

Emmanuel College (Prince Albert), 7

Emmanuel College (Toronto), 27

Empress of Britain, 145

Energy, Royal Commission on, 199

Engen, Fred, 30, 33

Engen Professor of Economics, salary and allowances, 33, 34

Engen research professorship, 47

Engerman, Stanley L., 41

England, Robert, 64–6

enrolment, 102, 192; economics courses, 57; in first year (1909), 6–7; and hard times, 96; increases, 82, 200; post-Second World War, 162, 200

'The Establishment of the National Banking System' (Swanson), 48

Estey, James A., 46

Estey, J. Wilfred, 47

evening class, introductory economics, 55, 57

extension services, 14, 59, 204, 208

Extractive Resources and Taxation, 41

Fabian Society, 94

faculty: isolation among, 103; reasons for coming to Saskatchewan, 212; recruitment, 16–17

Faculty Association, 191

Fairclough, Ellen, 176

Falconer, Robert A., 9, 10, 18, 19, 46, 140, 206

Farm and Home Week, 59

farm debts, reorganization and consolidation of, 68

farm machinery, royal commission on, 40

farmers: march on Ottawa in 1942, 132; reaction to Lewis Gray, 39; romantic view of, 187

farmers' movement, 133

Faucher, Albert, 182

Fay, C.R., 60, 135, 147

federal government, 81; Saskatchewan presence in study of, 208

'Federal Government in the British Empire and the United States' (Clokie, thesis), 113

federal-provincial financial relations, university scholars and, 209

Federal-Provincial Fiscal Relations (Royal Commission), for Federation of Rhodesia and Nyasaland, 197–8

'Federal Public Finances III: South Africa' (Allely in *CJEPS*), 164

Federation of Rhodesia and Nyasaland, 198

Ferguson and Richardson (law firm), 84

Fielding, W.S., 50, 123

The Financial Power of the Empire (Swanson), 49

First World War: Canada in, 100; effect on university work in Canada, 88; Oliver as chaplain during, 26

Flanagan Hotel, Saskatoon, 3–5, 11, 12

Flavelle travelling scholarship, Oxford, 93

Fleming, Donald, 198

Floyd, John, 160, 211

Fogel, Robert W., 41

Food Research Institute (Stanford), 64

Ford Foundation, 193

foreign-controlled companies, effects on Canada, 193

foreign investment in Canada, 192

Foreign Ownership of Canadian Industry (Safarian), 193

Forsey, Eugene, 174

Fort Walsh, 4, 18

Forty Friends, 130

4-H Clubs, 59

4th University Company, 98

Fowke, Helen, 185

Fowke, Vernon Clifford, 127, 130–2, 161, 171, 182, 184, 195, 206; academic degrees, 130, 131, 152, 207; academic rights, 190; and the administration, 189–90; and Britnell, 135, 195–6; Canadian Association of University Teachers (CAUT), 191; Crow rate, 200; Crowe case, 191; economics department, 74, 76–7, 147, 154, 155, 156, 189; Faculty Association, 191; on good teachers, 190; promotion, 189; Royal Society of Canada, 198; salary and allowances, 158; and students, 160; and Timlin, 183, 195–6; and University of Toronto, 207
fraternities and sororities, 16
free trader, Swanson as, 67
Freifield, Sidney, 76
freight rates, 188, 209
The Fully Processed Cheese (Ward), 174

Gaffney, Mason, 41
Gardiner, James G., 173–4
Gates, Paul W., 42
'General Equilibrium Analysis and Public Policy' (Timlin in CJEPS), 181
General Theory of Employment, Interest and Money (Keynes), 149
George Peabody College for Teachers (Nashville), 41
'The Gerrymander of 1882' (Dawson), 124
Gettell, Raymond, 143
Gilchrist Scholarship, Walter Murray, 8–9
Glaeser, Walter W., 75
Glazebrook, George de T., 70
Globe and Mail (Toronto), 109, 174

gold standard, 52–3
Gordon, Scott, 198
government, 108; assistance to from university, 208; commissions, 172; ownership, 44; problems of, 105; university, 141
Government in Canada (Ward), 173
The Government of Canada (Dawson), 125–6, 208; fourth edition 1963 (ed. Ward), 174; revisions of, 126
government work, Buckley, Fowke, and Britnell, 209–10
Governor General's Award for Non-Fiction, 125
graduates, return to university as faculty members, 127
Grain Commissioners for Canada, Board of, 47
grain elevators, co-operative system, 29–30
Grain Growers' Association. See Saskatchewan Grain Growers' Association
grain markets, commission of inquiry on, 23
Gray, Lewis Cecil, 31–42, 43, 58, 185, 204–6
Gray, Pearl, 34–5
Greats, at Oxford University, 93
Greenway, Samuel E., 89–90
Greig (superintendent of buildings), 6
grievances, among faculty in 1919, 89
Grimley, O.B., 132
Guggenheim award, 178, 183
Guthrie, John, 74

Haberler, Gottfried, 151, 179
Halifax Curling Club, 9
Hamline University, 88

Hansen, Alvin, 179
Hanson, Stan, 24
Harold Innis Visiting Research Professor of Political Economy, 199. *See also* Innis, Harold
'The Harrod Life of John Maynard Keynes' (Timlin in *Canadian Liberal*), 181
Harvard University, 96, 116, 147, 164, 178, 194; Department of Government, 113; salary schedules, 17
Haslam, John Heber, 23
Haultain, F.W., on MacKay, 91
Haultain Hall, 62
Hawkes & Co., 100
Heasman, Donald J., 191
Heaton, Herbert, 108, 137
Hébert, T.J., 115
Her Majesty's Mice (Ward), 174
Hertfordshire regiment, 99
Hicks, J.R., 150, 169
Higgins, Benjamin H., 74–5, 149, 180
Hilton, Helen, 132
Historical Statistics of Canada (Buckley and Urquhart), 167
history: of agriculture, 185; of economic thought, 55
History and Problems of Organized Labour (Carlton), 36
History of Agriculture in the Southern United States to 1860 (Gray), 41
History of the Canadian West to 1870–71 (Morton), 102
History of Economic Thought (Haney), 36
Hoffman, David, 172
Hogg, John L., 89–90
Homemakers' Clubs, 59
honours students: in economics and political science, 161; marked on

their English, 159; master's degrees, 159–60
Hood, William C., 153, 196
House of Commons, 144; Coyne debate, 199; Select Standing Committee on Banking and Commerce, 52
Howard, Earl Dean, 49–50, 54
Hudson's Bay store, 96

Ilsley, James L., 181–2
immigrants: British, 65; non-English-speaking, 60
immigration: effects on Canadian economy, 182; studies, 59, 181; Ukrainian, 50
'The Immigration Problem in Canada' (Carrothers in *Queen's Quarterly*), 60
'The Immigration Problem in the Prairie Provinces' (Swanson, paper), 71
Immigration and Settlement, Saskatchewan Royal Commission on, 65
Imperial Conference 1930, Canadian delegation to, 66–7
Imperial Order Daughters of the Empire, scholarship, 113, 133
In Search of Canadian Liberalism (Underhill), 102
Innis, Harold, 57, 64, 66, 82, 125, 137, 145–6, 150, 163, 172, 195, 207; and Britnell, 134–5, 142; and Buckley, 166; and Fowke, 152; fur trade, 103; McPhail's diary, 135–6; Social Science Research Council, 206; and Timlin, 152, 180; University of Saskatchewan, 57, 206, 209; on Wright, 147. *See also under* 'Harold'

Innisian economics, 187
interest rates, role in general equilibrium, 150
International Bank for Reconstruction and Development, 197
International Economic Association, 182, 200
International Federation of University Women, 182
International Journal, 179
International Labour Office (ILO), 163; Extra-European Studies, 153
'An Introduction to Agricultural History' (Fowke, paper), 152
Introduction to Public Finance (Plehn), 36
Irvine, William, 52

Jackson Press (Kingston, Ontario), 48
Jacoby, Neil Herman, 70
James, William, 85
job opportunities, for political science students, 161
Joerg, W.L.G., 70
'John Maynard Keynes' (Timlin in *CJEPS*), 181
Johnson, Harry, 151
Journal of the Canadian Bankers' Association, 49, 50
Journal of Commerce, 50
Journal of Farm Economics, 64
Journal of Political Economy (University of Chicago), 48, 151

'Kant and Idealism' (MacKay, essay), 84
Kautz, Robert W., 201
Keenleyside, Hugh L., 181
Keirstead, Burton S., 81
Kennedy, W.P.M., 124–5

Kerr, Don, 24
Keynes, John Maynard, 76, 149–50
Keynesian economics, and Canadian policy making, 149
Keynesian Economics (Timlin), 150–2, 178, 207
Khaki University, 26, 99, 100
Killam Fellow, 173
King, William Lyon Mackenzie, 107; Dawson as biographer of, 126
Kingston, Ontario, 48
Kirkendall, Richard S., 34, 42
Knight, Frank, 146
Knox College (University of Toronto), 19, 21
Knox Presbyterian Church (Saskatoon), 22
Kristjanson, Leo, 201
Kurihara, Kenneth, 181
Kylie, Edward A., 18, 94

Labour Party (United Kingdom), 194
laissez-faire, 68–9
land boom, opening of real estate offices, 213–14n6
land reclamation program, 42
Lange, Oscar, 150–1
Laski, Harold, 94, 133
Laskin, Bora, 191
Latin Prose Composition (Arnold), 86
Latvia, 53
Laughlin, J.L., 48
Laurier, Sir Wilfrid, 15
Laurier House, Underhill as curator, 111
law, 83; graduates, 47, 80, 141; University of Alberta, 58; at University of Toronto, 78
'The Law of Employers' Liability

and Workmen's Compensation in Canada' (Weir, thesis), 58
Leacock, Stephen, 105, 118; satire on the 'whodunit' book trade, 119
Leacock Medal for Humour, 174
League of Nations club, 105
League for Social Reconstruction, 110
Leddy, J. Francis, 11, 176
Lederman, William R., 75, 145
Leontiff, Wassily, 179
Lerner, Abba P., 151
Lewis, David, 85, 144
Liberal government, Regina, 210
liberals, 102
library: collections, 58–9; University of Saskatchewan, 23
Lightbody, Charles Wayland, 112–13
Lindsay, A.D., 94
Ling, George, 8, 20–1, 72, 114–15
Lippmann, Walter, 107
liquor control debate, 23–4
Liquor Dispensaries Which Recently Existed in South Carolina (under State Control), Royal Commission to Inquire into and Report upon, 23
Literae Humaniores (Greats), at Oxford University, 93
Lithuania, 53
local option vote (1910), 24
Logan, H.A., 67
London, England, 191
London School of Economics and Political Science, 56, 59, 72, 74, 76, 114, 120, 133, 160, 163, 166, 191, 193, 196
London Stock Exchange, 76
Lothian, John, 103, 104

McCaul Gold Medal (University of Toronto), 18
McCaul Scholarship (University of Toronto), 93
McCool, Charles, 166
Macdonald, John A., 109
McFarland, J.I., 66
MacGibbon, Duncan, 46–7, 56, 64, 66, 112, 114, 152
McGill University, 10, 85, 91, 110, 157, 176, 180, 189, 194; political science as academic discipline, 80
'The Machine Process in Agriculture with Special Reference to Western Canada' (Mahaffy, thesis), 58
MacKay, Ira Allen, 58, 83–91, 104, 112–13, 120
MacKay, Robert A., 114, 122–3
Mackenzie, A.S., 140
Mackenzie Fellowship (University of Toronto), 134
Mackinnon, Clarence, 9
Mackintosh, W.A., 70, 72, 114, 137, 144, 148
McLaurin, Robert D., controversy among faculty, 89–90
MacLean, J.A., 96
McMaster University, 19, 46, 148, 157, 168–9, 174, 176, 193
McMaster University Monthly, 19
Macmillan Commission on Banking and Currency, 69
McNaught, Kenneth, 110
Macnaughton, John, 48
McNaughton, Violet, 66
McPhail, A.J., 66, 67, 135
Macpherson, C.B., 80–1, 126, 168
MacPherson, Hector, 33
McQueen, David George, 56

McQueen, Robert (Pete), 56, 57, 71–3,
76, 130, 133, 135–7, 182
Macrorie, Saskatchewan, 132
Magill, Robert, 29, 30
Mahaffy, A.W., 58
maid service, 104
Mallory, James R., 153, 154, 173
Manchester Guardian, 100
Manitoba Agricultural College, 63
Manitoba Free Press, 97
Manitoba government, 29
Marshallian economics, 163
Martin (Premier), 90
Marx, Shaffner and Hart Award
(University of Chicago), 46
Maurice Cody Fellow, 170
Mavor, James, 44
Maxwell, W.R., 70
Mayfair Hotel, 66
Memorial Gates, 117
Methodist church union, 26
Methodist College, Belfast, 55
Meyer, John R., 41
Mice in the Beer (Ward), 174
Michell, Humfrey, 45
middlemen: farmers and, 39; wheat
economy, 206
Mikesell, Ray, 150
milk prices, arbitration board in
Saskatoon, 53
Mill, John Stuart, 48
Milner, William S., 94
Mitchell, Wesley Claire, 50
Modern Business (Howard), 50
Moe, Henry Allan, 183
monetary control, 69
monetary policy, 52
'Monetary Policy and Keynesian
Theory' (Timlin in *Post-Keynesian
Economics*), 181

Monetary Times Annual, 50
Monetary Times of Canada, 49
Money and Banking (Scott), 36
'Money, Prices, Credit and Banking'
(Swanson in *American Economic
Review*), 49
money supply, managed, 69
Montreal Harbour Commission, 50
Moose Jaw, 12
Morton, Arthur Silver, 9, 67, 84, 102–
3, 134
Morton, W.L., 186, 187
Mowat, Oliver, 78
Moxon, Arthur, 8, 20, 68, 86, 88, 91
municipal finance and taxation
study, 70
Munro, W.B., 113
Murray, Christina, 9, 11
Murray, Jean, 163
Murray, Walter Charles, 8–21, 24–5,
44, 50, 52, 62, 71–3, 131, 139, 140,
166, 175, 201, 203, 206, 208, 211;
accusations over funds, 89–90;
community service, 204; and Dawson, 115; economics department,
43–8, 204; extension service, 59;
faculty hiring, 16–18, 30–4, 43–7,
55–6, 61, 74, 112, 133, 204; and
Gray, 31–4, 37–41; and MacKay,
86; political science department,
105; and politics, 51, 101–2; postgraduate programs, 58; *Report*
1910, 83; *Report* 1911–12, 30; Royal
Society of Canada, 124; and the
students, 215–16n29; and Underhill, 95, 110; Wisconsin Idea, 28–
30
Murray Memorial Library, 62
'The Myth of the Self-Sufficient Pioneer' (Fowke), 184

Nashville, 37, 38, 41
Nation Canada, 100
National Bureau of Economic
  Research (New York), 196
National Conference of Canadian
  Universities, 153
National Energy Board, 199
National Oil Policy, 199
'The National Policy and the Wheat
  Economy' (Fowke), 186
nationalism, Canadian, 100
natural disasters, 1912, 96
natural gas, export controversies,
  199
Neatby, Blair, 126
Neill, Fr Robin F., 166, 206
New Brunswick, 8
New Democratic government, 189
New Democratic Party, 85
new economics, 76
New Europe, 100
New York, 196
New Yorker, 170
New Zealand, 191
Nicholson, J. Shield, 55
North-West Mounted Police, 12, 22
Northwestern University, 49
Nova Scotia, civil service, 123
Nova Scotia Commission on Provin-
  cial Development and Rehabilita-
  tion, 169
Nova Scotia Economic Council, 139,
  142
Nutana Collegiate, 7
Nyasaland, 198

Oklahoma Agricultural and Mechan-
  ical College, 34
Oliver, Edmund Henry, 3–5, 7–8, 12,
  15, 18–27, 39, 46, 58, 84, 182; off-
campus activities, 205; Royal Soci-
  ety of Canada, 124
Oliver, Mary, 21
On Contracts (Anson), 86
'On Some Appendices to the Rowell-
  Sirois Report' (Fowke), 152
Ontario legislature, 78
Ontario Royal Commission on
  Unemployment, 50
Order of Canada, 174, 182
Oregon Agricultural college, 33
organized farmers, confidence given
  to Fowke, Britnell, and Buckley,
  206
Orwell, George, 194
Oshawa, Ontario, 48–9
Ottawa, 153, 201
Outlines of Economics (Ely), 22, 36
Outlook College, 132
Overseas Livestock Marketing,
  Saskatchewan Royal Commission
  on, 53
Oxford model, 13
Oxford University, 93–4, 113, 147, 192

'Parliamentary Representation in
  Canada' (Ward in *CJEPS*), 170
Parry Sound, Ontario, 130
Partridge, E.A., 29
Partridge Plan, 29
*A Party Politician: The Memoirs of
  Chubby Power* (ed. Ward), 173
paternalism, of university govern-
  ment, 141
Paulson, Pauline May, 145
Paulson, W.H., 145
Penlington, Norman, 162
Phillips, Paul, 190
Pine Hill Divinity Hall (Halifax), 9,
  27, 141

Plumptre, A.F.W., 136, 150
Political Economy Club, 169
The Political Economy of the Canadian North (Rea), 193
political science, 78–83, 92, 105, 112, 119, 141, 143, 207; as academic discipline, 80; Americanization of in Canada, 83; as Dawson's life work, 117; and economics, 81, 157–8; law graduates as teachers of, 141; at Queen's University, 80; Shortt's definition of, 79; specialization in, 112, 161; traditionalists versus behaviourists, 82–3; Underhill's teaching of, 105; in the United States, 80, 83; at University of Saskatchewan, 82, 91–2
Political Science (Gettell), 144
Political Science Quarterly, 105
The Politician: Or the Treason of Democracy (Gardiner, ed. Ward), 173
politics: agrarian, 132; Confederation, 109; of the left, 110; in the twenties, 101
Politics in Saskatchewan (ed. Ward and Spafford), 173
population. *See* census
Post-Keynesian Economics, 181
postwar cohort, changes brought by, 200
prairies: living standards on, 135; universities, 102; upheaval, 101
Presbyterian church, 9, 25–6
'Present Problems in Canadian Banking' (Swanson in *American Economic Review*), 49
Preston, Howard H., 131
price: of acquisitions for library, 58; of Shortt's library of Canadiana, 59

'Price Determining Factors in the Wheat Market' (Davidson, thesis), 58
'Price Flexibility and Employment' (Timlin in *CJEPS*), 181
Prince Albert, 12
Prince Albert Collegiate Institute, 132
Princeton University, 147
The Principle of Official Independence (Dawson), 116
Principles of Economics (Taussig), 54
The Principles of Psychology (James), 85
Principles of Rural Economics (Carver), 36
'The Problem of Leadership' (Ward in *Sociology and Social Research*), 170
Problems of Modern Government (Dawson), 125
'Problems of Our Rural Debt Structure' (Britnell, radio talk), 144
Progressive Conservative government, 199, 210
Progressive Conservative Party, 84
Progressive movement, 100, 102, 104
prohibition. *See* temperance movement
protests, against financial interests of eastern Canada, 101
public affairs, role of university in, 208
Public Affairs, 170
Public Education League, 25
public opinion: economics professors' effect on, 204–6; pre-Confederation period, 108
public policy, 181

The Public Purse: A Study in Canadian Democracy (Ward), 173
public service, faculty members, 205, 208–9
Public Utilities Commission, British Columbia, 60

Qualter, Terence H., 191
Qu'Appelle Hall (men's residence), 15
Quarterly Journal of Economics, 41
Queen's Quarterly, 49, 60, 64–5, 70, 79
Queen's University, 26–7, 43–5, 49, 54, 72, 130, 136, 148–9, 157, 174, 176, 191, 195; and political science, 10, 33, 49, 79–80
Queen's University *Bulletin*, 49
Quinlan, Fr Leonard C., 155, 165

radicalism, 63; agrarian, 25; pre-Confederation period, 109
Rail, Road and River (Swanson), 70–1
Rayner, John G., 129
Rea, Kenneth J., 180, 193, 201
real-estate offices, and land boom, 213–14n6
'Recent Developments in Canadian Monetary Policy' (Timlin in *American Economic Review*), 181
Regina (city), 12, 156; cyclone, 96
Regina College, 12, 131
Regina *Leader-Post*, 144
Regina Manifesto, 110
registration day, University of Saskatchewan, 1909, 3
Reid, Archibald N., 149, 162–3, 197
'A Rejoinder' (Timlin in *CJEPS*), 181
'Rent under the Assumption of Exhaustibility' (Gray in *Extractive Resources and Taxation*), 41

Reserve Bank of Australia, 194
Restrictive Trade Practices Commission, 167
revenues, decline in 1930s, 127
'The Revision of the Canadian Bank Act' (Swanson in *American Economic Review*), 49
Rhodes scholars, 58, 86, 112–13, 136, 141
Rhodesia, 198
Riel, Louis, 22
Rife, Clarence, 88
Robbins, Lionel, 74, 163
Robertson, R. Gordon, 75, 141
Rogers, Norman McLeod, 112, 115, 141
Roman Catholic Church, 101
'Roman Economic Conditions to the Close of the Republic' (Oliver, doctoral thesis), 19
Roseborough, Harold E., 175
Round Table, 101, 103
Rowell-Sirois Commission, 60, 73, 82, 136, 139, 144, 149, 163, 188
Royal Air Force, 55, 56
Royal Canadian Air Force, 153, 162, 166
Royal Society of Canada, 27, 79–80, 111, 124, 173, 182, 184, 193, 209
rural social survey, Gray, 40
Russell and Palmerston Liberal Club, 94
Russia, 53
Rutgers University, 113, 115, 117

Safarian, A. Edward, 192–3, 196, 198, 201, 211
St Andrew's College, 26, 53
St Paul, Minnesota, 88
St Thomas More College, 155, 165

salaries and allowances, 33–4, 45, 47, 56, 95, 102, 115–16, 131, 135, 149, 171, 179–80, 189; improvements, 158; and pensions, 191; Saskatchewan (1918), 17–18; temporary instructor, 54; University of Toronto, 110

Sanderson Fellowship, 160, 166–7, 193–4, 196, 242–3n6

Sapiro, Aaron, 101

Saskatchewan, 40, 141, 171; government, 29; political scene, 171; provincial archives, 22, 102; provincial government and Britnell, 209; scholars, 209

Saskatchewan Archives Board, 197

Saskatchewan Commission on Agricultural Credit, 44

Saskatchewan Co-operative Elevator Company, 23

Saskatchewan Co-operative Wheat Producers, 66

Saskatchewan Economic Advisory Committee, 156, 188

Saskatchewan Economic and Technical Committee on Transportation and Freight Rates, 188

Saskatchewan Grain Growers' Association, 23, 29, 31, 33, 38–9; convention 1917, 50–1; Warman Local, 38

Saskatchewan Hall (women's residence), 15, 163

Saskatchewan History, 164

Saskatchewan University Act, 12–13

Saskatchewan Wheat Pool, 66, 101; travelling library, 129

Saskatoon, 3–5, 12, 97, 105, 166; comparison to Toronto, 108; land boom in, 95–6

Saskatoon Business College, 129

Saskatoon Collegiate, university space in, 7

Saskatoon Daily Star, 51, 90

Saskatoon Historical Society, 103

Saskatoon Public Library Board, 24, 197

Saskatoon Public School Board, 24, 53

'Saskatoon spirit,' 5

Saskatoon Star-Phoenix, 68, 166

Scott, Anthony, 36, 41

Scott, F.R., 110, 146

Scott, Walter, 10–11, 29–30

Second World War: declaration of, 145; effect on university, 152–3; federal support for teaching veterans, 153; postwar campus, 162–3; postwar instructors, 162

Seligman, Edwin R.A., 19

Senator Hotel, 5

settlement, lands suitable for, 65

Shackle, G.L.S., 151

Sharp, Mitchell, 181

Sheaf, 35, 38, 40, 98, 100

Sherriff, Annie Bell, 58

Shortt, Adam, 10, 22, 33, 44, 48–9, 52, 79, 117; library of Canadiana, 59

Sibbald, Andrew S., 47

Silhouette, 169

Simpson, George, 105, 108

Simpson: Robert Simpson Co., 108

Sintaluta, 29

Skelton, Douglas Alexander, 120

Skelton, Oscar Douglas, 33, 36, 43–9, 80–1, 112, 114, 120

Skelton-Clark Fellow, 173

Smith, Adam, 48

Smith, C.E., 4

Smith, David E., 174

Smith, Sidney, 72, 75
Smith-Mill-Marshall school of politico-economic wizardry, 210
Social Credit, 119
Social Credit in Alberta series, 186
Social Problems Club, 40
Social Science Research Council of Canada, 193, 198, 206
social sciences, 176; and agricultural policies, 42; autonomy in, 210–11; role in service of the state, 29; and specialization, 157
The Social Sciences in Canada: Two Studies (Timlin and Faucher), 182
Socialism: A Critical Analysis (Skelton), 36
sociology, 175, 211
Sociology and Social Research, 170
soil survey, provincial, 65
'Some Aspects of Currency Depreciation' (Allely in *CJEPS*), 164
sororities and fraternities, 16
South Saskatchewan River project, 181, 188; Royal Commission on, 167
Spafford, Duff, 173
Stanford University, 64, 201
state universities, 203; U.S., 30
students: insularity of, 194; and radicalism, 110
Students' Representative Council, 6
'The Study of Political Science in Canadian Universities' (Bourinot, address), 79
Stykolt, Stefan, 198
'A Survey and Study of Economic and Social Life in the Ethelton District' (Coates, thesis), 58
Swanson, Grace, 47
Swanson, William Walker, 33, 44–59,

63, 66, 119, 131, 134, 153, 155, 182; and Britnell, 139, 140; economic position of, 51–2, 67–71, 206; economics department, 147; and Fowke, 155; revision of Earl Dean Howard's text, 50; Underhill's relations with, 107
Swift Current, Saskatchewan, 131

Tarshis, Lorie, 147
Taussig, F.W., 54, 149
Taxation in Saskatchewan, Royal Commission on, 70
'Taxation in Saskatoon' (Creighton), 58
Taylor, Henry C., 31–2, 34, 36, 42
Taylor, Kenneth W., 43, 169, 178
Temperance Colonization Society, 4, 22
temperance movement, 24
'Theories of Welfare Economics' (Timlin in *CJEPS*), 181
Thiessen, Gordon, 161, 193–4
Thomas, Lewis, 164
Thompson, Walter Palmer, 62, 96, 141, 155–6, 157, 165, 176, 179, 190
Thomson, James Sutherland, 141, 145, 149, 152–4, 190, 208; Canadian Broadcasting Corporation 1942–3, 152–3; faculty hiring, 147; National Conference of Canadian Universities, 153
Thorburn, Hugh, 167, 194–5
Time on the Cross (Fogel and Engerman), 41
Times Literary Supplement, 100
Timlin, Cyril, 128
Timlin, James, 127
Timlin, Mabel Frances, 16, 74, 77, 127–30, 134, 142, 146, 155, 157–8,

167, 184, 201–2, 212; and Britnell, 195–6; correspondence program, 129, 152; economics department, 130, 147–8, 156, 159, 178, 209; and Fowke, 195–6; Guggenheim award, 178, 181; Harvard lecture, 179; honorary degree, 182; immigration study, 181–2; Order of Canada, 182; postgraduate studies, 129, 130, 149–51; promotions and salary improvements, 158, 179–80; Royal Society of Canada, 182, 198; and students, 160; University of Toronto, 207; Web site, 250n69; yellow-painted cottage on riverbank, 180, 183

Timlin, Sarah, 128

Todd, J.E., 116

Toronto, comparison to Saskatoon, 108

Toronto Mendelssohn Choir, 108

Tory, Henry Marshall, 10, 14, 16, 17, 26

trade barriers, 67

Transactions of the Royal Society of Canada, 182

transportation: and freight rates, 209; public ownership, 70

Transportation on the Mackenzie River System (Thiessen, thesis), 193

Transportation, Royal Commission on, 50, 188, 200

Trinity College (Dublin), 8

Turner, F.J., 34

The Unashamed club, 104

Underhill, Frank Hawkins, 88, 92, 93–111, 117, 120, 133, 174; academic career, 94, 97–8, 110–11; army career, 98–100; attachment to Saskatchewan, 104; and Dawson's book, 123–4; and Innis, 103; left-wing politics of, 110; and Lightbody, 112; marriage to Ruth Carr, 104; Morton's approach to history, 103; political science and history, 105; and University of Saskatchewan, 94–5, 212; at University of Toronto, 109–11

Union College (Vancouver), 27

United Church of Canada, 12; Oliver as moderator, 26–7

United College, Winnipeg, 189

United Farmers of Canada, 68, 146

United Kingdom, 76; imports of University of Toronto faculty, 43

United States: Bureau of Agricultural Economics, 42; civil service, 41–2; contacts made by Britnell, Timlin, and Fowke, 196; Department of Agriculture, 42; Division of Land Economics, 42; Midwest universities, 13; New Deal administration, 42

University of Alberta, 10, 56, 58, 88, 157, 176; adult education, 15; agricultural programs, 14; compared to University of Saskatchewan, 16; Department of Political Economy, 47; theology faculty, 25

University of Berlin, 21

University of British Columbia, 60, 157, 176, 192

University of California, 192; School of Business Administration, 70

University of Chicago, 19, 34, 46, 48, 56, 60

University of Chicago Press, 48

University of Edinburgh, 9, 29, 55

University of Manchester, 94

University of Manitoba, 55, 72–4, 96, 113, 136, 157, 189

University of Minnesota, 75

University of New Brunswick, 9, 29, 156

University of Pennsylvania, 201

university of the people, Murray's credo, vii, 13–14, 203

University of Saskatchewan, 20, 126, 129, 131, 139, 152, 164; American influence on, 207; buildings in 1909, 6; compared to University of Alberta, 16; Canadian Officers' Training Corps, 164; and the Depression, 62; extension department, 59; and faculty, 117, 212; law, 68, 88, 121, 133; location, 7, 12; and the pioneering community, 12–14; postgraduate degrees, 58; Toronto connection, 207; and wheat studies, 135. *See also* college of agriculture; courses (University of Saskatchewan)

University of Saskatchewan Faculty Association, 167, 191

University of Toronto, 43, 46, 72, 78, 82, 157, 163, 166, 168, 176, 193, 201; Britnell at, 135, 137; and Falconer, 206; Mackenzie Fellowship, 134; Edmund Oliver at, 18; political economy, 80–1, 125, 201; salary schedules, 17; school of economic history, 82; and Timlin, 180, 207; Underhill's appointment to, 109–111

University of Toronto Act (1906), 13

University of Toronto Press, 125, 137, 150

University of Toronto Quarterly, 173

University of Vimy Ridge, 26

University of Washington, 49, 75, 129, 131, 152, 185, 207; College of Economics and Business, 131

University of Western Ontario, 176, 191

University of Wisconsin, 28–32, 34, 83, 86, 201, 203

university world, changes in 1960s, 211

The Unreformed Senate of Canada (MacKay), 114

'Urban Local Government in the North-West Territories: Their Development and Machinery of Government' (Reid in *Saskatchewan History*), 164

Urquhart, M.C., 167

Value and Capital (Hicks), 169

Van Hise, Charles R., 28, 31, 32

Veblen, Thorstein, 48

Victoria elementary school, 7

Viner, Jacob, 73

Visitor, under University Act, 90

von Hayek, Dr, 75

'Voting in Canadian Two-Member Constituencies' (Ward in *Public Affairs*), 170

Waines, W.J., 185

Wakaw Lake, 171

Wallace, W.S., 117

Wallas, Graham, 114, 116, 117, 122

war veterans, return of, 162

Ward, Betty, 169, 172

Ward, Norman McQueen, 121, 123, 126, 162–3, 168–75, 192, 194, 195, 201, 207–8, 211; and Dawson, 170, 174, 208, 212; honorary degrees, 174; labour mediator, 173; Order of

Canada, 174; postgraduate degrees, 170; Royal Society of Canada, 198; and University of Saskatchewan, 212; writer of popular material, 170, 173

Wartime Prices and Trade Board, 146, 156, 169, 178

Washington University, 15

Watkins, Frederick M., 81

Weir, John, 58, 88

welfare economics, 181

Wesley College, 55

West, the: isolation of, 103; people and society of, 63; to Underhill, 95

western dissidents, and pre-Confederation radical politicians, 109

western movement, 101

Western Producer, 69, 133

Westminster Gazette, 95

Westminster Presbyterian Church, 18

What Is Political Science? (Ashley), 78

wheat: pooling, 101; and standard of living, 135; and University of Saskatchewan, 135

Wheat (Swanson and Armstrong), 63, 64

The Wheat Economy (Britnell), 137–9

Whidden, Chancellor, 169

William Lyon Mackenzie King: A Political Biography, 1874–1932 (Dawson), 126

Wilson, J.R., 5

Wilson, Tom, 151

Winch, David, 193, 197

The Winning of the Frontier (Oliver), 27

Winnipeg, 84

Winnipeg Free Press, 27, 73, 199

Winnipeg Grain Exchange, 64

Wisconsin Idea, 28–32, 39, 204

women: economists, 182; enrolment first year, 7; and life on the prairies, 31, 38; right to vote, 24, 218n.70; scholars, 179

Woods, H.D., 147

Woodsworth, J.S., 57, 97

Workable Competition and Monopoly (Britnell, Timlin, Fowke, Buckley, brief), 198

Working, Holbrook, 64

World University Service, 182

World War I. *See* First World War

World War II. *See* Second World War

Wright, C.P., 147, 148

Wrong, George, 94, 109, 110

Young Men's Christian Association, 6

Young Women's Christian Association, Lewis Gray's lectures to, 38